Documentary
Filmmakers
Handbook

Documentary Filmmakers Handbook

NED ECKHARDT

McFarland & Company, Inc., Publishers
Jefferson, North Carolina, and London

LIBRARY OF CONGRESS CATALOGUING-IN-PUBLICATION DATA

Eckhardt, Ned, 1940–
Documentary filmmakers handbook / Ned Eckhardt.

p.   cm.
Includes bibliographical references and index.

ISBN 0-7864-6043-4
softcover : 50# acid free paper ∞

1. Documentary films—Production and direction—Handbooks, manuals, etc.
I. Title.

PN1995.9.D62E35   2012   070.1'8–dc23   2011039669

BRITISH LIBRARY CATALOGUING DATA ARE AVAILABLE

Front cover design by David K. Landis (Shake It Loose Graphics)

Manufactured in the United States of America

McFarland & Company, Inc., Publishers
Box 611, Jefferson, North Carolina 28640
www.mcfarlandpub.com

This book is dedicated to all of the documentary students who have taught me so much about finding and telling compelling stories. Their passion and collaborative drive have been a never-ending inspiration.

My children, Giana and Bret, and wife, Didi, continue to make my family life an unending joy. To them I extend my deepest thanks.

Finally, the memory of my parents, who worked so hard to provide me with a positive moral, social, and educational foundation, has motivated me to aspire to excellence and hopefully make them proud.

Acknowledgments

This book is the culmination of many years of teaching television and documentary production. My own documentary production career has paralleled my teaching career and I am continually amazed at how much I have learned from my students. Their excitement, creativity, and dedication have inspired me both in the classroom and out.

In 1990 my first documentary production class was extraordinary. Those 12 students proved to me that the documentary form could give a voice to young production people who were looking for ways to tell their stories to others. The tradition of excellence they established lives on and thrives today. That class also allowed me to prove to myself that I could successfully teach a class dedicated to making socially-oriented documentaries. That class included Keith Gale, Michelle Decker, Scott O'Leary, Mary Weydt, Scott DePace, Jennifer Calhoun, Don Roman, Jill Stone, Scott Chew, Karen Thomas, Dave Friedman, and Lori Libutti. Tom Rosa, Pete Sandford, Bob Christensen, and Joe Truncale are also former students who have influenced my life in a large way.

My colleagues in the Radio/TV/Film Department at Rowan University have been wonderful sources of advice, inspiration, critical feedback, and fun. They are Mike Donovan, Joe Bierman, Ken Kaleta, Michael Desilets, Diana Nicolae, Keith Brand, Carl Frandino, Terry Coyle, Kathleen Murphy, Chris Winkler, David Bianculli, Tara Bennett, and Mary Gifford.

The creative problem-solving organization, *Odyssey of the Mind*, opened my eyes to the beauty and power of creative thinking and imaginative teamwork. I adapted many of its learning techniques into my own classroom, productions, and life.

The documentarians whose voices are heard in this book inspired me to begin the journey to write this book. They are diverse, yet connected to each other in their passion for finding and telling their stories. To Arnold Shapiro, Deborah Oppenheimer, Connie Bottinelli, Paul Gallagher, Keiko Ibi, Carolyn Scharf, Keith Gale, Heidi Ewing, Rachel Grady, and Michael DiLauro my deepest thanks.

The people in my personal life who have inspired and supported me include my best friend, Frank McLaughlin, whose mentoring and nurturing helped me find my way and stay on course, my wife, Didi, who taught me the value of blending work with family obligations, and thus enriched my life immeasurably, my daughter, Giana, who has always been a voice I listen to, and whose life continues to inspire me, and my son, Bret, who carries the creative torch along with the joy of parenthood, and has always been a source of originality and laughter.

Table of Contents

Introduction

This production guide can be used by anyone, student or independent, who would like to tell his or her story about the human condition in documentary form.

At the core of this book is a belief in the power of focused and committed production people to make meaningful documentaries that can have a positive impact on their local, regional, national, and global communities. Most of us rarely have an opportunity to express ourselves and address important issues. We are continually searching for our voices to tell our stories. When we discover our voices, we are capable of creating profound commentary on the world around us.

Documentary production draws on a wide range of creative and technical skills. Being part of a documentary team that is committed to meeting the challenge of solving all of the problems of production is an uplifting experience and great preparation for life. Reality production is on the rise throughout our culture. Digital technology has brought the tools of production into our homes as well as our schools. People have always been curious about the world around them. Now, they can document their explorations and share them with an audience.

STEP-BY-STEP PRODUCTION GUIDE

This book is a documentary production guide that starts with a quick study of the documentary form, progresses through a recommended viewing immersion, details how to research and write a documentary proposal, then explains how to design, shoot and edit a documentary. Equal attention is given to both creative and technical details and decision making.

In a college setting students are in a perpetual learning mode. They are searching for their voices so they can investigate the facets of life they find interesting. Independent, highly motivated documentarians are also ready to tell their stories. All of the information that is needed to create a successful documentary is in this book.

The design and technical chapters apply to all levels of productions. For those who are readying themselves for making a documentary outside a college setting, this guide should be invaluable in leading the production team through the various phases of production.

I've been teaching documentary studies and production at Rowan University for the last 20 years. Our students have made over 70 documentaries, many of which have won national awards and been honored at film festivals. Approximately 90 percent of these former documentary students are working in some form of media production today. Many work on documentary units full-time. This book is an out-

1

growth of teaching those classes and my own documentary production experience.

For 12 years I made an annual event documentary for a wonderful organization called Odyssey of the Mind. It teaches creative problem solving to hundreds of thousands of young people worldwide every year. I would document its annual world finals and find the inspiring stories from among the 15,000 people who attended the finals every year. I modeled many of the elements in my documentaries on Bud Greenspan's iconic series of Olympic Games documentaries. Bud Greenspan made full-length documentaries about the Olympic Games beginning in 1967. He was an often-honored documentarian who established himself as a master of the large-event documentary.*

I've also made historical documentaries for the New Jersey Historical Commission (*Seabrook Farms Remembered*), character study documentaries of famous authors (*Cheese, Chocolates, and Kids: A Day with Robert Cormier, Creativity around Us: Dr. Sam Micklus*), and cultural study documentaries for my own interest. I love the documentary form and the experience of making a contribution to our collective history. Over the years I have met many documentarians who have shared their production experiences with me. This book draws on many of their insights.

— INTEGRATING DOCUMENTARIES PAST AND PRESENT —

Throughout the chapters are detailed references to more than 100 documentaries. Most of these documentaries were made between 2000 and 2010. It is hoped that as you read a description of either an intriguing story or a creative production technique, you will be motivated to view the documentary and learn from it. The Web enables you to instantly find the documentary's home page, perhaps see a trailer, and often find a free viewing.

This modern explosion of creative reality storytelling has been wonderful for our global collective consciousness. Documentary viewing is rising on the scale of entertainment options. The human desire for knowledge and experience is driving more and more people to tell their stories. As I discuss technical and creative elements in the production process, I've tried to weave in many modern examples of the various ways documentarians have solved the same eternal problems and challenges.

Michael Moore is the most successful documentarian who ever lived, if you measure success by how much money a documentary makes. Arnold Shapiro's 1969 documentary *Scared Straight!* has probably been seen by more people than any other documentary. Academy Award–nominated documentaries *Spellbound, Supersize Me, Born Into Brothels,* and *Murderball* were made by first-time documentarians, shooting with small digital cameras, who found and struck a chord in our collective minds. All of these films and many others are referenced frequently. Our interconnected media world enables all of us to access films instantly. There are many places on the Web that offer a wide range of documentaries for free. Sites include hulu.com, vimeo.com, and freedocumentaries.org, or you can often rent the film on Netflix.

Because documentaries are personal stories, and the people in them are usually

*Bud Greenspan founded his own independent production company in 1967 and has been a prolific producer of sports documentaries ever since. He has won eight national Emmys and is recognized as one of our greatest documentarians. Bud Greenspan is still an active documentarian. His web site fills in a lot of the details: http://budgreenspan.com/index.html

interesting and memorable, it helps if you can watch them with other people in a setting that is quiet and comfortable. Documentaries, especially the ones that tell offbeat stories in new and creative ways, are often controversial and generate emotional reactions. We bring our own baggage to the experience, and as a result there isn't a set reaction to the story. Many times the documentary maker isn't sure exactly what he/she has captured. Michael Moore is a prime example of a documentary maker with a personal agenda. His ambush vérité style turns a lot of people off. But his passion is obvious, and he always generates heated discussions. His populist documentaries about social issues have shown thousands of younger audiences the documentary style of presenting societal problems that hopefully stimulates responses.

Classic documentaries are also referenced frequently. Pioneering documentary makers like Robert Flaherty, John Grierson, Leni Riefenstahl, Albert and David Maysles, D. A. Pennebaker, Barbara Kopple, Errol Morris, and Ken Burns are acknowledged for their innovation and creativity. Their use of the documentary form has influenced thousands of people, both audiences and makers. It is hoped that the reader will be motivated to watch these excellent documentaries. They will provide context for your own ideas and production. When you make a documentary the story is always yours; the frame into which you place the story can be influenced by those who have come before.

DOCUMENTARIAN INTERVIEWS

Over the years I have been fortunate to have met, worked with, and interviewed many documentary makers. Many of the quotes and references are exclusive to this book. These dedicated filmmakers speak in the universal language of humanistic production. They overcame problems and kept their passion. They all agree that the documentary process is a collaborative one, and the process of making a low-budget student/independent production or a $300,000 broadcast or theatrical production is strikingly similar.

This book is designed to give the reader a behind-the-scenes look at how award-winning professional, independent, and student documentary teams have addressed all of the creative and technical challenges their documentary-making experiences presented to them. Although crew size, budget, and time constraints may vary, every documentary production unit faces the same basic set of problems. Every documentary journey begins with critical research. Every documentary unit takes an emotional roller coaster ride, because dealing with real people in real-life settings is an unpredictable and problem-filled experience.

This book also reflects how the traditional documentary has morphed into the many hybrid forms now seen in first-run theaters and art houses, at film and video festivals, and on broadcast and cable television programming and the Web. These new forms of the documentary include varying budgets, mass or niche audiences, quick-turn-around production schedules, many types of video footage, varying production values, formulized structure, and often extensive use of special effects during the editing process. My philosophy is that this expansion and shifting of the traditional documentary form is healthy and exciting. Watching *Jesus Camp*, which was produced for the A&E Network, or *Tupac: Resurrection*, which was produced by the documentary department at MTV/VH1, is just as exciting and inspirational as watching Ken Burns's *World War II*, which was produced for PBS. Watching Michael Moore's *Sicko* in a first-run theater is just as exciting and enlightening as watching *The Weather Underground* on hulu.com on the Web.*

At least a passing knowledge of the giants and pioneers of the documentary form is highly recommended. Just like aspiring narrative filmmakers have iconic films they should see, like *Potemkin*, *Citizen Kane*, *To Kill a Mockingbird*, *On the Waterfront*, *Bonny and Clyde*, and *American Graffiti*, there are similar iconic documentaries like *Nanook of the North*, *Man with a Movie Camera*, *Olympia*, *Harvest of Shame*, *Salesman*, *Harlan County U.S.A.*, and *The Thin Blue Line*. The makers of these documentaries created the grammar of documentary filmmaking. It is from their foundation that modern documentary makers have created the hybrids we see today. If you want to begin a documentary library, these classic titles are a great way to start.

DOCUMENTARY REFERENCES AND ENDNOTES

As mentioned above, this book has hundreds of references to documentaries that have been made during the last ten years and earlier. When I am making points or describing examples, I always refer in detail to contemporary documentaries that have used a technique or style successfully. There are hundreds of documentaries being made every year at every level. Many of them are outstanding, and use creative approaches to presenting their story. The goal of this book is to gather into one place examples of all of the many different styles and techniques documentary makers have used to produce and tell their stories. The spectrum goes from the famous, such as Spike Lee, Ken Burns, the Maysles Brothers, Werner Herzog, and Errol Morris, through lesser-known Emmy, Oscar, and film festival award-winning producers and directors, to innovative independent and student documentary makers. They all have something to share with the reader, and their solutions to problems can enlighten us all. The endnotes are meant to add information to the narrative. The endnotes expand the point being made in the narrative, and they often include specific references to other documentaries and resources.

At the end of each chapter is a list of the documentaries that are referenced in the chapter. As you advance through the chapters many of the documentary references repeat. That is because documentaries are organic and I chose them because they contain all of the elements involved in creating an interesting, meaningful story.

THE 12 BASIC ELEMENTS

Another singular aspect of this book is the breaking out of the content of a documentary into 12 basic elements. Documentary makers always need to address the structure, production style, and design decisions that go into creating a documen-

---

Free Documentary Web Sites — The rise of the documentary form and the huge increase in viewership of documentaries has resulted in many websites where you can view documentaries for free. Four of the biggest and most viewed are: http://www.hulu.com/; http://www.freedocumentaries.org/; http://www.documentary-log.com/d215-google-documentary/; http:/www.vimeo.com. These four sites have free viewing for many of the best documentaries over the past ten years. They are a great way for you to immerse yourself in the documentary form in your favorite quiet setting. The sites below have large catalogs of documentaries, but not always the most famous or popular: http://quicksilverscreen.com/videos?c=44; http://www.freedocumentaries.org/; http://onebigtorrent.org/search.php?realsearch=1&search=documentary&cat=14&orderby=0&ordertype=DESC&dead=ok

tary. The story will always be there. How you frame the story and creatively use production techniques is what gives each documentary its uniqueness. The 12 basic elements are like a creative toolbox for storytelling. Depending on the story, you will make your choices of tools and how to use them. The 12 basic elements also help you to analyze existing documentaries and help you understand how other documentarians have grappled with these production decisions. As you watch more and more documentaries, you will begin to decide which styles and techniques you like. This is the evolution of your documentary storytelling aesthetic. As you pass through your research phase and near your production phase, you will decide on your own style and technique. It is always a leap into the unknown when you do this, but a well-thought-out plan is always better than no plan at all. You are the artist when you are making your documentary and should always believe in yourself.

PRODUCTION EQUIPMENT

My philosophy is that an outstanding documentary can be made with a wide variety of equipment. The chapter on equipment lays out the full spectrum of choices as of the writing of this book. Film and digital cameras, sound systems, production lighting and accessories, and editing software are all presented and discussed. You always try to use the highest level of equipment available to you and within your budget. But don't put off making a documentary you are burning to make just because you are short on funds or high-end equipment. The technology is so diverse and capturing pictures and sound can be done on so many levels that there is always a camera and sound system that you can use to capture your story.

How you use the equipment available to you is the key. The chapter on equipment should help you determine what is necessary for successful production. Academy Award-nominated documentaries like *Born Into Brothels*, *Jesus Camp*, and *Spellbound* were shot on consumer-available equipment.

CREATIVE B-ROLL

Often what makes a documentary exceptional are the choices of cutaway shots, archival footage and/or reenactments. There is always an entertainment element in making a documentary. How you sustain interest and enhance the spoken story is critical to your documentary's success. The chapter on B-roll explains the many ways you can use your imagination to find these visual and sound enhancements. There are many descriptions of how other documentarians have achieved success in this area. When you have read this chapter, hopefully you will be inspired to find ways to use these techniques to help you tell your story in a creative way that reflects your aesthetic.

The modern use of the term "B-roll" comes from television news of the 1960s and '70s, when the field crews were still shooting in 16mm film. The interview would be shot on one roll of film called the A-roll, while the cutaway footage that showed what the talking head was talking about was called the B-roll. During editing, clips from these two rolls would be combined into the finished story.

I worked as a television producer in the programming department for NBC affiliate WCAU-TV, Channel 10, in Philadelphia,

PA, for seven years in the 1980s and B-roll is the term I prefer for the footage that is shot to complement interviews, narration, conversations, and montages in documentaries. Classic film-oriented production people often don't like the term B-roll because it has television origins. They prefer using the terms "cutaway" and "cut in." Both references are correct. I just prefer B-roll because today there are so many people from different educational and production backgrounds making documentaries that everyone knows instantly what you are talking about if you use it.

MEETING THE DOCUMENTARIANS

There is a wonderful book of interviews with topflight documentarians that should be a treasured resource for all aspiring and veteran documentary makers. The book is *Documentary Filmmakers Speak* (2002, Allworth Press) and the author is Liz Stubbs. The author interviewed almost all of the living legends of the documentary form as well as many new, successful documentary makers. They are wildly diverse in their philosophies and approaches to finding and telling their stories. They represent the many styles and techniques that continue to be emulated and to evolve. They are also inspiring. It is clear that passion for the story is the universal driving force. This inside look at the documentary-making process, and the creativity that emerges from it, is priceless.*

As you watch documentaries, you will probably find documentary makers whose style of storytelling you like. If you research their work through the Web and the special-features extras on documentary DVDs, often you will hear them describe why and how they put their personal mark on their documentaries.

There is also a very informative DVD called *Capturing Reality: The Art of Documentary*. It was produced by First Run Features and the National Film Board of Canada in 2008. It features short interviews with another group of successful documentarians. Once again, they do not agree on every point of producing and directing a documentary story, or even what a documentary is. But they tell you why they make the documentaries the way they do, and this is eye opening. There are clips from their documentaries to illustrate their points. Both Stubbs' book and this DVD are available on Amazon.[†]

These two resources should tell you that finding your own voice and style are very important. There is not just one way to tell your story. There are many. You must find *your* voice, style, and structure ... just like these documentarians did.

SHOWCASING YOUR STORYTELLERS

The chapter on capturing interviews and conversations covers a wide range of approaches that can be used to showcase your storytellers. Whether you are using a real-world, stylized, or abstract design approach, you will find many analyses and descriptions of how to use the interview setting to further your story. Mixing vérité

---

*Liz Stubbs is a writer/producer with a specialty in documentary and independent film. Her book, Documentary Filmmakers Speak, is a collection of interviews with the giants and contenders in today's documentary world. A must read. Allworth Press, 2002.

[†]Capturing Reality is a DVD that contains video interviews and B-roll examples of 38 documentary directors. These 38 documentarians include most of the greatest living documentarians. There are 163 film clips and over five hours of features. The documentarians often disagree. Lots of food for thought and fascinating. National Film Board of Canada. 2008.

and directed styles is becoming popular, and there are many examples of how modern documentarians have used this mixed style. When you have read the chapter on interviews and conversations, you should be able to see what is possible and what is effective.

CREATING A LOOK

The "Design and Aesthetics" chapter focuses on how you create your own personal style and look through use of light, color, sound, the camera, and pace. Every documentary has its own look and feel, which is a reflection of both the maker and the subject. Sometimes we know the design aesthetic we would like to bring to the story from the start. Other times we aren't aware of the aesthetic we will bring to the storytelling until we are deeply into the production experience. Documentaries are such collaborative experiences that both storytellers and crew usually begin to think alike. And out of this symbiotic relationship a common aesthetic can arise.

When you have finished reading this book, you should understand what it takes to make a documentary. You will have a reference guide to production, with hundreds of suggestions and tips for ways to visually and aurally enhance your story. There are observations by experienced, award-winning documentarians that help put the information into perspective.

FOUR DOCUMENTARY VOICES

Four award-winning documentarians are frequently referenced throughout the book. These seasoned veterans understand what it takes to conceive, begin and complete a documentary. Their voices are heard throughout the chapters as they share their wisdom and passions.

Connie Bottinelli is a veteran of documentary production who has made many award-winning documentaries for the Discovery, History, and Learning channels. She always finds ways to infuse creativity and art into her documentaries. Her style is full of color and sound. *Paul Gallagher* was the supervising producer for MTV/VH1's pioneering documentary series *Behind the Music*. For a six-year period (1997–2003), *Behind the Music* was the most-watched program in prime time on VH1. He brings insights from the world of TV documentary series, where a tight story structure impacts how the stories are told. *Arnold Shapiro* directed a classic documentary, *Scared Straight!* (1978). He is a champion of the social-issue documentary and has many important observations to make concerning how to create this kind of documentary. Shapiro has made over 150 documentaries, and won an Academy Award and seven Emmys. *Deborah Oppenheimer* produced the Academy Award-winning documentary *Into the Arms of Strangers* (2000). This intensely personal story is a touching study of a little-known program of salvation and redemption that saved the lives of 10,000 Jewish children during World War II. Her experience of finding people and archival sources so the story could be told is inspirational.

Hopefully, you will read all of the statements by all of the documentarians as enlightened commentary on the process and meaning of making a documentary. These documentary makers are speaking directly to you in a language we can all understand.

Documentaries are personal stories of the human condition. They tell their stories by capturing reality. Your ideas will always be present in some way in your completed work. This is a good thing. The pursuit of truth is an individual journey, and the world will be more enriched when your honest story becomes part of the documentary tradition.

CHAPTER PROGRESSION

This book is a step-by-step guide for documentary production. Each chapter guides the reader through a critical phase of production. There are 11 chapters in this book. Although each chapter addresses a specific area of importance, they can be arranged into three parts:

1. Preproduction (chapters 1–4)
2. Field and Studio Production (chapters 5–7)
3. Postproduction (chapters 8–11)

FINAL THOUGHTS

Creating a documentary is one of the most challenging experiences in life. Your story must capture reality in such a way that a clear story emerges. You become part of your own production as the people in the documentary meet and mix with you and your crew. There is always a transformation as the production experience unfolds. It is a strange, wonderful, compelling ride. When the last edit is made and you have screened your story for your storytellers, crew and a wider audience, you will see that the experience is incomparable.

Part I: Preproduction

1. The Documentary Tradition and Getting Started

History of the Documentary: A Brief Chronology

Note: The four primary literary sources for this chronology are *Documentary: A History of the Non-Fiction Film* by Erik Barnouw; *The Documentary Idea: A Critical History of English-Language Documentary Film and Video* by Jack C. Ellis; *Directing the Documentary* by Michael Rabiger; and *A New History of Documentary Film* by Jack C. Ellis and Betsy McLane. These well-researched and thought-provoking works are highly recommended for anyone interested in the history of the documentary form.*

Documentaries are part of humankind's attempt to understand the world and people in it. From Robert Flaherty's *Nanook of the North* (1913, 1922), to Dzigu Vertov's *Man with a Movie Camera* (1929), to Leni Riefenstahl's *Olympia* (1936–7), to David Lowe's *Harvest of Shame* (1960), to Frederick Wiseman's *Titicut Follies* (1967), to the Maysles Brothers' *Gimme Shelter* (1969), to Barbara Kopple's *Harlan County U.S.A.* (1973), to Michael Moore's *Roger and Me* (1989), to Spike Lee's *4 Little Girls* (1999), to Errol Morris's *The Fog of War* (2004), to James Marsh's *Man on Wire* (2008), film and video documentary makers have been trying to discover the meaning of life. Documentary making has a long and vital tradition, and everyone who sets out to tell a story about the human condition in sound and pictures shares in this tradition.

Documenting reality in moving pictures was made possible by the invention of the film camera and the creation of local cinema houses for viewing films. For over 60 years (1895–1960s) film was the medium that captured the life that was presented in documentaries. A key turning point in the history of the documentary was the emergence of television as a showcase in the 1950s and 1960s. The new mass TV audience created a demand for tightly structured informative entertainment. The advent of professional portable video in the late 1970s, the accessibility of portable video systems to the general public in the 1980s, and the digital revolution of the

The publishers of these four seminal works of documentary history are Documentary: A History of the Non-Fiction Film *by Erik Barnouw (Oxford University Press, 1993);* The Documentary Idea: A Critical History of English-Language Documentary Film and Video *by Jack C. Ellis (Prentice Hall, 1989);* Directing the Documentary *by Michael Rabiger (Elsevier Inc and Focal Press, 2009); and* A New History of Documentary Film *by Jack Ellis and Betsy A. McLane (The Continuum International Publishing Group, 2005).*

1990 and 2000s are technological discoveries that have had a profound impact on the documentary form. The tools of production and postproduction are now available to everyone. While many documentary makers continue to use film in the traditional way, the video revolution has created many hybrid forms that also document reality. Throughout this book there are references to and examples of these new hybrid forms. But all of the many forms and styles of documenting reality today have their roots in the past. Only the tools have changed.

Below is a brief chronology of the evolution of the documentary form. This is in no way a complete history. It is rather a historical context in which it is possible to see the birth, growth and development of documenting reality. The highlighted people and events are just a scratching of the surface. But, hopefully, the reader can see that capturing reality and giving it meaning has always been important for the people who have a desire to make documentaries.

1895–1919

1890s–early 1900s: In 1895 Louis and Auguste Lumière recorded the simple comings and goings of life in Paris on silent film. These slices of life became the first publicly projected films. Soon other filmmaking pioneers in Europe and the United States began to make these documentations of life and screen them in theaters built to showcase them. The public was fascinated and showed up in droves. The real world was becoming a subject of entertainment.

1910–1919: Newsreels, human-interest films, and travelogues became the most popular forms for filming and depicting reality. The public continued to attend movie houses and enjoy the films they encountered there. A new form of entertainment was being born. Documenting reality was as popular a form as fictional storytelling.

1913–1948

American Robert Flaherty pioneered the modern documentary form. He began with a naturalist period in which he recorded culturally based stories of exotic people struggling against nature. These personalized stories revealed the nobility of the human spirit. *Nanook of the North* (1913, 1923) is a study of the primitive Eskimo culture seen through the life of one family. It is generally considered to be the first documentary. *Moana* (1926) is a study of life in Samoa that centers on the coming-of-age ritual of tattooing. *Man of Aran* (1934) is a study of primitive shark fisherman of the Aran Islands. *Louisiana Story* (1948) is a story of two worlds colliding. A backwoods Cajun family encounters oil-rig drillers in the bayou along which they live. In Flaherty's documentaries a family is at the center of the story. His style is to present primitive or isolated people and

Robert Flaherty's style of documenting reality in the '20s and '30s is the origin of the "vérité" or observing camera style of telling a dramatic story, although the terms "cinéma vérité" and "direct cinema" weren't coined until the 1960s. He is generally considered to be the first great American documentary maker and continues to influence both scholars and makers of documentaries *(The Criterion Collection, 1998).*

their worlds so we can admire their beauty and spirit. These people are passing into history, but their spirit is our modern legacy. Flaherty loved the new medium of film and composed his documentaries so they revealed not only the story he was telling but also the raw, primitive beauty of our natural world.

Technically Flaherty always used a tripod and employed telephoto lenses as much as he could. He spent lots of time with his subjects and would win their trust. This trust enabled him to become part of their lives. He created a reality where he could use his camera to observe subjects in action. Often he would ask them to redo something or try something else. His story often went beyond authentic reality. Because his subjects were comfortable with him and trusted him, they would cooperate with him, without compromising their actions.

1920s

The documentary form exploded around the world. Russia pioneered newsreels and social and historical documentaries. In Europe, the documentary form became an art form. The avant-garde art movement led to experimentation with surrealistic and impressionistic documentaries.

1930s

In England the Empire Marketing Board (EMB) made work-oriented documentaries with strong social and political messages. The leading documentarian at EMB was John Grierson, a Scot who learned to shoot documentaries in Chicago and was a fan of Flaherty's films. While in Chicago he coined the word "documentary." When he returned to England he headed a documentary unit at EMB that was dedicated to making documentaries that had definite social and political mes-

sages. Grierson always put a political message in his studies of working-class life. He saw the documentary form as a voice for political and social change and a way to educate the viewer and send a specific message. His philosophy was "Art is a hammer, not a mirror." He is responsible for training many young documentarians who would go on to produce many classic documentaries. He later moved to Canada and established the Canadian Film Board (CFB), which to this day has a well-respected reputation for documentary filmmaking. His socially responsible approach to documenting and explaining reality continues to have an impact on the world.

In Germany, Leni Riefenstahl made documentaries within the political setting of Hitler's Nazi regime. She created two documentary masterpieces, *Triumph of the Will* and *Olympia*, which is a study of the 1936 Olympics in Berlin. She was primarily a visual artist who practiced her art within the confines of a repressive political environment. One of her contributions to the documentary tradition was a new visual language that often idealizes and celebrates reality. She pioneered the use of many technologies to capture large panoramas of people and settings. She also pioneered the use of cranes, camera balloons, blimps, massive platforms, flagpoles and multiple cameras to capture events that would only happen once. She developed an underwater camera as well. Riefenstahl is one of the first female documentary filmmakers to achieve a worldwide reputation. Scholars and practitioners are still debating whether she was a willing collaborator of the Third Reich. But there is no doubt about her talent.

In the United States, government-sponsored, politically-oriented documentaries were made for *The March of Time* film series that was shown regularly in local theaters. These tightly formatted, 20-minute documentaries studied the important issues of the times. *The March of Time* series introduced the concept of a totally directed, tightly structured format for a documentary series. The format was to tell the story in four acts (Act 1: The Problem Presented, Act 2: The History of the Problem, Act 3: Complications of the Problem in the Modern World, Act 4: The Future of the Problem). Elements that recurred in each documentary included the deep-voiced narrator, lots of stock footage, dramatic musical scores, and fast (for the times) editing. At the height of its popularity, over 20 million Americans watched the series each week in over 9,000 local theaters.*

1940s

The countries involved in World War II used the documentary form to make many films to advance their causes. The Canadian National Film Board, the BBC, and the U.S. Army made documentaries, narratives and informational films using Hollywood and film community directors, writers and actors. Seven narrative films made by Hollywood director Frank Capra were compiled into a series called *Why We Fight*. After the war, there were thousands of hours of film footage of the war itself. This footage became part of a worldwide archive that is still being used to tell stories. *Night and Fog* (1955), a classic Holocaust documentary made by French filmmaker Alain Renais, was one of the first postwar documentaries to use footage from both sides of the war.

1950s

The emergence of television as a mass medium enabled documentaries to be seen by the mass audience. *See It Now*, *The March of Time* and *CBS Reports* were pioneering, issue-oriented television programs that dealt with a wide range of America's problems, including segregation, migrant worker exploitation, union conflict and poverty. The form of these TV documentaries followed the previously established format for *The March of Time* film series made for theaters. The networks had documentary units that included many of the best independent documentary makers in the country. (Frederick Wiseman, Robert Drew, Richard Leacock, D. A. Pennebaker, and the Maysles Brothers are some of the more famous documentarians who started during this era in either commercial or public television.) Edward R. Murrow often hosted the introduction and afterword for these documentaries on CBS, thereby fusing two formats into one show.

1960s

ABC created *Close-Up!*, a documentary program with an immediate, edgy style. In 1968 CBS created *60 Minutes*, which is still one of the highest-rated programs on television. By the 1960s two "schools" of documentary making had been established: the cinéma vérité style and the directed style.

"Cinéma vérité" was the term given to the style that used what Frenchman John Rouch called the "participatory" camera. In this shooting style the documentary maker and the camera are often acknowledged by the subjects and often stimulate the action. Rouch believed it was impossible for the documentary maker to be objective, since the presence of the camera alters reality in the first place. So the agenda of the documentary maker is al-

---

*Back in the 1930s when The March of Time series (1935–1951) was making short form documentaries for exhibition in local movie theaters the producers created a formula that enabled them to tell their stories using familiar, on-going elements. As documentary historian Jack Ellis states: "Structurally, each episode had four parts, with titles announcing each part. The first established the magnitude and urgency of the problem being dealt with. The second offered a historical survey of its origins and causes. Part three presented the immediate complications, confirming its newsworthiness. The concluding part looked to the future, stressing that the problem was a matter for continuing and serious concern" (Jack Ellis, The Documentary Idea, Englewood Cliffs, NJ: Prentice Hall, 1989).

lowed to impact the capturing of reality. The camera becomes a stimulant and causes people to behave differently than they "normally" would. Rouch's subjects talked about themselves a lot to the camera. The documentary maker made the documentary because he/she had an opinion and could exert an influence on the content. Michael Moore and Morgan Spurlock are direct descendents.

"Direct cinema" was the term given to the American version of cinéma vérité. The American style made the camera mostly observational, but occasionally the cameraperson and/or the director could participate in the action by asking a question or making a comment. This approach involved finding a meaningful story that had its own dramatic arc built into it. The documentary crew would spend a lot of time with the subjects and become part of their world. Consequently, the documentary subjects accepted the presence of the crew and acted "naturally." The documentary camera was noninvasive and therefore able to capture the reality. This echoed Robert Flaherty's use of the camera. Robert Drew and Richard Leacock, who had worked on the ABC series *Close-Up!*, became practitioners and spokespeople for this style and approach. Leacock had been Robert Flaherty's cameraman on *Louisiana Story* and was continuing the Flaherty tradition. Individuals were usually the centerpieces of this approach.

If a political message was the driving force behind the documentary, and a socially significant message was important, then followers of the John Grierson approach would use this direct cinema approach to focus on the issue and the message. Albert and Robert Maysles pioneered using this direct cinema approach. Their groundbreaking documentaries of the '60s, *Salesman* and *Gimme Shelter*, became the archetypes for finding a story and staying with it over time. As the '60s unfolded and the technology improved (the film cameras were smaller and better, the sound systems were simpler and better, and television allowed instant presentation to a mass audience), the practitioners of documentary making began to combine direct cinema and cinéma vérité approaches into what Jack Ellis calls cv/direct.

In this new hybrid form of documentary making, the subject can acknowledge the camera and react to it, as well as be caught in a personal moment that would only occur after the camera and crew had gained his/her trust. This approach is now referred to simply as the vérité style of capturing a nonfiction story. Some older documentarians still prefer the term direct cinema for the American version of cinéma vérité, and you still encounter the term in college film schools. But vérité is the quick reference term that almost everyone uses to refer to a documentary in which the camera and the director don't know what will happen when they arrive on the scene, or where the story will lead them.

The vérité style developed alongside a more controlled form of storytelling that was made first for movie theaters, then television. This is the directed style of making a documentary, in which all elements of the production, except what people say during their interviews, are controlled by the producer/director. In 1960 a directed documentary called *Harvest of Shame* aired on CBS television. The documentary told the story of the plight of migrant workers in the United States using the format established in the 1950s on *CBS Reports*, whose format had been modeled on *The March of Time Theater* series in the '30s and '40s. In chapter 2 of this book, the elements of a documentary are discussed in detail. Modern-day documentarians have discovered that a highly structured story shot to conform to a format and a budget can still captivate audiences. While some scholars, theorists, and documentary makers continue to argue about which "reality"—vérité, direct cinema, or directed—is more real, the makers of documentaries continue to experiment and use the documentary form to capture the increasingly complex examples of the modern human condition.

In Liz Stubbs's remarkable book *Documentary Filmmakers Speak*, she interviews many of the leading documentary makers from both past and present. As they all try to articulate their thoughts on documentary creation, there is often disagreement about the terms cinéma vérité, direct cinema, vérité, and controlled direction. What the documentary makers do agree on is that they are all filmmakers trying to capture reality and tell nonfiction stories. The style they pick to frame the story allows them to create a signature of their own.*

1970s

Portable video became another way to document life. Although originally designed for television-news gathering, the mobility, flexibility and economy of shooting on tape changed the documentary landscape. The tools of production became available to more and more people. The cost of making a documentary was reduced significantly. The television audience had developed a strong appetite for "true life" stories, especially ones that focused on attractive, compelling individuals. Documentary series continued to thrive on television. In the art theaters, social-issue, vérité documentaries like *Harlan County U.S.A.*, which showed the devastating effect a strike at a coal mine in Kentucky had on the miners and their families, became an entertainment option for filmgoers.

1980s

Film and video continued to cover the amazing number of subcultures that were developing in the United States and the world. Because there was so much "histor-ical" footage available, many documentaries took advantage of this resource, either in the form of straight historical subjects, or by intercutting historical footage into a modern subject. Vérité and directed documentaries coexisted and were often made by people who didn't know the terms or the history of the documentary, but had the desire and ability to document reality.

Television continued to be the most popular showcase for documentary viewing. Art theaters often showed long-form documentaries, but the new suburban multiplexes for the most part ignored the documentary form.

1990s

Digital technology and personal computers put the tools of documentary making in high schools, colleges and the home. The cable network explosion, with its addition of hundreds of channels, stimulated growth of the documentary form because it is relatively inexpensive to produce. Americans found the documentary form integrated into the music, sports, information and entertainment channels they were watching with more and more frequency. *COPS*, *The Real World*, *Survivor*, *Dateline*, *Biography*, *Hard Knocks*, *Behind the Music* and the PBS documentaries of Ken Burns (*The Civil War*, *Baseball* and *Jazz*, to name a few) became part of the American TV programming mainstream. In the theaters, documentaries like *Roger and Me*, *Hoop Dreams*, and *4 Little Girls* kept the more traditional documentary form alive and vital. The makers of documentaries also began to combine the vérité and directed styles. Now you would have directed interviews in controlled settings with vérité B-roll. The MTV-made, 2005 Academy Award–nominated documentary, *Murderball*, which is a fast-paced study of the men who play wheelchair rugby, and the 2004

---

*Documentary Filmmakers Speak *(Allworth Press 2002)* is a must read for everyone interested in first hand commentary by living documentarians on the importance of documentaries and why they make them.*

In 1989, Michael Moore made his influential documentary *Roger and Me*. His everyman approach to the social problem of unemployment in the auto industry created a new hybrid form of vérité. Because he was taking a personal journey and on-camera a lot, Michael Moore could create dramatic or funny reality moments while he searched for the president of General Motors. By stepping in front of the camera and being his own narrator, he opened up a new way to study a social problem. Documentarians like Morgan Spurlock in *Supersize Me* and Bill Maher in *Religulous* would carry this banner in upcoming generations *(Warner Brothers Entertainment, 2003)*.

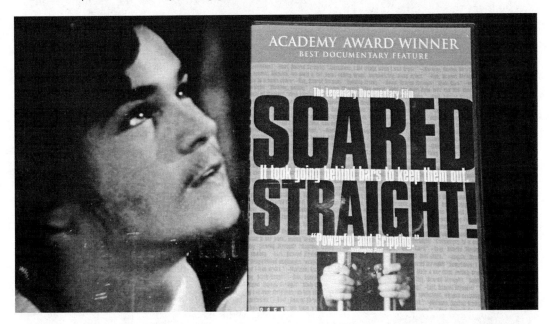

Arnold Shapiro's classic 1978 vérité documentary *Scared Straight!* was made on a small budget and shot in Rahway State Prison in New Jersey. It is still making a difference in young people's lives today *(Arnold Shapiro Productions, 1978)*.

Academy Award-nominated *Born Into Brothels*, which is a heartrending story about the children of prostitutes in Calcutta, mix both styles to compelling effect.

2000s

In the 2000s, the documentary form often merged with "reality" programming, sometimes for the better (ESPN's *The Life*, MTV's *Made* and *True Life*, PBS's *Frontline* and *The American Experience*) or for worse (*American Idol* and *Fear Factor*). But the fascination of exploring and documenting the human condition continues to attract a wider and wider cross section of our multifaceted, multicultural society.

HAVING A DOCUMENTARIAN ROLE MODEL

The documentary tradition includes many different types of people from many backgrounds. Arnold Shapiro was there when documentary programming was in its infancy on television. He has made over 150 documentaries on a wide range of subjects, but the common theme through all of them is focusing on a social problem. He has addressed child abuse, juvenile delinquency, drug addiction and many other societal issues. In an interview with me in 2001, he explained where his social consciousness comes from and why he loves the documentary form.

> In the 1950s and '60s I was watching the classic documentaries that the networks were airing at that time, like NBC's *Project 20* and *CBS Reports*. Those two networks would air dozens of hours of documentaries every year. The documentaries that really influenced me were the ones about the civil rights movement. Exposés were coming out on how blacks were being treated. These classic documentary studies were being done by the documentary units at NBC and CBS and I was fascinated. Early in my career, when I traveled to New York I would meet and talk to the producers of these documentaries.
>
> The reason I was so into this line of thinking was because of how I was raised. My parents were people with a social conscience. They owned a beauty parlor, but they spent time giving money to charity and raising money for charities. I can remember two incidents in particular that are symbolic of this: one I can re-

> member standing out in front of a supermarket collecting money for The City of Hope charity. The other I can remember is when the Korean War broke out [1950] asking everyone in my elementary school class to bring in supplies that we sent on to a chaplain to be distributed to the soldiers. Why did I do that, instead of playing baseball? It goes back to my parents trying to help other people.
>
> My parents imbued me with an overactive conscience. It's hard for me to hear about a social problem, have it eat at me, and not want to do something about it. Other people would volunteer their time; I want to make a TV documentary about it. I decided I needed to do that. I had to make documentaries to enlighten and educate people, and change society for the better. That's what led me away from entertainment programs into nonfiction.*

Arnold Shapiro has become one of the most honored and successful documentary and television producers of all time. He has blended the nonfiction film with the format-driven demands of television. He has been honored with 16 Emmys, an Academy Award, and many lifetime achievement awards. He has created programs for all of the broadcast networks and 14 cable networks, including MTV and HBO. He is an encouraging voice throughout this book. He understands better than most what it takes to make a meaningful documentary that fulfills its goals and entertains audiences. Shapiro is heard throughout the chapters, sharing his expertise and advice.

---

*I interviewed Arnold Shapiro on March 26, 2001. His quotes are drawn from the transcriptions of that interview.

─────────── STARTING OUT ───────────

Making a new documentary, whether as an independent production, a professional project for hire, or a class project, is an action that is filled with passion, dedication, and the unknown. This book has been designed for students and independents who are willing to learn the basic skills of documentary production and accept a life challenge that sets the bar high. Dedication, a strong work ethic, and a positive attitude are all qualities that are needed for success. The payback is the wonderful feeling of accomplishment when the final documentaries are premiered, and then go on to a productive life after production.

One of the best ways to begin the process of learning about the art and craft of documentary production is to share the experience of viewing a diverse group of documentaries. This includes professionally made classics, independent stories, and student-made documentaries.

During this documentary study phase, it's important to balance watching and analyzing professionally created documentaries made in the traditional way with modern documentary hybrids that are proliferating today in movie theaters, on the Web, and on television channels.

The study of student-made documentaries is also critical, because they send the message that making a quality documentary in a college setting is possible. All of the decision making and production challenges that professional and independent documentaries pass through apply to student documentaries as well.

One of the goals of this documentary immersion is to learn that there are certain basic elements present in all documentaries, whether professional or amateur. Another goal is to confirm that first-time documentaries can attain success within a short production time frame and small budget.

Finding Your Critical Voice

There is rarely unanimous agreement on the value and effectiveness of a documentary. So you need to develop your own "voice." Voice is the ability to articulate why you like or dislike the ideas and elements of a production. Many times there are no right or wrong answers, only solid reasons why you think a particular style or approach worked.

Shared Viewing

It's always a good idea to share viewing a documentary whenever possible. Documentaries usually leave strong impressions, positive or negative, and having someone with whom to discuss the impressions made by the documentary enables everyone to see the impact of the viewing experience. These impressions can be feelings, specific likes and dislikes, or memorable moments. From these random subjective reactions you can move on to more specific analysis of the message and the specific production elements. Agreement is never the goal. Expressing how the documentary impacted everyone is.

Gradually you will not only learn about what you like and don't like in specific documentaries, you will also learn about each other. Down the road this will help you decide who you would like to work with on your documentary.

Viewing Immersion

Finding a nice mix of documentaries to share is critical. Group viewing and discussion is one important way to learn about the documentary form. Viewing documentaries on television can also be beneficial. The key is to create a documentary-viewing immersion that exposes everyone to as diverse a group of documentaries as possible. Documentary making is an old and honorable art form that has a tradition of concern for the human condition. Understanding the tradition of concerned documentary makers helps instill a special feeling of worth. Production confidence is a quality that needs to be developed through understanding and motivation.

• **Using the Web** • There are thousands of documentaries on the Web. Sites like hulu. com, vimeo.com, and others have large documentary libraries that are all free. After you view a documentary, check the Web for home pages and commentary about the documentary. It is easy to become informed about not only the story but also the makers. This is a good thing. You have to sift through the information with a critical eye, but if you are discerning you can know all the details of production as well as the story behind the story.

• **Starting DVD Library** • I strongly recommend you buy the DVDs of any documentaries you like a lot. Not only will the documentary look better when you play it, but the special features often have the documentary makers explaining where they got their ideas and how they made the documentary. For instance, the comments from director Terry Zwigoff concerning the creation and filming of his documentary *Crumb* are very provocative and revealing. Errol Morris's commentary on *Standard Operating Procedure* is thought provoking and philosophical. A well-stocked documentary library is also a resource for your friends and family. The stories are real and often can open eyes and perceptions in others.

A QUICK-STUDY DOCUMENTARY PRIMER

Documentary study requires a basic knowledge of the documentary art form and the design decisions needed to facilitate the production. Every documentary will always have the documentary team's personalized stamp on it.

What follows is some basic information about the documentary form. This primer includes creative and technical techniques that are tools for the documentary maker. A lot of production is instinctive, but if you can articulate why you have decided to do what you are doing, you have increased your understanding of the potential of your art.

The Documentary Style: Three Choices

• **Directed Documentaries** • These are planned experiences that the producer and/or director create according to an overall goal for the documentary. The documentary is segmented and written before the crew shoots any footage. Interview subjects are selected and preinterviewed. The music, graphics, narration, recreations, and postproduction effects are thought out in advance. A written proposal that lays the documentary out step-by-step has been created so everyone taking the documentary journey knows what the purpose of the documentary is. That doesn't mean there can't be any changes or improvised shooting. But there is a solid plan that has been broken down into segments, subjects, shooting days and schedules. If you are looking for funding, this preproduction proposal can help explain your idea and goals to potential funders. Chapter 4 is dedicated to explaining how to create a proposal for your documentary.

ROLE OF THE CAMERA

The camera is controlled by the producer/director. It may be handheld or on a tripod or a mixture of both, but how it makes pictures in every situation is thought out. Interviews are set up, lit and miked as part of a plan. Subjects do not address the camera. They look off-camera at an unseen listener. The camera is an observer of important happenings. Hopefully, the subjects have become accepting of the camera and crew, and the result is authentic action.

Does the presence of the camera alter reality? Yes. Does that make the reality captured any less real? That is a question that has been debated since *Nanook of the North* and the first documentaries. The documentary maker has to address this abstract thought throughout the making of the documentary. Postproduction can add to the captured reality with music, visual effects, and additional information via graphics and/or narration.

• **Vérité Documentaries** • These are more free-form than directed documentaries. In this style, the camera arrives at various events and scenes and never knows what is going to happen. Subjects live their lives and the camera catches the action. Everyday talking and conversations unfold and are captured by the camera, and eventually the larger story or stories are revealed. For the most part the director/producer stays in the background, but occasionally he/she becomes part of the action when addressed by his/her subjects or heard off-camera asking a question, commenting on the action, or explaining something. Sometimes he/she is caught on camera. During editing, the choice must be made whether to include this breaking of the fourth wall.

Vérité documentaries usually have a naturalistic, raw look to them. Low production values and minimal technology often result in "amateurish" looking and sounding footage. But this nitty-gritty look can give the footage power and a powerful authenticity. This style of documentary usually generates a lot of footage because so much shooting time is spent waiting for something significant to happen.

ROLE OF THE CAMERA

In vérité documentaries the camera is trying to stay as unobtrusive as possible. Often the action in front of the camera is moving and the camera must move too. This leads to directors selecting smaller cameras and mobile shooters who can manipulate through unfriendly environments. Crews need to be small and know how to stay out of the story action unfolding all around them.

The vérité camera can be on a tripod if all it is doing is recording what is in front of it. The vérité documentarian Frederick Wiseman would often set up his camera on a tripod in a school, hospital, or courtroom, turn it on, and let it record whatever unfolded in front of it. He crafted some classic documentaries out of hundreds of hours of footage. *Titicut Follies* (1967) is his most famous and shows how a dramatic story can emerge from simply recording the life and people in front of the camera.

The vérité camera can also be handheld if there is the need to follow a subject and change vantage points. It has no restrictions. Only natural lighting is used. Microphones are put on the subjects or sound is gathered with a shotgun mike. The look and feel is mostly "natural." The viewer is right in the middle of reality; he/she accepts low production values because of the compelling story unfolding. The popular documentary *King of Kong* (2007) was made on a low budget with minimum production values. But the story of two opposite personality types competing for the title of world champion of Donkey Kong is compelling and involving. The style is almost completely vérité, and enables the viewer to see into the lives of the obsessed video gamers.

Postproduction doesn't alter reality in any way other than cutting scenes and mixing shots from different angles. The story is usually told without narration and takes a lot of on-screen time. The liberated camera can whip pan, snap zoom, Dutch angle, "float," change angles or be steady.

• **Directed and Vérité Mixed** • Since the early 1990s, hybrid forms of documenting reality have developed. Television has been the driving force in this evolution. Now, we often see these two basic approaches in combined form. But the predominant approach for television and film/theater documentaries is the directed documentary. Because time and money bear so heavily on almost all productions these days, funders of documentaries demand thought-out, controlled proposals before they invest in the project. Often, within the directed documentary there will be vérité-style scenes.

Examples of Documentary Styles

On the A&E Network there is a prime-time documentary program titled *Investigative Report*. This weekly show explores problems and issues in American society. The filmmakers' approach combines the tightly controlled, preproduction fact-finding/research phase with a vérité shooting style. Small, two- and one-person production crews fan out across the country to find and record examples of the issue that is being addressed. They shoot on digital video and travel light.

COPS, a television show that has aired continuously since 1989, is probably the best example of the weekly television "reality show" that uses a pure vérité shooting style. There is no narration, no script, no music, and no director—just a shooter and sound person. The fact that each episode of *COPS* has to be 22 minutes definitely shapes the postproduction phase of producing the show, but each "story" is a mini-vérité-style documentary. Subjects sometimes acknowledge the camera. Often they play to the camera, but the reality of the situation is genuine. The fact that everyone has to sign a release, including the bad people, tells you something about the power of being on television.

The *Real World* on MTV (1992–2011) mixes its vérité recording of the social and personal minutia of the young roommates with the more directed confessionals. More than any other show on television, *The Real World* has used a documentary approach to spark an awareness of the documentary style in the current generation of young adult Americans. It has fallen victim to contrived situations and casting for conflict, but when it first aired in 1992 it was fresh and raw. It began the reality show craze that is so prevalent now on television. Vérité spin-offs like *Road Rules*, *True Life*, *Made* and *Cribs* continue to feed the reality appetite of young people. *Survivor* and *Big Brother* have taken reality into the realm of pseudo-reality, where the people are prescreened for conflicting personalities, and the environments are artificial; but there is no discounting the fact that the growing acceptance and enjoyment of nonfiction programming and documentary-style production owes a big debt to these early reality shows.

Television documentary series are a very popular form right now. The national cable networks have rediscovered the extended biography documentary. A&E's *Biography* series began the trend in 1991. The series uses an on-camera host who doubles as narrator to present 44-minute, in-depth, directed biographies of the interesting and famous. These biographies are usually shot using the traditional approach to production values.

E! network's *True Hollywood Stories* is another example. Because the target audience is younger, the host is younger, appears on camera, and has more of an edge. The production elements are adjusted to fit the audience. The freestyle approach of the camera work, editing and special effects creates a faster, more hip look. This documentary series has over 500 episodes and has been running continuously since 1996.

ESPN has two current documentary

series called *The Life* and *Hard Knocks*. Both take an inside look at sports figures and trends. The stylistic approach is very loose and free. The series are shot in digital video, have relatively low budgets, are turned around quickly, and use all of the MTV-style shooting, editing and special effects techniques. This freestyle approach in shooting and editing is in direct contrast to the documentary series ESPN produced in 2000 called *The Century*. This series of extended profiles features the top athletes of the 20th century. The one-hour documentaries were shot in film, had big budgets, used long production schedules, and look like top-level PBS documentaries. Episodes from all of these documentary series continue to air on ESPN every day and make for excellent viewing and learning.

The History Channel and the Discovery Channel turn out hundreds of documentaries each year. Most of them are traditional in their look. On the other side of the design street are the freestyle documentaries on the MTV, VH1 and E! networks. There is a reality series on A&E called *Intervention*. Each one-hour episode tells the story of a person who is suffering from an addiction. We begin the episode by learning that the addict is deep into his/her addiction and on the brink of serious consequences. The camera follows the addicts through their chaotic worlds, then shows the heartbroken families that are living with the addicts. Eventually the program builds to interventions in which the families confront the addicts with their addictions. It is always emotional and if the addicts agree, they are sent to rehabilitation centers. The last act follows the addicts through rehab and a graphic tells us if they were able to stay clean. This is authentic reality and the vérité cameras are there to record everything. Watching authentic reality shows like *Intervention* can help you understand the vérité camera and see how a story emerges from that style.

Four Documentary Classifications

Documentaries usually fall into one of four four basic genres or types of documentaries. Each genre requires a specific approach. Often the genres overlap and you find elements of two or more of the types blended together. But, to get your bearings and focus on a specific subject, it's good to begin the critical viewing journey thinking of one of these four types.

• **The Event Documentary** • This type of documentary presents to the viewer an interesting, compelling event that creates action, drama, comedy and/or viewer involvement. The event documentary has to tell a story that reveals something about the world and our place in it. The event serves as the catalyst for self-discovery and enlightenment.

The producer of an event documentary must have a direct connection to the event and a reason for capturing the action and people involved. This type of documentary demands extensive background research, strict planning of the shooting days, and careful selection of who will tell the story of the event, both on and off camera. Usually there are a lot of short interviews with people who represent specific parts of the event. Collectively they tell the whole story. The documentary maker's reasons for making the event documentary should be part of the story. Narration can greatly help to shape the story and explain elements of the event. Some examples follow:

Bud Greenspan's *Olympiad* (1976–2008) series is a state-of-the-art example of this type of documentary. He made eight one-hour documentaries of nine Olympic games. Each hour tells a dramatic story that focuses on one of the competitors. He shot with a million-dollar-plus budget and eight cameras. For each documentary, the whole project took two years. But the stories he told of the athletes are compelling and enhanced because the subjects are performing on a world stage. His passion for humanizing these world-class athletes and revealing the inspiring journeys many of them have taken is obvious. When you finish watching one of the hours you feel uplifted. The human spirit on the field of sport is noble and life affirming.

Spellbound (2002) is another example of an event driving the storytelling. It is centered on the annual national spelling bee. The producers shot interviews with many of the finalists, then climaxed the documentary with the actual competition.*

Jeff Blitz and Sean Welch shot all of the profile segments with a high-end con-sumer digital camera, a Canon XL-1. They shot 160 hours of interviews, B-roll, and competition footage. The documentary is one hour and 37 minutes. For the national finals in Washington, DC, they hired additional crews and had five cameras rolling. They edited the documentary on Final Cut Pro, and it took two years. They launched the documentary at film festivals and were nominated for an Academy Award in 2002.

Spellbound is a great example of how you can get an idea for a documentary, do research, structure it before you shoot, train yourself to operate a camera, lights, and a sound system, then do it yourself. The production style is a mix of vérité B-

Producer/director Jeff Blitz got the idea for *Spellbound* while he was in college in 1997. He was a big ESPN watcher and when he saw the spelling bee ESPN airs each year a light bulb went on. In 1999, he and a friend, Sean Welch, decided to follow 12 kids as they made their way through their local and regional competitions. From the 12, they picked the best eight stories and created a classic that was nominated for an Academy Award. *Spellbound* is a great example of how you can get an idea for a documentary, structure it before you shoot, do research, train yourself to operate a camera, lights, and a sound system, then do it yourself *(Jeff Blitz, 2002)*.

*Spellbound *is a great example of how an idea can grow quickly into a full blown, award-winning documentary, even though the two people who are creating the documentary are inexperienced and don't have much of a budget. SOURCES: Spellbound DVD, Director's Comments.

roll and bites, directed interviews and conversations, and graphics that advance the story.

Spellbound is also a good documentary to watch because it contains all of the elements for good storytelling: an involving story, compelling characters, conflict, suspense, climax, and resolution. The documentary is also about the American dream because many of the champion spellers are the children of immigrants.

Best in Show (2000) is a satire or "mockumentary" of the crazed dog lovers who train their pets for competition in the annual Westminster Dog Show. The filmmaker uses the documentary form to poke fun at a collection of off-the-wall fanatics who obsess over their dogs while they focus their lives on a once-a-year dog show. The tongue-in-cheek approach, obviously improvised interviews, and bizarre action lend a feeling of cheesy surrealism to this vérité-style spoof.

Twinsburg, Ohio, by Susan Marcoux (1991), a charming and moving documentary about the annual gathering of twins in Twinsburg, Ohio, for a celebration of "twinness," focuses on the documentary maker's own problems with communicating with her twin sister. As the upbeat spirit of the Twinsburg celebration unfolds, the documentary maker's quest for happiness and the resolution of her problems with her sister takes on a poignant power of its own. Humor and pathos are mixed together in a "slice-of-Americana" setting. This 15-minute student documentary won a student Academy Award in 1991.

I have shown this documentary to my documentary classes for several years and it has always gotten a warm, positive response. It was shot for the most part in a rough, vérité style. The many pairs of twins who were interviewed on the fly give us a complete look at the event and insight into the unique twin experience. It doesn't pull any punches. The conflicting emotions that the documentary maker feels are there

for all of us to see. At the end, the twin sisters still haven't resolved their differences. But there is hope.

Leni Riefenstahl was the pioneering, controversial German film director who made two seminal documentaries based on large events: *Triumph of the Will* (1935), which captured a mammoth Nazi rally in Nuremberg, and *Olympia* (1937), which showcased the 1936 Olympic games in Berlin. She created many innovative uses of the camera and combined art with documenting. Although she has been labeled a propogandist for the Third Reich, she advanced the art of event documentary making by finding new ways to enhance her storytelling. These two documentaries are considered two of the best documentaries ever made.

CONCERT DOCUMENTARIES

These are documentaries about musical artists that are built around one concert. *Leonard Cohen: I'm Your Man* (2005) is a documentary about the Canadian poet and songwriter. The documentary captures a tribute concert in Sydney, Australia, in 2000. A variety of well-respected singers performed to honor Cohen. Interspersed with the performances are interviews with Cohen shot in Toronto that trace his history and creative process. Cohen was also filmed in London singing with the rock group U2. The result is an interesting character study of Cohen framed by a tribute concert.

The Last Waltz (1978) is a documentary about the final concert of a Canadian rock group called The Band. There are a wide variety of songs by the group with many more songs by special guest performers, who form a who's who of rock music at the time. The interviews were shot later at a recording studio. Martin Scorsese directed this documentary using seven 35 mm cameras for the concert and a borrowed stage set from an opera. It has become a classic and is visually beautiful.

• **The In-Depth Character Study** • This type of documentary presents to the viewer a person or group with a fascinating experience to tell about. Often the profiled person or group provides all or most of the narrative, so you need to find interesting and creative visuals to help explain the story and give the viewer something more stimulating to watch than a talking head. Shooting might occur in many locations on many different days. Testimonials/commentary from people who are either familiar with the documentary subject or are qualified to comment on the subject's impact on society help flesh out the story and give it different points of view.

The key to this type of documentary is the documentary maker's ability to find the person/group, win their confidence and draw them into the documentary-making process. Eventually, the entire documentary crew will become part of the subject's world for a while. This is always a challenge. One of the keys to winning the confidence of the subject is to have a researched and written documentary proposal that presents the idea and goals of the documentary to the subject.

Grizzly Man (2005) is an in-depth study of an obsessed naturalist who loved grizzly bears. It was made by renowned documentarian Werner Herzog. *Grizzly Man* is a fascinating look at a man who convinced himself that his obsession to save grizzly bears was his life's mission. Timothy Treadwell, the grizzly man, shot over 100 hours of video footage of himself in the Alaskan wild with grizzly bears. It is interesting to see how Herzog, using only 40 minutes of the Treadwell archive, crafts a bizarre story of a man out of control for both the right and wrong reasons. There is a moment when Herzog is sitting on camera with a woman who has an audiotape of the last minutes of Treadwell's life, just before he was eaten by a grizzly bear. As Herzog listens to the recording in a headset he agrees with the woman that it is too gruesome to include in the documentary. What would you have done if you had been in Herzog's place and been given permission to use the death recording? Include the recording or not? There is also a mini–documentary on the DVD of Herzog working with musicians to create the soundtrack. It is also fascinating.

Overnight (2003) is a wild ride and a good example of first-time documentarians realizing in mid–production that they have a different story than they started out telling. Instead of documenting the rise and success of their subject, Troy Duffy, they realized they were capturing the ugly, emotional fall of a former friend. Visually, the footage they shot is in the vérité style and the look includes a mad mix of 16 mm color and black-and-white film, video, stills, and postproduction colorization. The hectic, unpredictable life of their subject is mirrored in the use of the camera and the editing. The story played out over seven years and is a testament to the dedication of the two men who made the documentary, Tony Montana and Mark Brian Smith.

Overnight is a fascinating study of how a compelling story can overcome technical mistakes and inexperience. Sometimes just capturing the story trumps everything else.

The Personals (1998–9) was made by producer/director Keiko Ibi as her graduate thesis at NYU. This study of a group of older folks who are living on the lower west side of Manhattan turns into a rare glimpse of the loneliness and pathos that come to many of us when we find ourselves alone at the end of our lives. This group of eight 70-plus-year-olds meets every week at their local Y to rehearse and star in a play called *The Personals*. As they work with the director, they become a troupe of actors who learn to improvise on stage as well as off. The documentary team becomes a part of their world and records their lives in intimate detail. A mixture of vérité and directed production, *The Personals* is a slice-of-life documentary that fascinates and saddens.

The documentary is long, and whether this works for or against the effectiveness of the piece usually generates interesting discussion. This documentary won both the prestigious Dore Schary Student Achievement Award in the documentary film category and an Academy Award in 1999.

MTV/VH1's *Behind the Music* series of rockumentaries is a good example of how a documentary series can be formularized and still provide a fascinating look into the lives and times of rock bands around the time of the 20th century. Currently, a *Behind the Music* spin-off is VH1's *Bands on the Run* (2001–2011), which is an interesting series that contrasts multiple pop bands competing with each other to see who can be the most "successful." Other series like *The Real World* and *Road Rules* are fascinating studies of the ongoing mutations the documentary form can undertake. Whether these entertainment-driven documentaries are artistic or uplifting in any way is usually a good starting point for lively discussion.

• **The Cultural Trend, Issue or Phenomenon** • These documentaries are in-depth looks at our culture that require a knowledge of current sociological happenings, as well as extensive background research into the historical influences that have contributed to the trend/issue/phenomenon. Social-issue documentaries like *The Cove* (2010), which exposed the slaughter of dolphins in Japan, and *Lake of Fire* (2006), which studied the controversial issue of abortion, fit here. Politically focused documentaries, like *Why We Fight* (2005), and economically focused ones, like *Enron: The Smartest Guys in the Room* (2005), also are part of this type. In these types of documentaries the documentary maker must decide if he/she wants to walk the neutral line, or pick one of the sides and advocate for it.

Hard Choices (1982), a low-budget documentary shot on home video, looks at a small town in Pennsylvania that is suffering from massive unemployment because the local steel mill has closed. As the stories of the idle steelworkers play out we see how large corporations no longer make decisions with the best intentions for their workers. As the out-of-work steelworkers struggle with trying to create new lives, we get a sad glimpse of the modern, uneducated, blue-collar worker with limited skills who has been cast out into the employment cold. Although the production values are relatively low, this documentary gains power as the people of Midland, PA, relate their stories. The honest portrayal of innocent workers being caught up in forces beyond their control or understanding makes a powerful statement on one vanishing sector of today's workplace.

It is easy to appreciate the plight of the people of Midland, but they themselves don't always agree on what should be done to solve the townspeople's and the country's labor problems. This documentary usually stimulates a lot of discussion on work in general. Whose responsibility is it to train unskilled workers?*

Dogtown and Z-Boys (2002) is a raw look at the history of surfing and skateboarding as they evolved in a rough section of Los Angeles from the 1970s through the '90s. It is a wild mix of music, archival footage, special effects, and interviews. It captures the aesthetic and the history of the early rebel surfers and skateboarders from Dogtown.

Harlan County U.S.A. (1969) is a long, lingering look at a coal miners' strike in Harlan County, Kentucky, made by Barbara Kopple. It's a heartbreaking record of the people who stood up to the coal company in one of the poorest communities in the United States. The music track is a classic of coun-

---

*Hard Choices *was produced and directed by Marian Lipschutz in 1984 as her master's thesis project at NYU. It was shot on VHS video and edited into a 30-minute documentary. It is narrated by Ernest Borgnine and captures the sad story of out of work steelworkers in Midland, PA.*

This classic vérité documentary captures the stress and danger of a coal miners' strike in Harlan County, Kentucky, in 1976. Producer-director Barbara Kopple won an Academy Award for the documentary *(Cabin Creek Films, 1976).*

try and bluegrass music. This is one of the first American documentaries to show in vérité style what exploited, underpaid workers had to go through in order to get a few-cents-an-hour raise. The small crew often lived with the miners during the strike and gained extraordinary access to their lives.

• **The Historical Documentary** • This type of documentary targets a specific time in recorded history and presents information in an exciting way. People, places and events are woven together to create a story with a clear point. One of the visual challenges is shooting still photos and artwork. Often they can be enhanced using the technique called photomation, which is explained in detail in chapter 7. Displays of items that are artifacts and/or ephemera connected to the time/event can help add creative life to the piece. Reenactments and recreations can also be effective. Abstract sequences that reflect the mood or feeling of an event can often work in the place of a reenactment.

Obviously, research, writing, factual accuracy and credibility are very important. It is a good idea to always double-

check historical facts. Experts need to be found and woven into the history.

The story you are telling needs to be tightly defined before the search for eyewitnesses, commentators, survivors, and experts can begin. Historical documentaries usually include a narrator who can quickly relate historical events, make smooth subject transitions, and introduce talkers and experts.

Sometimes it is possible to tell your historical story with only statements from your subjects. Spike Lee's *4 Little Girls* (1998) accomplishes this difficult approach. But the traditional approach is to have a narrator as the calming presence that leads the viewer through the historical documentary. The historical documentaries of Ken Burns are outstanding examples of traditional historical documentaries. *The Civil War, Baseball, World War II,* and *The History of Jazz* are four of his best and are available on DVDs and Netflix. The History Channel is full of these types of documentaries. HBO has created some outstanding documentaries. *Letters from Vietnam* (1987) is one of the finest.

Historical documentaries often feature music as one of the most creative components. Original scores and "mood tracks" can greatly enhance the impact of a historical documentary. Vocals can also be effective. Bill Moyers created a one-hour documentary entitled *Amazing Grace*, which was a history of the origin of the song and what it has meant to different groups within our culture. The singing of the song throughout the documentary, which is in the public domain and therefore free, is moving and extremely effective.

Documentary Subject Selection and Self-Discovery

Documentaries are personal statements on the human condition. All of us have strong feelings about the world around us. We are all products of our upbringing and environments. If you are burning to make a documentary about a subject you are passionate about, then you can begin the production journey immediately. Sometimes people discover the documentary form and develop a passion for making a documentary, but aren't sure of a specific subject.

Because documentaries are personal statements by the documentary maker, everyone should first look into his/her own life and psyche for his/her documentary subject. There might be a cause you are interested in, a tragedy that has affected you in some profound way that you would like to make a statement about, a cultural phenomenon you have a personal interest in, a historical event you are attracted to, a societal issue that you feel strongly about. These subject areas are the traditional starting places for documentary subject searches.

The next step is a look into yourself in an attempt to dis-

cover *why* you are so interested in the subject. Self-discovery is very important. The experience of defining a worthy subject area and beginning preliminary research is also important.

Five of the Best

Often it can seem overwhelming to make choices for documentary viewing and studying. I have been teaching a documentary studies course for more than 20 years. My students and I screen many documentaries in their entirety, and screen the beginnings of many more. I try to keep the documentaries current while honoring the past. Here is a list of the documentaries that have been immensely popular. The audience doesn't always agree on the success of the documentaries, but they always admire the makers. Most in the audience have only seen a few documentaries and have yet to learn the rich history of the form. Here they are in the order I show them.

• *Gimme Shelter* (Albert and David Maysles, 1969) • This vérité classic shot in 16 mm film works for a number of reasons.

Albert and David Maysles made *Gimme Shelter* in 1969. Originally, it was supposed to be a concert documentary featuring the Rolling Stones. Then the brothers realized they had a larger story to tell. Albert Maysles is still making vérité documentaries in his 90s. His web site (http://www.mayslesfilms.com/) is a wonderful exploration of a career that has endured for almost 50 years. (Maysles Films, Inc., 1970.)

It features the Rolling Stones performing many of their classic songs. It shows 1960s hippie/flower-power kids at the peak of their influence. Technically, it shows what two crew people can accomplish after they win the trust of their subjects. It plays with linear time as a storytelling device. It uses archival footage to advance the story. George Lucas was a cameraperson on the big Altamont concert shoot at the end. *Gimme Shelter* always generates a lot of thought and discussion. It's a great way to begin a documentary journey. Albert Maysles is still making vérité documentaries in his 90s.

• *American Movie* **(Chris Smith and Sarah Price, 1999)** • This in-depth character study, shot in film with a mostly vérité style, of a midwestern filmmaker trying to get his films made while his life falls apart has become a modern, semiunderground classic. The struggles of Mark Borchardt to find funding for his films involve his family and community in a way that takes the character study into cultural and lifestyle areas. The two young, unknown documentarians spent a year filming Borchardt's life, went heavily into debt, and were discovered at the 1999 Sundance Film Festival when their documentary was awarded the Grand Jury Prize for Documentary and was bought by Sony Corp. for $1 million. This documentary always generates lively discussion about how much influence the documentary crew has on the story. Also, the midwestern setting provides a sympathetic backdrop for a character like Mark. Could he have been as compelling if he lived in New Jersey? The documentary makers made money on the documentary, but Borchardt did not. Is that fair?

• *Man on Wire* **(James Marsh, 2008)** • This combination historical and in-depth character study features the legendary Philippe Petit, who wire walked between the two World Trade Center towers in 1971.

The directed documentary uses archival footage of Petit when he was younger, controlled interviews (sometimes in sets), graphic animation, and black-and-white reenactments to capture the essence of the story. The passion and dedication of the core conspirators, who sneaked into the towers and pulled off one of the great pranks of all time, are fascinating. The beauty and art of Petit's unique, death-defying wire walking is mesmerizing. The reenactments within the towers are handled like a "heist" film, and the creative cinematography, acting, and editing are stunning. This documentary won an Academy Award in 2008. It has almost every element that a director can bring to a nonfiction story. The sum total of the elements is brilliant. This is a rare documentary that succeeds as story, art, and craft. Because of the cultural significance of the Twin Towers and 9/11, *Man on Wire* works on many levels and discussion about what appeals to each viewer is interesting. The reenactments have a creative aesthetic that warrants discussion and analysis on why they are so successful.

• *Jesus Camp* **(Heidi Ewing and Rachel Grady, 2006)** • This cultural study of the modern phenomenon of Pentecostal evangelical Christians training kids to prepare themselves to fight the advancement of Islam is a vérité cautionary tale. Becky Fisher, the leader of a group of evangelical Christians, shows the viewer how young people must commit to a Christianity that needs to be more militant in this world of radical Islam. Three young preteens are followed as they begin to be missionaries for this point of view. The directors labored hard to stay objective in the story. After the first cut of the film, they felt a need to balance the radical evangelical point of view and included Mike Papantonio, a moderate Christian who hosts a daily religious radio talk show. The content is controversial and generates a lot of emotional discussion. The vérité style captures the evangelicals well, and is a testament to how documentary directors can win the trust of their subjects and have them reveal themselves perhaps more than they realized. *Jesus Camp* was shot on a Panasonic DVX100 digital prosumer camera that costs approximately $3,500. It was nominated for an Academy Award in 2007.

• *The Thin Blue Line* (Errol Morris, 1988) •
This revolutionary documentary changed how documentarians tell stories. The film investigates the murder of a Dallas police officer, and interviews all of the players in the investigation, trial, and aftermath of the murder. Along the way Morris recreates the murder over and over again. Each time it is from a different vantage point or point of view. Each reenactment is different in action, to correspond with the different ways people involved remember the event. Morris is making a statement about the impossibility of everyone agreeing on the "truth." Is it possible to ever know the real truth? Meanwhile, the recreations are stylized visually and presented with a scored musical sound track by composer Philip Glass. The interviews take place in nitty-gritty work settings, while the B-roll reenactments are often stylized and artistic. *The Thin Blue Line* so bewildered Academy Award judges that they didn't want to classify it as a documentary. They called it a nonfiction film and refused to consider it for an Oscar.

The documentary is totally directed. Every minute is controlled by Morris except for the content of the interviews. It is one of the first documentaries to bring art to the telling of a crime story. Because of the impact of the documentary and the new details revealed by many of the major players in the story, the man who was convicted of the murder got a new trial and was freed. This documentary opened the doors of self-expression to documentary makers and continues to influence the documentary form. Morris has made many other interesting and off-beat documentaries and all are recommended. He finds powerful and/or fun stories, then uses his artistic sensibilities to enhance them. He won an Oscar in 2005 for *The Fog of War*, and his latest documentary, *Standard Operating Procedure* (2009), deals with the dramatic occurrences at Abu Ghraib prison in 2003. He runs his own Web site and it is far-reaching and informed.

FINAL THOUGHTS

The documentaries I've described have hopefully wakened your interest in discovering how everyday people, inspired by their imaginations, have told the stories they felt compelled to tell. Next up is the process of learning the elements of telling a story in documentary form.

DOCUMENTARY REFERENCES

Each of these documentary references was chosen because it has a creative element or technique that stands out. Some of the most creative filmmaking has occurred while a documentarian is telling his or her story. It is hoped that the curious reader will be motivated to watch many of these documentaries not only for enjoyment, but also for inspiration.

The Boys of Baraka. 2005. Rachel Grady and Heidi Ewing, Loki Films. Winner of many prestigious film festival awards including Silver Docs, SXSW, and Cine Golden Eagle. A moving look at a group of inner city kids who travel to a special school in Kenya to find themselves. A digital vérité documentary that also features diary cameras for the kids when they are in Kenya.

Dogtown and Z-Boys. 2001. Stacy Peralta. Vans, Inc. and Sony Entertainment. Double Sundance winner. Sean Penn narrates this fast-paced, creative telling of the origins of skateboarding. Peralta uses his 16mm skills to add a jumpy, layered look to his B-roll and montages. He mixes black and white interviews with color B-roll and home movie archival footage.

Enron: The Smartest Guys in the Room. 2005. Alex Gibney. Magnolia Home Entertainment. An informed look at the corruption and far-reaching consequences surrounding the fall of Enron. The interviews are shot creatively, often using reflections to provide a second, upside down image of his storytellers and reinforce the feeling of dislocation the complex drama generates.

The Fog of War. 2003. Sony Pictures Classics, Inc. Errol Morris's Academy Award winning study of the psyche of Robert McNamara as he relates his take on recent military history. The interview settings are disorienting and artistic. They provide an ironic contrast to McNamara's cocksure attitude that his version of history is the right one.

Food, Inc. 2008. Robert Kenner. Perfect Meal LLC. This eye-opening, Academy Award nominated look at US agribusiness makes the case for more environmentally friendly and health conscious processing of our meat, grain, and vegetables. Interesting on-location interviews, and some clever transitions using graphics and beauty shots.

Grizzly Man. 2005. Werner Herzog. Lionsgate Films, Inc. This documentary was compiled from over 100 hours of personal video footage shot by Timothy Treadwell, the tragic subject of the film. Herzog narrates and appears in this unique, Academy Award nominated documentary.

Hoop Dreams. 1994. New Line Home Entertainment, Inc. This 3-hour, vérité-style documentary took 5 years to make (1989–1994) and generated 250 hours of raw footage. It was shot on video using a Betacam video camera. This documentary remains a classic example of dedicated vérité filmmaking. It captures the lives of its two subjects as well as the inner city life of Chicago.

Into the Arms of Strangers: Tales of the Kindertransport. 2000. Deborah Oppenheimer and Mark Jonathan Harris. This moving, inspira-tional story of how 10,000 children, mostly Jewish, were sent by their families to England to avoid the Nazis in Germany. Spectacular, pristine archival footage is presented from a child's point of view. Judy Dench narrates this Academy Award winner.

Jesus Camp. 2006. Heidi Ewing and Rachel Grady. Loki Films, Inc. This intense, vérité film about evangelical Pentecostal Christians preparing for religious warfare by running a religious camp every summer is shocking and a cautionary tale. It was shot on digital video over a seven-month period. It won many film festivals and was nominated for an Academy Award.

Lake of Fire. 2006. Anonymous Content. Tony Kaye. This beautifully shot black and white documentary deals with the controversial issue of abortion. Both sides are strongly presented and the filmmaker leaves it up to the audience to decide for themselves. It was a labor of love and took eight years to make.

Murderball. 2005. Henry Alex Rubin and Dana Adam Shapiro. ThinkFilm LLC. The documentary was made by the documentary division at MTV/VH1. This mostly vérité cultural study of the members of a wheelchair rugby team uses sound during the competition sequences in a creative and interesting way. It was nominated for an Academy Award.

My Architect. 2003. Nathaniel Kahn. Louis Kahn Project LLD. This vérité documentary follows illegitimate son Louis Kahn as he searches for clues to the mystery of his world famous architect father. Some creative on-camera hosting sequences, this personal journey documentary was nominated for an Academy Award.

Overnight. 2004. Tony Montana and Mark Brian Smith. DNP Productions. This wild profile of a young director self-destructing in Hollywood took eight years to make. It is a mad mix of film, video, special effects, and home movies. At one point the subject fires the director.

Spellbound. 2002. Jeff Blitz. Blitz/Welch. This first-time documentary was conceived while Jeff Blitz was a student. Almost all of the footage was shot with a low-end digital camera and a crew of two. It is a prime example of how a good story can be told with a minimum of cost and technology.

Supersize Me. 2004. Morgan Spurlock. Kathbur Pictures. Morgan Spurlock channels Michael Moore and takes on the overweight epidemic in the US. He lives on McDonald's food for 30 days and lets the viewer keep him company.

Wasted Youth. 2000. Carolyn Scharf and Rasheed Daniel. Rowan University. Binge drinking and its tragic consequences are the subject of this social issue documentary that has been viewed by tens of thousands high school and college students.

Who Killed the Electric Car? 2006. Chris Paine. Sony Pictures Classics. This well researched look at the auto industry's love/hate affair with electric cars is narrated by Martin Sheen.

Why We Fight. 2005. Eugene Jarecki. Charlotte Street Films LLC. This Sundance winner is a cautionary tale about the dangers of America's evolving military machine that now includes political and corporate interests.

2. The 12 Basic Elements of a Documentary

All documentaries contain basic structural and content elements. Though these elements may appear in different manifestations, as you begin the study of the documentary form, understanding what these elements are will help you appreciate documentaries more. When you are ready to make your own documentary, reviewing the elements and deciding how they will impact your production should help you with a lot of your decisions.

Here is a list to keep in mind as you view and study documentaries. Whether the documentary maker is successful or not is often debatable. Articulating the reasons why the elements succeeded or failed is part of the development of production awareness and finding your own voice. Soon you will be in your own documentary unit and all of these elements will have to be addressed. Depending on the documentary subject and the production style you've chosen, some elements will become more important than others. But awareness of the range of elements will better prepare you for your decision making. As each element is explained, there are examples drawn from popular documentaries that illustrate the element. Almost all of these documentaries are available for free viewing on the Web or for a small fee at Netflix. If your interest is piqued, please don't hesitate to watch the illustrative documentary.

ELEMENT ONE: STORY STRUCTURE AND SEGMENTING

Like a good story, all documentaries must have a beginning, middle, and end. Hopefully the characters are compelling, there is some conflict, and your story builds to a climax. Your story must also have an articulated reason for being. Documentaries are personal statements and have obvious points of view. Part of the preparation for making a documentary is to break the proposed documentary into theoretical segments or chapters. Just like the larger documentary itself, each segment has a specific purpose and goal.

As mentioned in chapter 1, the documentary *Spellbound* (2002) is a good example of how you can establish a simple but effective structural format for your story. This documentary follows eight young spelling bee contestants as they win their regional tournaments and move on to the national finals in Washington, DC. After the documentary's opening sequence and title, the director, Jeffrey Blitz, visits all eight kids in a row in their hometowns. Each of these biographical segments is between five and seven minutes long. Each segment is structured the same. We first meet the middle-school child; see B-roll of his/her hometown; meet a mix of parents, siblings, teachers, and schoolmates; and get to know who the child is through conversations with him/her. After meeting our eight spellers, we move to the national finals in Washington, DC, for the climactic spelling bee competition and conclusion. The balanced structure enables the director to present the storytellers with equal impact, while the editing presents us with their best sides and draws us into their lives. Their candidness and innocence are compelling and the director is able to build emotional involvement to go along with the suspense of whether one of them will win the national championship. *Spellbound* is a great example of a character-driven story telling itself while the camera watches.

Arranging segments into an order that tells an effective story is vitally important. Sometimes producers write a detailed treatment of the purpose of each segment within the documentary as the research phase leads into the shooting phase. In the Oscar-winning documentary *Into the Arms of Strangers* (2000), producer Deborah Oppenheimer tells an uplifting story about the thousands of young children from Germany and Austria who were sent to England by their parents to escape the Nazi terror just prior to World War II. These children survived the war and were adopted by their second families. Deborah's mother was one of these children and the documentary was inspired by her connection to this untold story. In 2001, in an interview I had with Deborah Oppenheimer, we discussed the entire evolution of the documentary. One of the areas she felt was essential to telling this historical story was having a firm grasp on its basic structure.

> Before we began shooting we had an entire script. That's not to say we didn't diverge from it but I think documentaries have everything to do with structure. You can throw things out that you didn't succeed in getting and add stuff that were discoveries made along the way, but there has to be some kind of structure. For our project we knew the story we wanted to tell and there was a tremendous amount of research done to support that story before we began. We were always evaluating what we were getting and discussing if it contributed to telling the story. We were always asking if we had all the elements in place. We knew before we did any interviews what elements of the story we hoped to capture and we made certain that we selected interview subjects who could contribute to that portion of the story. We knew that there were no guarantees that once we interviewed them they would come through, but we certainly knew which part of the story we were hoping they would tell.*

Your outline of your story will become more specific after interviews are shot and transcribed. As the documentary moves through production and postproduction, segments may get revised, moved, or dropped, but the documentary will always be comprised of segments that have specific goals. Organizing by clearly defined segments helps enormously in controlling the footage and telling your story in a comprehensible way. In directed documentaries the ordering of content before production is more obvious than in a vérité documentary when you aren't sure where the story is going. In vérité documentaries, a lot of the structuring comes after the footage is shot and you are preparing your story for editing.

Errol Morris's historical documentary *The Fog of War* (2004) organizes the con-

---

*I interviewed Deborah Oppenheimer on August 15, 2001. The quote is taken from written transcripts of the interview.

tent into an opening and 11 "lessons." These lessons are announced with a graphic text on a black background. This organi-

Errol Morris created an abstract setting for Robert McNamara, the star of his documentary *The Fog of War.* This off-balance set contrasted with the total confidence of McNamara's recollections and explanations. By dividing his documentary into 11 chapters, Morris creates the illusion that a war as complex as the Vietnam War is capable of being explained simply *(Sony Picture Classics, Inc., 2003).*

zational tool allows Morris to present his storyteller, Robert McNamara, as someone who thinks he has history compartmentalized and under control. Whether this is really possible is what Morris leaves up to the viewer.

In the vérité documentary *Hoop Dreams* (1994), which follows the lives of two teenage, inner-city basketball players for five years, we see the evolution of their lives, conflicts, events, family relations, and inner struggles. The documentary follows a linear structure, and we advance through their stories year by year.

Sometimes a linear approach to time isn't the right way to go. In the character study of journalist Hunter Thompson, *Gonzo,* by director Alex Gibney, Hunter's life skips around as various friends and relatives explain their relationship with Thompson. Since he was such an iconoclast and rebel, Gibney uses the abstract, mosaic approach to slowly fill in his life story. Gibney takes a daring, stylized approach to the elements in this fascinating directed documentary.*

Tip: As you watch a documentary, it's a good idea to mentally note when a segment ends and a new one begins. How the documentary maker makes the transition between segments helps the viewer understand the design and pace of the piece. One of the biggest creative challenges of designing a documentary is how to order the segments and create the transitions.

───── ELEMENT 2: THE OPENING AND TITLE ─────

Because documentaries are a form of storytelling, the beginning is important. You've got to interest the viewer and launch the story. As you watch the opening, you might make a few mental observations. Are moods and feelings dominant, or does the story begin immediately? What is the role of the storytellers, B-roll, narration,

and music in the opening? How long is the opening segment before the title? Or does the title appear first? Getting started is one of the biggest challenges in a documentary. It takes a lot of thought. Sometimes you take a risk.

The in-depth character study documentary *Overnight* (2003) chronicles the

Gonzo is one of the most creative documentaries to be made in the past decade. Director Alex Gibney commits to a wild, abstract approach in his B-roll sequences, but balances this with beautifully composed, calm interview settings. Aesthetically his reenactments of Hunter Thompson writing on his typewriter feature an actor and special effects generated images that create an impressionistic feeling of the chaos of Thompson's life and writing style. Gibney states in the director's comments on the DVD that his goal was to recreate the "spirit" of Thompson. As director he wanted to embrace the mix of fantasy and fact in Thompson's life, much like his subject did in his writings.

wild, self-destructive trip a young Hollywood director, Troy Duffy, takes over an eight-year period. The opening is a montage of grainy black-and-white film shots of Duffy alone in various locations. Many of the shots are out of focus, and the handheld camera floats and jerks as it captures the director, often looking at the camera. There are two audio bites at the end of the sequence that capture the arrogance of the director. The music has a mournful, metallic quality, and the overall effect is that something scary is about to happen. The lowercase title

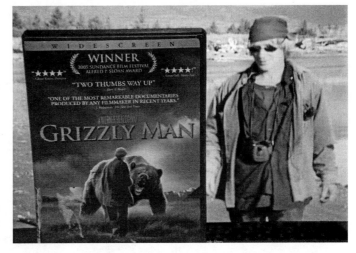

Werner Herzog's documentary *Grizzly Man* was compiled from over 100 hours of personal video footage shot by Timothy Treadwell, the tragic subject of the film *(Lions Gate Films, Inc., 2005).*

letters move and jerk in a way that reinforces the feeling that something is out of control. The visual aesthetic has been established and the mood is dark and foreboding. All in one minute and 23 seconds.

Often the opening is the last decision that is made, even after all of the footage has been reviewed and all of the other segments have been edited. During the opening, sequence themes and imagery that will recur throughout the documentary are often presented. Pace and your sound track (music and/or natural sound) are usually established.

In the cultural study documentary *Jesus Camp* (2006), directors Heidi Ewing and Rachel Grady wanted to establish the setting of the rural Midwest, with lots of space, not a lot of people, fast-food restaurants sprinkled here and there, and religious talk radio going 24/7. All of these elements appear in the opening, and they recur throughout the documentary. In Werner Herzog's in-depth character study *Grizzly Man* (2005), the documentary begins with subject Timothy Treadwell's own archival footage of himself talking to the camera in Alaska with grizzly bears in the

background. As he describes why he is fascinated with bears, he makes a cocky statement that unwittingly foreshadows his own death. Music is introduced that is used throughout the film. Werner Herzog also introduces himself as the involved, curious narrator. Those three elements, Treadwell's archival footage, personal narration, and original music, compose most of the film.

Into the Arms of Strangers producer Deborah Oppenheimer wanted to evoke the World War II era as she began her courageous story of Jewish German parents sending children to England so they could survive the war and begin new lives.

> Our original idea for the opening was to go to Berlin and shoot modern-day children playing in a playground with their parents. We searched all of Germany to find a playground that had an elevated track running beside it so that we could pan off the children on the playground and up to the train racing by. We timed out the shot very carefully and did it over and over until we got it beautifully. We brought the footage home, edited it, took a look at it, and decided that it was too intellectual. It didn't bring the viewer into the story fast enough. So we threw out

the opening and we came up with the idea of an arrangement of children's objects, which was inspired by the film *To Kill a Mocking Bird*. Once we came up with that idea, then I was quite determined, again in respect for my mother and for the survivors, that there would be absolute authenticity. None of those objects would be simply antiques found in an antique shop. They would be authentic objects taken by the children on the train and saved for 60 years, so every single object you see is historic, irreplaceable and authentic, and I am glad to say people seem to respond to it. When we added the children's choir on the sound track the opening worked.*

In Alex Gibney's documentary *Taxi to the Dark Side* (2007), which is an investigation into the United States using torture tactics during interrogations in Iraq and Afghanistan, he opens the story with beautifully composed scenes of the Afghanistan countryside. Into these beautiful settings, he introduces surviving friends of a taxi driver, Dilawar, who died after being unjustly arrested and tortured in prison. They make short statements about who he was and how innocent he was. Finally, in a long shot, a taxicab slowly drives through the scenic vista toward the camera. This peaceful opening is in high contrast to the chaotic, tragic story that is about to unfold. The documentary ends by returning to the peaceful, rural setting, thus bookending an out-of-control story of deceit, hypocrisy, torture, and death.

> **Tip:** As you watch the beginning of a documentary, try to monitor your reactions to how the story is being set up. How are you impacted by the opening? Are you drawn in? Are you teased into wanting more? After the viewing experience is over, can you articulate how effective the opening was? Could it have been better?

───── ELEMENT THREE: TRANSITIONS ─────

How does the documentary flow from one segment to another? The decision to create a format for segment/chapter transitions is important. Some of the standard transitions are

Fade to/from Black

When one segment/section of the documentary ends, there is a fade to black, then from black into the next segment. The reason behind this technique is that the slow fades to and from black give the viewer time to reflect and prepare for a content shift. Historical documentaries often use this technique. Ken Burns is the master of finding the right moment to end a segment and fade to black.

A (Slow) Dissolve

This moves the documentary from one segment to another. Like the fade to/from black, the slowness of the dissolve creates time for reflection. But the fact that the pictures remain on the screen means the documentary maker doesn't want you to disconnect from the piece.

Graphic Title

This is an announcement of what is next. Sometimes these graphic announcements are white letters over black, other times they are lettering superimposed over still photos, freeze-frames, artwork, moving footage, or special effects imagery. As mentioned above, in Errol Morris's documentary *The Fog of War*, he has divided

---

*I interviewed Deborah Oppenheimer on August 15, 2001. The quote is taken from written transcripts of the interview.

the documentary into 11 lessons about war, as explained by former Secretary of War Robert McNamara. White letters on a black screen announce each lesson. Historical documentarian Ken Burns often uses white letters on black screens to title his segments. Sometimes he will add a red underline for effect.

In the documentary *Food, Inc.* (2008), which is an eye-opening look into the world of processed food, each chapter is announced with a title consisting of animated lettering over a black background, with a wide variety of music underneath that helps get us into the mood of the next segment. The investigative revelations in each chapter are usually startling, and the transition titles give the viewer a chance to take a deep breath and integrate the latest information into the larger story. Similarly, in the documentary *Taxi to the Dark Side*, there is a recurring graphic sequence that announces either what is coming or informs us of who is about to speak. The elements in the transition are military-colored letters that are moving amid layered color effects that are also moving.

Short Bridge Sequence

A brief segment that repeats throughout the documentary is another transitional device. It might be a special effects sequence with or without music. In the documentary *Dogtown and Z-Boys* (2001), Stacy Peralta uses a high-energy, image-layered, moving screen that always includes the jumpy black-and-white countdown numbers to a film. This recurring imagery keeps making his point that skateboarders lead fast, exciting, unpredictable, and risky lives. Another technique is an on-camera stand-up transition by a host/narrator. Morgan Spurlock in *Supersize Me* (2004) often appears on camera to reflect on what just happened or to provide a lead-in to the next segment. Michael Moore will also often provide the link between segments by appearing on-camera in his controversial documentaries.

> **Tip:** As you view documentaries, you will begin to see how the documentary makers have segmented and ordered their stories. The transitions become vital to the flow and effectiveness of the storytelling. Discussions on how successful the segmenting, ordering and transitioning are should reveal how there are no "right" answers. But successful documentaries are always thought-out works, and their design elements are used to hopefully enhance the whole piece.

───────── ELEMENT FOUR: STORYTELLERS ─────────

These are the people who will tell the story of the documentary. As the documentary maker begins to assemble the people who will be in the documentary, he/she should have an idea of what the final story will be. A first draft of a *treatment* that outlines the story, presents the wished-for group of storytellers, and notes other elements and actions is usually written before production begins. It inevitably goes through revisions as the documentary unfolds. But this first attempt at a *narrative line* is the glue that holds the piece together. Failure to write a first-draft treatment of the narrative line before production starts might result in a lot of wasted effort and confusion. This is a huge challenge for the producer/director, but it forces him/her to organize and think out the piece. A directed documentary lends itself to preplanning and a detailed treatment. A vérité documentary needs preplanning also, but most of the specifics of the story will still be unknown. If you are making a directed documentary, having a first draft of the voice-over narration (if you are using this device) also makes it easier to discuss the documentary during production meetings. There are three basic types of storytellers.

Narrator/Omniscient Voice-Over

This is a pleasing, "right-sounding" voice of a person that the viewer never sees. This voice supplies the documentary with background information, transitions, interview subject introductions, and other vital information. This voice-over is entirely scripted and must be grammatically correct, easy to understand, and clever/entertaining/dramatic depending on the need of the piece. In *Dogtown and Z-Boys* (2001), Sean Penn is the narrator. Because he was born and raised in Dogtown, and is famous and a rebel himself, he was a good choice for the narration. In the cultural documentary *Who Killed the Electric Car?* (2006), Martin Sheen is the narrator because he is often identified as a green-issue spokesperson. In the World War II historical documentary *Into the Arms of Strangers* (2000), British actress Judi Dench brings a warm, dignified, friendly tone to her role as the narrator of an inspiring story of sacrifice.

Often securing a "name" narrator can help fund and sell the film. But the person has to match the subject matter and tone of the film. Historical documentaries almost always have an omniscient narrator who has a professional-sounding vocal quality. In the documentary *Wasted Youth* (2001), which is a social-problem documentary that focuses on binge drinking in college, one of the college-age crew members provided the narration. His vocal quality and age added authenticity to the story. In both *Grizzly Man* (Warner Herzog) and *Taxi to the Dark Side* (Alex Gibney), the documentary maker provides the narration. The stories are powerful and different, and the "everyman" feeling the "nonprofessional-voice" narration gives the documentaries authenticity.

Deciding on who will narrate a documentary is a BIG decision. In a college setting, there are a wide variety of "voices" to pick from. Local media outlets also have people who might be available for narration. On the other hand, when a documentary is exploring a subject that is youth oriented, perhaps an "everyday" voice or voices is best. Today's audience is much more accepting of "real-sounding" voices. Personal journey documentaries feature the subject's voice in both a narration and on-camera role.

Over twenty years ago HBO made a documentary called *Dear America: Letters Home from Vietnam* (1988). This creative, moving piece had famous movie stars reading letters written home by soldiers in Vietnam, while we see footage from the war and the soldiers' lives. The producers used a mixture of male and female voices and it was very effective.

Until recently, male voices dominated narration tracks because they were culturally identified as "authoritative." But female narration is on the increase. More and more documentary subjects reflect female issues and stories, and a female voice often has a softer aesthetic quality than a male voice. In documentaries that are personal journeys in which we see the central character, there is a mix of on-camera sequences and self-narration. If the story is strong and enticing, the quality of the voice isn't important. We accept the voice of the main character and are interested in the story.

The Academy Award–nominated documentary *My Architect* (2001) is about a son searching for biographical details of his dead father, world-famous architect Louis Kahn, whom he never knew. The story unfolds as the son tells us why he needs to know about his father. He visits his storytellers and various places around the world. The son has many on-screen ruminations and encounters, as well as providing all the narration. Kahn's voice is not a professional-sounding voice, but because it is his story and a fascinating one, we accept his voice with no negative reactions. Bill Maher's *Religulous* (2008) is a lighthearted personal journey exploring various religions. He effectively hosts and narrates.

The actual recording of the narrator is one of the last events on the documentary timeline. A scratch track or reference audio track is usually recorded and used for off-line editing. This voice doesn't need to be professional sounding. Someone on the crew can do it. As the final segments are being edited, the narration goes through its final tweaks. When the entire documentary is picture complete and video locked, then the finalized narration can be recorded and added to the documentary, replacing the reference audio track.

> **Tip:** As you watch narrated documentaries, see if the chosen voice works for the mood, feel and pace of the piece. Often famous people with good voices are recruited for the narration. Do they fit the theme and story? Sometimes an "amateur"-sounding voice can add vulnerability and/or authenticity to a documentary.

Subject Storytelling

In this style of narrative, the people in the documentary supply the needed spoken information. The producer creates a structure and list of questions/content areas that lead the crew in pursuit of the desired information. There may be directed on-camera statements/interviews mixed with vérité slices of life. You must know the information you need to see/hear in order to create the questions/

situations that will draw out the proper comments.

If you are making a directed documentary, then you need to identify your subjects, decide on your interview locations, design your "look," prepare your questions, schedule the filming/taping, and then execute the interviews.

If you are making a vérité style documentary, then you need to know what you need in terms of story line and hope your on-the-fly conversations and eavesdropping with your subjects will supply the story. This approach is the hardest type of narrative to achieve, but can be very effective. *Lake of Fire* (2006), an eight-years-in-the-making labor of love that examines the issue of abortion, and *The Boys of Baraka* (2005), a heartbreaking, three-years-in-the-making story of the struggles of a group of inner-city kids who get a chance to go to school in Kenya and then lose it, use this vérité style of storytelling very well.

The producer/director needs to constantly review all footage as it is shot so whatever parts of the story line are missing can hopefully be found and shot. This approach usually results in longer shooting time and finished documentaries that need

The Boys of Baraka was created by vérité documentarians Rachel Grady and Heidi Ewing. It tells the story of a group of inner-city kids who get a chance to attend a school in Kenya. Their lives are changed forever *(Loki Films, Inc., 2005).*

an extended time frame to complete. Sometimes there are "surprises" on-camera that reveal something new and can change the course of the documentary. Often in this style of documentary, the producer can target one or more subjects for extended vérité minutes. By finding a way to ask your subjects the same questions as well as individually oriented questions, you generate footage that tells both individual stories and common stories. Once again, this style of gathering narrative requires constant familiarity and interaction with your subjects, and constant review of the footage.

On-Camera Reporter/ Narrator

This type of narrative line is more in the television-hybrid style of the mini-documents that appear on *Dateline*, *20/20*, and *60 Minutes*. More traditionally produced series like *Biography* on A&E, the BBC *Nature* series on the Discovery Channel, and PBS's *Front Line*, *Now*, and *The American Experience* series hosted by Bill Moyers are prestigious, big-budget, hosted documentary series. But as the documentary form continues to morph, there is a whole group of programs on VH1, MTV, HBO, E!, ESPN, The Travel Channel, The Food Network, The Learning Channel and many others that use the on-camera host as narrator. These documentaries have all of the essential elements of the documentary form. They are also usually tightly formatted in their content and timeline.

When using this approach, you need to match the right "looking and sounding" on-camera talent/host/reporter with your documentary subject. Scripting is essential, but often improvising can be effective. The reporter/host addresses the camera and if there is anyone else with the reporter, the camera should always be part of the "three-way" discussion. Camera acknowledgment should be consistent. If the host speaks to others, they should respond and acknowledge both the host and the camera. Michael Moore uses this type of host/narrator approach to make his agenda-filled documentaries. His "ambush" interviews are controversial, but they are quintessential vérité style.

Usually, an on-camera host creates a "personality" that contributes to the overall effectiveness of the piece. Wardrobe, body moves, attitude, camera shooting style and location can all help create a successful on-camera personality. Morgan Spurlock, who created and starred in *Supersize Me*, his documentary about obesity in America funneled through the fast-food prism of McDonald's, leads us through his personal story with on-camera stand-ups and vérité sequences with his doctors and friends.

Mixing Them Together

More often than not there is a mix of these various types of storytellers. It is up to the documentary maker to decide how to tell the story and who will tell it.

ELEMENT FIVE: SOUND TRACK: MUSIC, VOICE, NATURAL SOUND, AND SWEETENING

The sound track of your documentary is very important. Gathering voice and natural sound needs to be thought out and planned. In directed documentaries where you can control the environment of the interviews, you want to choose locations that don't have any competing ambient sounds like heating and air conditioners, airplanes, traffic, or other distracting sounds. Homes, workplaces, hotels, and studios are typical locations. Always scout the locations first and listen for unwanted sound. You can't always do this, but audiences are much more forgiving of poor quality sound in a vérité documentary than they are in a directed documentary.

Voice

Without a doubt, gathering clear, crisp audio from your subjects is of primary importance. In directed interviews your subject is still, so you can decide which of the two basic systems (lavalier or shotgun) you want to use. A small lavalier mike can be clipped onto clothing. The general rule is to place it one foot from the sound source. This can't always be achieved because of what people are wearing. The next decision is whether you want the mike seen. If it is OK to see microphones, then try to make them as unobtrusive as possible. Hide the audio cables under clothing. If you don't want to see microphones, then you need to hide them under clothing. See chapter 5 on production equipment and chapter 6 on shooting the interview for more details on miking. If you use a shotgun mike on either a boom pole or pistol grip, make sure you are within three feet of your subject.

Audio decisions are often not thought out and the voices come out distant sounding and tinny. As the producer/director of the documentary, you should always listen to a sound check in headphones so you can hear the sound quality. The camera mike was not made for primary sound pick up. It is there for gathering natural sound for B-roll shooting and as a backup for your primary miking system. Always shoot room tone for at least one minute after an interview.

Music

Music can greatly enhance a documentary. However, because the copyright laws that affect all music registered with ASCAP, BMI and SESAC are now being strictly enforced, documentary producers often have to pay top dollar for registered music. These fees are usually beyond the budget of college or first-time productions. As a result, you will probably have three options for music.

• **Original Music** • This is music that has been composed and recorded by a person or group that owns the rights to the music and is willing to sign a standard release that will assign you the rights to use the music in the documentary. There are usually a lot of local musicians who are looking for recognition and résumé items. They are often willing to become involved in a documentary project. It is exciting to work with original music composers. The creation of a musical score usually works two ways.

MOOD TRACKS

The composer is drawn into the project and views a lot of the raw footage. From conversations with the producer and crew, the composer forms an accurate perception of the themes, moods and goals of the documentary. The composer then scores and records a number of tracks that match the mood/themes of various sections/segments of the documentary. Each track might be one to three minutes long. Maybe there are some slower, mellow, "thoughtful" tracks. Maybe some fast-moving "upbeat" tracks. Maybe some "inspirational" tracks. The producer will select the times the music will be used. Depending on the rapport developed between the producer and composer, the composer may or may not become part of the editing process. Most of the time, music selection and mixing is best left to the producer, director, and editor. One of the special features on the DVD of the documentary *Grizzly Man* is a mini-documentary of Werner Herzog working with musicians as they create mood tracks for the documentary. It is fascinating to see how Herzog tries to articulate what he is looking for, shows the musicians clips from his rough cut, then listens and comments as the musicians create musical themes and melodies for the documentary.

SCORE TO ACTION/PICTURE

This approach is much more complex. Here the composer works with final cuts of the documentary. The footage and music are timed to be synchronous. The music fits the action on the screen. This requires the composer to be an intricate part of the production team, and the creation of the entire music track is delayed until near the end of the editing phase. This is risky, complicated, and stressful, but usually worth it. Errol Morris often has composer Philip Glass score his documentaries like feature films. The carefully matched sound to action creates an emotional response to dramatization sequences, transition sequences, and even his interviews. The *Thin Blue Line* (1988) is a classic scored documentary.

• **Music Libraries** • Music libraries have become very popular with independent producers because you get a lot of prerecorded music tracks for your money, and the rights to use the music are granted when you purchase the library. If you are in a college setting, you can find music libraries in music departments and at the college radio station. You can buy a 20-CD, 20-hour library that has over 1,000 tracks for as little as $500. The CDs are themed and have the same tunes in thirty-second, sixty-second, and two-minute tracks. Purists and students don't like music libraries, but professional documentary makers use them all of the time. On the Web there are sites like garageband.

com, freemusicarchive.org, ccmixter.com, and jamendo.com where there are thousands of free music tracks and songs.

• **Negotiated Rights** • Sometimes you can contact the music publisher, composer and/or proper agency and negotiate special, "once only" rights to a specific song or track. A contract is drawn up between you and the proper party on the music end, then signed by official representatives of both parties. This is a long journey of phone calls, e-mails, letters and faxes. But it can be done. The key to success is tenacious communication and selling the artist/composer on the merit of the project.

As mentioned above, there is so much free music on the Web that you might find what you need there. The Web site apple.com/ilife/garageband/ is a warehouse of original music. Some of it you can create yourself on the site, other tracks are there for the taking. Web sites like royaltyfreemusic.com and mobygratis.com also offer large libraries of free music.

> **Tip:** As you listen to the music in a documentary, try to figure out how the music was added to the piece and where it came from. Sometimes there is a mixture of these three music sources. Usually, music is underscored in documentaries and doesn't have a strong presence. But not always.

Natural Sound

This is the sound of the shooting environments. The grunts in a boxing gym, an ambulance siren, the rustle of leaves, the gurgling of a baby, the clanging of a prison door, the street sounds of a neighborhood, the stomping of a horse's hoof, the yells on a playground, the frying of food, the clacking of a computer keyboard. Natural sound helps you present the reality of the world you are capturing. It makes the viewer "feel" your story. Natural sound gives a documentary soul. This is a very important element in a documentary and demands special thought and microphoning in the field. In the documentary *Murderball* (2005), the crunching sounds of the wheelchair rugby players as they collide and compete in their matches help add to the excitement and emotion of the story.

The documentary *Murderball* was made by the documentary division at MTV/VH1 in 2005. This mostly vérité cultural study of the members of a wheelchair rugby team uses sound during the competition sequences in a creative and interesting way *(ThinkFilm LLC, 2005)*.

Tip: As you watch a documentary, learn to hear it too. Many times the documentary maker will create montages of pictures and music. Are the natural sounds there too? Do they need to be? Often montages are created with natural sound only. Newscasts use natural sound bites a lot because they grab attention. If the station is doing a story on road repair the first edit in the story is usually the sound of a jackhammer with a picture, then the voice begins. If the story is on a fire, the package will begin with natural sound of the chaos at the scene. A sports story will begin with crowd and/or competition sound. This technique of shocking the viewer with a natural sound bite can be used in documentary making. Look for it and decide if it works in the context of the piece.

Sweetening

This is a technique of adding natural sound and/or sound effects in postproduction. If you are shooting an interview in a park and there are no birds chirping on the interview tape but you wish there were, you can add the bird chirps in post by using a sound-effect library or taping a bird chirping yourself at a different time/location. There might be some ethical problems with some sweetening, because you are altering reality too much. Well-done sweetening is almost impossible to detect, but sometimes it sticks out. Sweetening almost always adds to the storytelling experience. If we see a train, why not hear it also, even if you didn't capture the sound when you shot the footage? Ken Burns, the historical documentarian, has sound techniques he uses all of the time. As he is showing the viewer a still photo, he adds a corresponding sound effect. The audio reinforcement of the message of the photo helps him tell his story and get the viewer more emotionally connected to the moment.

Discussion on how far you can go with sweetening is always interesting. This subject can easily lead into a discussion on the ethical boundaries the production crews will have to set during production and postproduction. In chapter 9 there is an expanded discussion on how much liberty a documentary maker can take in order to include elements that weren't there originally.

ELEMENT SIX: MOVEMENT

Movement involves the viewer in the action. As you watch a documentary, notice how much movement has been put into the piece. Movement can be big (a race car drives through the frame), medium (a child walks through a flower garden), or small (a prisoner rubs his eyes in a close-up). Most of the time it is hard to generate movement in a sit-down or stationary interview setting. If emotion is revealed it is good to create a close-up so the facial movements of the emotions will be accentuated.

Subject Movement

Many times the documentary director will shoot B-roll shots of the interview subjects as they move through their worlds. These types of shots are called walk-bys in the television world and they are usually wide shots of the subject walking through the frame in a setting/location that helps you learn more about the subject. (A coach walks through a locker room, a doctor/nurse walks down a hospital corridor, a teacher walks in front of a school, a dancer walks down the street in leg warmers.)

Often these shots take up to ten seconds to unfold and can serve as introduction shots to lead into the interviews. A narrator might voice over an introduction of the person by name and title/occupation that is timed to fit this action. Other times the interview begins on the audio track during the walk-by.

Shooting B-roll of your subject often allows for your subject to be doing something revealing. Movement can enhance the shot, make it more involving and interesting. Often conversations and B-roll shot in a moving vehicle can provide visually interesting footage. In chapter 6 there are many examples of how to be creative with interviews.

Lens Movement

This can also add to the interest of the documentary. Pans, tilts, zooms, trucks, dollies, arcs, cranes, whip pans, snap zooms, and depth-of-field shifts can all draw attention to some person, action or thing. Old school documentary makers often don't like to rely on these shooting techniques to supply movement and action. Still, used properly, they can enhance a piece. Today the "floating" camera is popular because the camera movement keeps the frame alive and interesting. During editing, motion can be added to still imagery by using the picture-in-picture or pan-and-scan special-effects tool that creates pans, tilts, and zooms. Moving graphic letters within the screen space is also a way to achieve motion. The eye is drawn to motion because it is dynamic. A shot of an empty playground is static. A child swinging on a swing in an otherwise empty playground is dynamic. You will need to think about ways to add movement to your story without it seeming unnatural or forced. And there are times when no movement works.

> **Tip:** An eye for movement is very important in creating a dynamic story. There are exceptions to this rule, but not many. Train yourself to notice how the director, camera operator, and editor create and use movement. Soon you will be deciding how to make your documentary active and exciting.

ELEMENT SEVEN: THREE BASIC SHOOTING STYLES

As you watch more and more documentaries, you will train yourself to become aware of how the camera is being used. There are three basic shooting styles.

Traditional

This visual approach results in the shots looking steady and square to the horizon. There is limited camera movement and interviews are shot on tripods. All shots are "composed." You don't break the traditional head-framing rules of eyes in the upper third of the frame and no one looks off-camera at more than a 30-degree angle so we always see two eyes. B-roll shots are composed and handheld shots are "rock steady." There is no manipulation of the image in postproduction. The traditional camera is calm and always unobtrusively observing what is in front of it. All Ken Burns documentaries use a traditional camera, and watching one of his documentaries will give you a precise idea of how the traditional camera works.

Freestyle

This is the "free" camera that is allowed to break the traditional rules and draw attention to itself. It is almost always handheld, and sometimes it "floats" as the shooter slowly rocks the camera from one side to the other. Whip pans and snap zooms are often added to the visual content of an interview. High- and low-angle camera positioning might be employed. Multiple cameras are often used, with one of the cameras manipulated during postproduction. This could result in black-and-white, sepia-toned, blue, and/or strobed shots mixed in with the color shot from the other camera. MTV pioneered this freestyle approach to interviews. Now these rule-breaking techniques are seen everywhere. The documentary *Overnight* achieves a unique freestyle camera aesthetic.

Mixed Shooting Style

Sometimes mixing shooting styles can create a unique look. This approach must be thought out. One way is to double shoot an interview and/or B-roll with two cameras. One is a tripod, traditional camera and one is freestyle. You cut back and forth between the two looks. *Murderball* employs this mixed use of shooting styles.

Tip: Discussions on how effective the director's choice of shooting style is and whether another style might have enhanced the documentary more are usually lively. Beginning documentarians are often more conservative than you might think they would be. On the other hand, sometimes they can create a "look" that is very effective. One thing is for sure, there are always many points of view on what determines a successful shooting style. Watching a wide array of styles used in successful documentaries is the best way to arrive at your preferred style.

ELEMENT EIGHT: PACE

Pace is a rhythm the documentary generates. This rhythm usually includes some or all of these elements: the rate at which shots change, the tempo of the music, the number and nature of the interviews, B-roll sequences, montage design, and the type of movement within the frame. Pace is a created element and has always been consciously addressed by the documentary maker. Often the pace can change within the piece, especially if the documentary is building to a climax. But the overall pace of the documentary should be thought out in advance. Will fast editing with quick cuts and special effects be part of your plan? How will you use your camera to gather your B-roll? In the documentary *Murderball*, the quick cuts and freestyle camera used in the competition sequences of the wheelchair rugby players are contrasted with calm interview sequences that allow the viewer to get to know who the players are. An in-depth profile of an artist, like in the documentary *Crumb* (1994), will have a different pace than a study of the cultural phenomenon of skateboarding, like *Dogtown and Z-Boys*.

Music, editing rhythm and frequency, interview settings, B-roll sequences, and use of montages usually lead to an understanding of the pace of a piece. Pace is often an unconscious thing for the viewer and only during discussion after viewing does an understanding of the pace reveal itself.

ELEMENT NINE: GRAPHICS

Graphics are the letters, numbers, symbols, artwork, backgrounds and screen locations used to present lettered and/or symbolic information to the viewer. Graphics are electronic and the documentary maker has a huge selection of characters and color palettes. There are four graphic areas that documentary makers have to make decisions on.

• *Title Sequences* • These include the opening title, up-front credits, and segment/chapter titles, if used. The most common documentary opening title graphic consists of white letters over a black background. The opening title often appears after an opening sequence, and it might be on top of moving video, a freeze-frame, manipulated video, special video effect or original artwork. Up-front credits usually include the name of the director, producer, and distribution company and/or the production company. Often there are segment or chapter titles which can be simple or complex. Either can work.

In the documentary *Devil's Playground* (2002), which is a study of the Amish tradition of rumspringa, we follow four Amish teens as they take a year to decide if they want to stay in the Amish community or strike out on their own. The documentary begins with text graphics over montages of Amish life. These words tell a brief history of the Amish people and acclimate the viewer to the basics of Amish life. Throughout the documentary text is used to update the viewer on what has happened to the four main characters.*

Storyteller Identification

Some documentaries don't put the subject's name and title on the screen. The subject is introduced by the narrator/voice-over or introduces him-/herself. This is the more traditional approach. Some documentaries will use letters/words to announce the name and title. Screen position; selection of fonts, edges, drop shadows, and colors; and consistency are usually important factors to consider as graphic titling is decided. Often a visual picture that relates to the story accompanies the letters.

We have all been living for over 20

*DVD Special Feature, *Devil's Playground*, 2001, Stick Figure Productions.

years with the television screen full of words and letters. Traditionalists don't like the screen cluttered with printed information and believe the viewer is interested in the documentary enough to concentrate and remember who people are. Modern documentary makers often like to use lettered IDs because they figure they will help the viewer remember who is who, thus insuring that their stories will be better understood. Either way, you need to think out in advance which method you are going to use.

Credits

Credits are the acknowledgements at the end of the documentary that give everyone involved written, on-screen credit for their work. Once again, the most common credit design is white letters over black. However, sometimes credits appear over outtakes, freeze-frames, artwork, video clips and/or special-effects sequences. The subject matter and pace usually dictate what fits for the credit sequences. Credits can roll, appear as single pages, with one or more names and titles on the page, or be a mixture of both.

In the documentary *Taxi to the Dark Side*, director Alex Gibney pays homage to his deceased father by including a clip in which his father expresses his disgust with the U.S. military for using torture tactics during interrogations in Iraq and Afghanistan. We learn from a graphic that his father was a military interrogator during World War II and the Korean War. This information is a coda to the story and lets us into Alex Gibney's life a little bit.

The effectiveness of credits can be undermined if letters are too small, thin letters become unreadable because they break up on screen, or inter-credit spacing is too little or much. Credits are always the last element done, and often they are overlooked. There are some traditional rules for credit creation that you should know.

1. *People are more important than jobs*. This means a person's name should be at least one size larger than the job title letters.

2. *White letters over a picture background should be edged and/or shadowed*. If they aren't, they will be unreadable if they appear over any white on the screen.

3. *Creative jobs go first, technical jobs second, special thanks last*. Producers, directors, writers, and talent lead off the creative jobs. Camera operators, sound and light people, editors and graphics people lead off the technical jobs.

4. *Choose centered or flush left/right*. Credits are either centered on the screen or even with the left or right side of the screen. There are exceptions, often because of background visuals.

5. *Choose continuous roll or single page*. This decision is often made with time in mind. It takes a lot longer to use single pages.

Information Blocks

Often there is vital lettered information beyond titling that is important to the documentary. Historical information, statistics, poetry, document excerpts, action and character commentary, and other forms of information appear full screen. Once again, the background decision helps make the information effective. Black can be used. Freeze-frames, moving video, layered graphics, and artwork are all candidates for backgrounds. Clever use of graphics can not only provide important information, but also enhance the story.

Tip: As the graphics unfold during the documentary, keep a critical eye for their design aspects. White lettering is the traditional documentary letter color, but if the letters end up over a white shirt, they

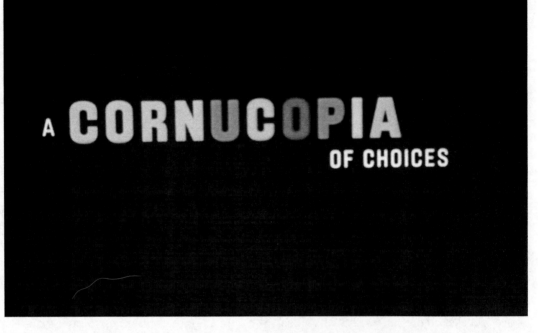

Each chapter of the *Food, Inc.* story of how our processed food gets from farm to table is introduced with a moving graphic title, music, and specific colors *(Perfect Meal, LLC, 2008).*

become unreadable. "Mistakes" like this are often made in documentaries. This is another area where people have strong and conflicting opinions. What is your point of view on lettering, text, and graphics?

ELEMENT 10: MONTAGES

A montage is a short, stand-alone segment that includes some or all of these elements: visuals, music, voice and natural sound. Montages are always themed. They have a specific purpose that advances the point of the documentary, or a segment of the piece. Montages are often emotional in nature because they generate a "feeling" about their subject. They are often used as bridges between one segment and another. Montages present vivid examples of what people are talking about. In *Hoop Dreams*, there are often montages of exciting basketball action; in *4 Little Girls* (1997) and *Into the Arms of Strangers*, there are montages of historical, archival film clips; in *Behind the Music* episodes, there are artist performance montages using shots from music videos. For the documentary maker, creating montages that help give the story variety and art is an exciting challenge.

Tip: Montages are exercises in creativity, and give the producer a chance to reinforce the themes and sentiments within the story. Music usually plays a large role in the power and effectiveness of montage. As you watch documentaries, become aware of how the producer is using the technique of montage. Documentaries often begin and end with montages. Pace is also affected by the use of montage. Where montages appear, and the form they take, is usually food for strong, opinionated discussion.

ELEMENT 11: RESEARCH

Documentaries are long looks at subjects, not quick glances. In order to create a context for the viewer to learn something of value, the documentary maker must search diligently for information that will give the documentary credibility and life. The subjects in a documentary speak for themselves, but the producer/director is responsible for the accuracy of the narration and the arrangement of the subject matter. Sometimes research leads to firsthand involvement.

For the documentary *Devil's Playground*, the producers traveled many times to Lancaster County, PA, to scout the Amish community and find their main characters. Eventually the producers hired another producer to live with an Amish family for seven weeks. While she was embedded with the family, she found the four teens who would be the main characters of the documentary.*

In historical documentaries traditional research sources like libraries, collections, and Web sites can yield archival stills and film/video of your subject. Personal archives from people associated with the documentary subject are an even better source. The National Archives in College Park, MD, has the largest collection of historically oriented media in the United States. Research is usually the starting point of preproduction for historical documentaries.

Often when you are location scouting you meet people who can lead you to information and resources you didn't know existed. Documentaries always seem to take on lives of their own. Along the way you meet new people who know information that might be valuable to the production. In chapter 4, there is further discussion about the research phase of the documentary process.

Tip: As you view documentaries become aware of those moments that reflect research. Most of the time, research-heavy segments are obvious because the narrator will be voicing the information or the screen will fill with researched information. But research is also reflected in the choice of talkers and locations, use of B-roll, and the arrangement of the segments. The lack of research is also often obvious. A strong point of view always needs real-world verification. The success of the documentary often hinges on the results of research.

ELEMENT TWELVE: TONE

Tone is hard to define, but is always a presence in documentaries. Tone includes the style and approach the documentary maker takes toward his/her subject. Tone is a result of the use of the elements, although knowing your tone from the beginning can help you choose and use the elements. Michael Moore takes a direct, in-your-face approach, and the tone of his documentaries is loud and aggressive. Other documentaries are slower and more intimate in tone, like *Born into Brothels* (2004). Some are obsessed and unrelenting in tone, like *Lake of Fire* and *Overnight*. There are documentaries that are neutral in tone, like *Jesus Camp* and *American*

*DVD special feature, *Devil's Playground*, Stick Figure Productions, 2001.

Movie (1999), and others with a sentimental tone like *Man on Wire*. There are documentaries that have an upbeat, fun tone like *Woodstock* (1970) and *Spellbound*, and others that have a dark tone, like *Crumb* and *Salesman* (1969). Some documentaries have dramatic conflict built in, like *King of Kong* (2007) and *Murderball*. Tone impacts all creative decisions and usually reveals itself early on in the production journey, often after long discussions with the crew. Tone can emerge when you are deciding how you will frame your story with the elements.

These 12 elements form a critical prism through which the merits of a documentary can be viewed. You don't want to risk missing the power and effectiveness of a documentary because you are so busy dissecting the parts of the whole. But, hopefully, recognizing these essential elements will become second nature, and the viewing of a documentary will be enhanced for you.

DOCUMENTARY REFERENCES

Each of these documentary references was chosen because it has a creative element or technique that stands out. Some of the most creative filmmaking has occurred while a documentarian is telling his or her story. It is hoped that the curious reader will be motivated to watch many of these documentaries not only for enjoyment, but also for inspiration.

Born into Brothels. 2004. Zana Briski and Ross Kauffman. Red Light Films. This is a personal story of how a woman with a camera can make a difference to neglected kids being raised in the red light district of Calcutta. This Oscar winner was shot with a small digital camera and a lot of love.

The Boys of Baraka. 2005, Rachel Grady and Heidi Ewing. Loki Films. Winner of many prestigious film festival awards including Silver Docs, SXSW, and Cine Golden Eagle. A moving look at a group of inner city kids who travel to a special school in Kenya to find themselves. A digital vérité documentary that also features diary cameras for the kids when they are in Kenya.

Crumb. 1994. Terry Zwigoff. Crumb Partners. This Sundance winner was shot in 16mm color film and has a vibrant, dark aesthetic, not unlike the subject, Robert Crumb. Its vérité style captures the strange, intense life of an iconic artist. The director's comments are interesting as Zwigoff explains how odd it is to make a documentary about a friend and iconic cultural figure.

Devil's Playground. 2001. Lucy Walker. Stick Figure Productions. This was an HBO low budget project that follows four Amish teens in Lancaster, PA, as they go through a coming-of-age period called Rumspringa. It was shot in digital video by a young crew that lived with the Amish community, won the trust of the subjects, and captured a fascinating story.

Dogtown and Z-Boys. 2001. Stacy Peralta. Vans, Inc., and Sony Entertainment. Double Sundance winner. Sean Penn narrates this fast-paced, creative telling of the origins of skateboarding. Peralta uses his 16mm skills to add a jumpy, layered look to his B-roll and montages. He mixes black and white interviews with color B-roll and home movie archival footage.

The Fog of War. 2003. Sony Pictures Classics, Inc. Errol Morris's Academy Award–winning study of the psyche of Robert McNamara as he relates his take on recent military history. The interview settings are disorienting and artistic. They provide an ironic contrast to McNamara's cocksure attitude that his version of history is the right one.

Food, Inc. 2008. Robert Kenner. Perfect Meal LLC. This eye-opening, Academy Award–nominated look at U.S. agribusiness makes the case for more environmentally friendly and health conscious processing of our meat, grain, and vegetables. Interesting on-location interviews, and some clever transitions using graphics and beauty shots.

4 Little Girls. 1998. Spike Lee. Home Box Office. This sensitive, well-researched, historical documentary retells the tragic story of the civil rights church bombing in Birmingham, AL, in 1963. The parents and families of the

four slain girls relate the story in intimate interviews.

Gonzo. 2008. Alex Gibney. HDNet Films LLC. An artistic, gritty study of rogue journalist Hunter Thompson. Director Gibney uses a green screen in his recreations that is creative and effective. How time is presented is also interesting. He chose to not tell Thompson's story chronologically.

Grizzly Man. 2005. Lionsgate Films, Inc. Werner Herzog's documentary was compiled from over 100 hours of personal video footage shot by Timothy Treadwell, the tragic subject of the film. Herzog narrates and appears in this unique, Academy Award–nominated documentary.

Hoop Dreams. 1994. Steve James. New Line Home Entertainment, Inc. This three-hour, vérité-style documentary took five years to make (1989–1994) and generated 250 hours of raw footage. It was shot on video using a Betacam video camera. This documentary remains a classic example of dedicated vérité filmmaking.

Into the Arms of Strangers: Tales of the Kindertransport. 2000. Deborah Oppenheimer (producer) and Mark Jonathan Harris (director). This moving, inspirational story of how 10,000 children, mostly Jewish, were sent by their families to England to avoid the Nazis in Germany. Spectacular, pristine archival footage is presented from a child's point of view. Judy Dench narrates this Academy Award winner.

Jesus Camp. 2006. Heidi Ewing and Rachel Grady. Loki Films, Inc. This intense, vérité film about evangelical Pentecostal Christians preparing for religious warfare by running a religious camp every summer is shocking and a cautionary tale. It won many film festivals and was nominated for an Academy Award.

King of Kong. 2007. Seth Gordon. LargeLab. This low-budget, digital documentary explores the world of arcade gaming by following the top two scoring gamers as they compete for the highest score. Production values are low but the story is compelling.

Lake of Fire. 2006. Tony Kaye. Anonymous Content. This beautifully shot black and white documentary deals with the controversial issue of abortion. Both sides are strongly presented and the filmmaker leaves it up to the audience to decide for themselves. It was a labor of love and took 16 years to make.

Murderball. 2005. Henry Alex Rubin and Dana Adam Shapiro. ThinkFilm LLC. The documentary was made by the documentary division at MTV/VH1. This mostly vérité cultural study of the members of a wheelchair rugby team uses sound during the competition sequences in a creative and interesting way. It was a low-budget, digital film that shows if you have the story, production values don't have to be huge. It was nominated for an Academy Award.

Overnight. 2004. Tony Montana and Mark Brian Smith. DNP Productions. This wild profile of a young director self-destructing in Hollywood took eight years to make. It is a mad mix of film, video, special effects, and home movies. At one point the subject fires the director.

Salesman. 1969. The Maysles Brothers. This ground-breaking, vérité documentary follows four salesmen as they go door-to-door selling bibles. The Maysles brothers were able to penetrate the lives of the salesmen and record an everyman slice of life. This intimate style of extended filming with your subjects set the stage for all of the vérité documentaries that followed.

Spellbound. 2002. Jeff Blitz. Blitz/Welch. This first-time documentary was conceived while Jeff Blitz was a student. Almost all of the footage was shot with a low-end digital camera and a crew of two. It is a prime example of how a good story can be told with a minimum of cost and technology.

Supersize Me. 2004. Morgan Spurlock. Kathbur Pictures. Morgan Spurlock channels Michael Moore and takes on the overweight epidemic in the United States. He lives on McDonald's food for 30 days and lets the viewer keep him company.

Taxi to the Dark Side. 2007. Alex Gibney. Jigsaw Productions. A powerful look at the U.S. policy of torture and questionable interrogation methods being used in the Middle East wars. It uses the sad case of an innocent Afghan taxi driver's torture and death as the springboard. Some interesting interview setups and creative B-roll.

The Thin Blue Line. 1988. Errol Morris. Third Floor Productions. Perhaps the most influential and groundbreaking documentary of the last 22 years. Morris tells the story of the murder of a police officer in Dallas and reveals that the wrong man is serving a life sentence. Morris brings art to the film by using a score by Philip Glass and using stylized recreations to make the point that the truth is often hard to find.

Wasted Youth. 2000. Carolyn Scharf and Rasheed Daniel. Rowan University. Binge drinking and its tragic consequences are the subject of this social issue documentary that has been viewed by tens of thousands of high school and college students. Creative use of a recurring surreal party reenactment enhances the message.

Who Killed the Electric Car? 2006. Chris Paine. Sony Pictures Classics. This well researched look at the auto industry's love/hate affair with electric cars is narrated by Martin Sheen. It's a good example of how a well known narrator can add impact to your documentary.

Woodstock. 1970. Michael Wadleigh. Wadleigh-Maurice. This Oscar winner pioneered the genre of concert films. The use of multiple images on the screen, creative B-roll, excellent sound mix, and shooting with many cameras resulted in an event being captured for entertainment, historical, and cultural purposes. It harkens back to Leni Riefenstahl's work and presages Bud Greenspan's Olympic Games documentaries.

3. Design and Aesthetics

There has been a visual revolution going on for over 30 years that is just now beginning to be recognized. You can probably date the revolution to August 1, 1981, which was the day MTV went on the air. The young, creative minds who designed the "look" for this new music network, whose target audience was 12- to 22-year-olds, remind me of what was going on during the late Renaissance. In those days, new technologies were opening up new ways to do old things. Just as the improvement in paints, brushes and canvas gave the Renaissance painters the ability to work larger and deal with light in a different way, the arrival of computer animation and graphics made the creation of an edgy, in-your-face "look" for MTV exciting and new.

During the Renaissance, new instruments made new sounds and rhythms possible for the orchestras and composers. New dyes, fabrics and improved weaving technology made clothing brighter and enabled fashion to change more quickly. If you were walking down the main street of Florence, Italy, in 1623, you would see painted and sculpted images, hear sounds, and see fashions that often had been created together, by the same core group of people. This merging of art forms energized the Renaissance culture and stimulated younger members to learn these new art forms and experiment with them.

In 1981 hip-hop was just emerging from the niche culture of the Bronx, NY.

MTV hadn't discovered it yet, but a lot of the same forces were driving both phenomena. Most people agree that hip-hop originally contained four basic elements: graffiti art, break dancing, DJ backup record scratching, and an emcee rapping. Today, hip-hop is a lifestyle and culture unto itself. MTV was able to translate many of these elements onto the screen. Graffiti art became the MTV logo that changed every day and many other graphic symbols and images. Break dancing moved into music videos, then new dance and body moves originated in the music videos and migrated back out into the youth culture, black, Latino, and white. VJs replaced DJs and slowly, then quickly, rapping moved into suburban white neighborhoods where it thrived right along with its urban audience.

New technologies were changing how art and music were used. Music videos were creative visual artworks that showcased new sounds in music. Special visual and sound effects along with fast-cut editing techniques made listening to music a new visual experience. There was freedom in the way musical artists dressed and looked. They could recreate themselves any time they wanted. Think MC Hammer's pants, grunge flannel shirts, Michael Jackson's glove, the Go-Gos' outfits, ZZ Top's long coats and beards, Bono's bandana, Adam Ant's earring, Pink's hair, Britney Spears' belly-button ring, Seal's bald head, Billy Idol's bleached hair, or

Madonna's raggedy, unmatched clothes. Like the main street in Florence in the 1620s, sometimes fashion changed rapidly, and sometimes it stuck around.

Rap and R & B were discovering the sampling technique of using distorted playback of some other music as part of a new song. They were incorporating the process of making sounds into the final composite sound. Record scratching, sampling, and techno reverb became a favorite of most artists in their teens and 20s. Lots of times different artists would sing different tunes as they sang together. New electronic sounds were becoming part of the sound of a song. Clothing became part of the hip-hop "look." Poetry and spoken word carried big messages that sometimes took multiple listenings to decipher. Dance and body moves were part of the performance. Hip-hop was a lifestyle that included music, poetry, fashion, technology, message and soul. You did a lot of things all at once. You were in perpetual motion. You had a language that came out of your lifestyle. Our society was going through a cultural renaissance. So much of this emergence happened because MTV was combining art and technology, just the way the Renaissance did.

The arrival of the printing press in the late 1400s enabled composers to score and print their music so they could share it with other countries and cultures. As a result the first musical superstars began to emerge. The modern equivalent is our ability for the last 20 years to listen to our music anywhere, anytime. We download music and share it with anyone, everyone.

One of the new discoveries of Renaissance artists was perspective. Depth in the image and the corresponding shift in size became part of artistry. The modern equivalent of this revolutionary discovery is "layering." Just as Botticelli and Giotto created sculpture and paintings that had merged foregrounds and backgrounds, now sources as diverse as Disney, Hollywood, MTV, and the advertising industry use moving images to create multilayered images via computer animation and digital layering. When you watch a classic music video like Peter Gabriel's "Sledgehammer," you are watching abstract expressionism in a moving, layered setting enhancing the music.

Even conservative television producers like ESPN, MSNBC, the Weather Channel, and Bloomberg Television are trying to make the talking heads exciting by layering and moving a diverse set of images through the screen. The creative and technological freedom of the '80s and '90s has led to today, when we don't have to wait to see what the cutting-edge video gamers, Industrial Light & Magic wizards, or MTV creative services department folks are doing. We can do it ourselves at home with our cheap video cameras and editing software.

MTV and the Renaissance are/were all about breaking the old rules and inventing new ones. The camera-on-a-tripod mentality of creating pictures that were level to the horizon and rock steady was unfun and counterproductive to a revolutionary approach to program content design. Handheld cameras were everywhere: in the studio, in the field, in the music videos. The "floating" camera that gently rocked and rolled while a crazed band member gave you a short bite on world hunger became the norm. The liberated camera also gave us whip pans, snap zooms, 360-degree spins and the feeling that life is in motion most of the time, which it is.

MTV just about invented the mainstream use of the editing techniques of the jump cut, rapid-fire edits, multiple screens, and layered imagery that we accept today without a second thought. The advertising industry, ever hungry to connect with young target audiences, realized the effectiveness of this new, fast-cut, image-creation style and jumped right in.

Just as hip-hop music often has two or more rhythms, beats and tunes going on, MTV invented the two-camera interview/coverage visual technique. Now, if you want to interview Lady Gaga, you bring two cameras and they both roll during the interview. One camera is a more-or-less normal, handheld camera, but the other camera is trying to be totally different. Maybe it is a low-angle, jittery camera, or maybe it runs through snap-zoom sequences, or maybe it tapes the other camera shooting the interview, or maybe it will be strobed when the piece is edited, or maybe it will be colorized blue or black-and-white. MTV opened up the process of making pictures and enabled people to be independent and creative. The possibilities became endless rather than limiting, just like they did for the visual artists of the Renaissance who broke out of their picture frames and let their imaginations go.

As you design your "look," don't feel restrained in any way. Although the vast majority of documentaries are traditionally shot and edited, incorporating a new use of the camera or a layered screen effect or a behind-the-scenes aesthetic might work for you and your story.

Here are some critical areas that should be addressed before shooting begins. These design decisions should be organic to the story you are telling. The feel and tone of your documentary will help you decide on how to proceed. Obviously, a documentary on the cultural phenomenon of professional wrestling will look different than an extended character study of a Nobel Prize–winning physicist. Or will it? Creativity is a subjective force in all of us. There is no "right" way to design your documentary. There is only your way. Trust your instincts, but give everything a lot of thought before you proceed.

Your "Look"

As you begin to solidify your idea for a documentary and locate the people who will tell your story, there is a need to address the "look" and "sound" of your completed documentary. As the analysis of the 12 elements in the previous chapter reveals, you must customize your use of the elements to your subject matter.

Here is an overview list of design and aesthetic decisions every documentary maker should make before shooting begins. Design and your personal aesthetic are the way art becomes part of your documentary. Documentary makers are filmmakers. Film has always had an art component. You may not perceive yourself as an artist, but if you are telling a story you are passionate about, then bringing artistic design elements to your story enhances it and enables you to entertain while you document reality.

Shooting Styles

As discussed in chapter 1, there are three ways to approach capturing the content of your story. Each involves how you use the camera, as well as how you tell your story.

• **Vérité Documentary Making** • This approach can be best defined as when the camera arrives on the scene no one knows what will happen. The camera is observing reality and trying to stay as innocuous as possible. Often this style is called "fly on the wall." Many documentary makers who shoot in this vérité style don't like this term, because they realize that no matter how hard you try to stay out of the action, you will always influence people and events to some degree ... unlike the fly.

Albert and Robert Maysles, the great vérité documentary makers, began working in the 1960s. Albert Maysles was still making vérité documentaries in 2010. Both can often be heard off camera talking to their subjects and generating action/reaction. In *Gimme Shelter* (1969) and *Grey Gardens* (1975), they became part of the story as they won the trust of their subjects and followed the story.

In this photo, David Maysles appears on camera explaining a detail to Rolling Stone member Charlie Watt. His brother Albert is operating the camera. The documentary is the vérité classic *Gimme Shelter (Maysles Brothers Films, Inc., 1970).*

Vérité documentary making requires time, patience, and trust. By using the camera to observe their subjects for long periods of time, documentary makers become entwined with their subjects. Most of the time the respect and trust the documentary makers earn result in a positive relationship with their subjects. Vérité documentary makers don't know where the story is going, but document the action as it happens. Eventually a story emerges with all of the elements of storytelling, including compelling characters, emotion, conflict, climax, and resolution. Because vérité documentaries often lead the makers into uncharted waters, decision making isn't easy both during production and editing.

Jesus Camp and *The Boys of Baraka* are two vérité documentaries made by Rachel Grady and Heidi Ewing. *Jesus Camp* explores the world of evangelical Pentecostal Christians while focusing on the woman who runs a summer camp for Pentecostal children, and three of the kids who attend the camp. In *The Boys of Baraka*, a group of inner-city kids from Baltimore go to a school in Kenya in an attempt to change their negative life patterns. This documentary took three years to make. Both documentaries allow the subjects to show and tell us their stories. However, how to edit the stories wasn't always clear.

Heidi Ewing and Rachel Grady took one year to research, create, shoot, and edit *Jesus Camp*. They didn't always agree on certain design and aesthetic elements. The opening originally was going to be a montage of the Pentecostal evangelical members during their highly emotional worship services. After many discussions and rough cuts, Ewing and Grady agreed to use the existing opening, which shows a Midwestern townscape of fast-food businesses surrounded by vast spaces and has a radio newscast on the sound track. Another area they initially disagreed on was the music sound track. They commissioned an original music score that features a low-base synthesized sound that sets a mood some viewers might interpret as ominous. They debated about whether this sound would be interpreted as a negative editorial comment by them. In the end they used the music.*

*Four times during the period of 2007 to 2010 directors Heidi Ewing and Rachel Grady (*The Boys of Baraka* and *Jesus Camp*) participated in a visiting artist series at Rowan University. In a lecture during the spring 2008 semester they discussed how they sometimes disagreed on production and creative elements and had to find a way to settle the disputes. They used the problem of deciding on a music score for *Jesus Camp* as one of their hardest disagreements to resolve.

Scared Straight! is a riveting 1978 vérité documentary shot in a prison in one day. *Scared Straight!* captures the raw intensity of a group of lifers at Rahway State Prison in New Jersey while they give 17 at-risk teenagers a heart-stopping glimpse of what life is like in a maximum-security prison. Director Arnold Shapiro was given one chance to capture the frenetic interaction of the kids and the lifers. He shot four extra days of B-roll in the kids' neighborhoods. More than almost any other vérité documentary, *Scared Straight!* captures the pure actions and emotions of a small group of people in a confined place. *Scared Straight!* is highly recommended for the use of its vérité cameras and its effective yet unobtrusive editing.

Scared Straight! has been seen by millions of Americans. It debuted on PBS in 1978 and won two Emmys and an Academy Award in 1979. Since then it has continued to air regularly on television, and has been seen in thousands of high schools throughout the country. It is worth examining *Scared Straight!* in detail because it is a seminal social-issue documentary. In a 2001 interview with me, Arnold Shapiro discussed the background and experience of making *Scared Straight!*:

> In January 1978 I read an article in *Reader's Digest* about Rahway Prison's lifers program for at-risk juveniles and I was blown away by it. I called the prison and asked if a similar program was going on in California. They said it was only going on here in New Jersey and they asked me to come and see them in action.
>
> I talked to management and said I wanted to take a research trip to the prison because I thought this could be a really powerful documentary. I went, watched the sessions with the kids and met with the lifers. It was a very scary situation. I'd never been inside a prison and here I was in a maximum-security prison alone with

the lifers. No guards around or anything. They are intimidating guys.

> I went back and met with the station management and said this could be the most astounding documentary ever. But you have to understand there will be all this obscene language in it. You can't bleep it out. It would have to be there.
>
> The auditorium stage in the prison where they held the sessions would be lit before we began shooting. We'd have two cameras going. We'd pre-interview the kids and get signed releases from the kids' parents. We'd show the kids before they went in. Cocky and boastful. We would show the whole session and do a follow-up with the kids six months later. We'd get their reactions right after they came out from the prison. We'd get a celebrity host.
>
> Not counting my salary, $600/week, the budget for *Scared Straight!* was $39,000. Most of that was for 16 mm film stock. They gave me permission to do it. In the course of April and May, 1978, *Scared Straight!* was produced.*

But occasionally the relationship between maker and subject goes sour, even though a worthy documentary arises. *Overnight* and *The Wonderful, Horrible Life of Leni Riefenstahl* (1993) are two examples. In both cases the documentary maker set out to capture a strong personality, and in both cases the personalities

Overnight **is a study of an artist self–destructing in Hollywood. The documentary makers used many kinds of cameras, including a 16 mm film camera that shot in black and white. The result was a grainy, jumpy look that mirrored the downfall of the subject, Troy Duffy** *(DNP Productions LLC, 2004).*

*These words were transcribed from an interview I had with Arnold Shapiro on March 26, 2001.

fought and argued with the makers. In the case of *Overnight*, the subject, Troy Duffy, fired the documentary makers. Vérité documentaries are high-risk projects that challenge the makers to stay with the subjects and find the story. Before embarking on a vérité documentary, it is a good idea to watch documentaries like the ones mentioned above.

Before you commit to a vérité approach you need to ask yourself a few questions about the story, time, flexibility, and expenses.

THE STORY

A vérité approach means you don't know how the story will end. You have found some interesting people or issue or event, and you are following them or it hoping you will discover compelling characters, interesting action, a climax, and a natural ending. This is a risk that plays out over time. *The Devil Rode on Horseback* (2007) and *American Movie* are two very different vérité films that paid off for the makers with built-in drama and climaxes. Vérité documentaries are exciting, scary, and anxiety filled, but have a huge payoff because they are as close as documentary making gets to capturing unaltered reality.

TIME

Plan to spend a lot of time researching your subject and people before you are ready to begin shooting. Your subjects need to get to know you and understand your objective isn't exploitative or self-centered. Once you begin shooting, you must follow the story wherever it leads. Often the storyline changes and you get rerouted in concept, space and time. Your commitment and dedication get tested as much as or more than your subjects'. Your life becomes consumed by your story. There are low points, maybe even conflicts between you, the subjects, and your crew. You must push through these times until you follow the story to the end. What

keeps you going is the thought that you are contributing to the collective knowledge of the human condition, and that is a beautiful thing.

FLEXIBILITY

Vérité documentaries are constantly shifting course and moving down new roads. You must accept this and ride the wave of your story. Although you may have done extensive research prior to shooting, external forces usually require your adapting to new situations. The unknown is always a force in vérité documentaries.

EXPENSES

Since vérité documentaries unfold over an unknown amount of time, you must stay with the story and this will cost money in terms of travel, storage, crews, and equipment. So factor all of this in before you begin the vérité journey.

• **Directed Documentary Making** • A directed documentary is one where all the elements of the documentary, except what people say, are controlled by the documentary maker. For instance, in a directed interview the subject is asked/told to sit in a certain area, the camera is positioned by the director, the shot is composed, production lights might be used, a microphone is strategically positioned, and a series of questions are asked by the director off-camera.

Errol Morris, who has made classic documentaries like *The Fog of War* and *The Thin Blue Line*, is a good example of a director who uses this style. Before he begins shooting his documentaries, he thoroughly researches his story, creates a detailed treatment of it, finds and screens his talkers, creates sets/places where they can be interviewed, and then uses graphics, recreations, archival B-roll, and mood music to enhance his story. The impact of the director is total. Only the words the subjects use are unknown. When the interviews are complete, Morris crafts his documentary.

In a similar manner, Ken Burns, the master of the historical documentary, controls all aspects of his stories including the interviews. He carefully crafts questions that lead his storytellers through the content they are providing to fill in the larger story. His use of research, archival footage, recreations, music, narration, and interviews forms a story that informs, inspires, and entertains.

When Spike Lee decided to make *4 Little Girls*, he was able to plan all aspects of the documentary: interviews, interview settings, use of archival footage, and creative B-roll locations and sequences. Lee researched the tragic event and first contacted his storytellers in 1993. But it wasn't until 1998 that he finally got permission from his last storyteller. The documentary was a labor of love. When Lee was shooting the interviews, there were only two people present beside the interviewee: Lee and his camera operator.*

Because so much of the directed documentary process is controlled by the director/producer, the production process is usually shorter and more controllable. All aspects can be planned, so a shooting schedule is possible. Locations can be determined, B-roll can be planned, and a finish deadline can be established. Directed documentaries have a much better chance of being pre-sold, because the essence of the story is known, and all of the steps toward completed product can be fixed into a timeline.

• **Directed and Vérité Mixed** • A relatively new hybrid of these two styles of production is created by mixing the vérité and directed styles. This mix includes vérité shooting for B-roll and perhaps some spontaneous interviews, while directed sequences include some/all of the interviews, use of archival footage, and recreations.

Murderball is a good example of this hybrid mix. The action sequences of the wheelchair rugby competition and some B-roll of the athletes are shot vérité style, while many of the interviews and some B-roll sequences are composed and directed.

Similarly, in Michael Moore's documentaries his on-camera ambush sequences are vérité, while his narrated sequences are directed. In *Bowling for Columbine* (2002) he enters a bank to get a free gun from a teller and the camera observes it all vérité style. Later on in the film Moore creates directed sequences about guns through a mix of archival footage, animation, film clips, graphics, and voice-over narration.

Michael Moore is a controversial documentarian. He sees the documentary form as a means to promote his populist agenda. He sees himself as the champion of the common person. He thinks that America needs fixing in many areas and he sets out in his hosted documentaries to present the problems and find solutions. His documentaries have been seen by more people than any documentaries ever. *Roger and Me* (unemployment in the auto industry), *Fahrenheit 9/11* (the aftermath of the Twin Towers tragedy), *Bowling for Columbine* (gun control), *Sicko* (health care), and *Capitalism: A Love Story* (the stock market crash in 2007) have earned him millions of dollars and world renown. He doesn't like the way capitalism has eroded our lives and values. He wants the United States to find the way back to honest politicians and ethical businesses. Along the way he has upset many citizens.

Personally, I like Michael Moore and his documentaries. He is a healthy voice in

*DVD Special Feature. *4 Little Girls*. Spike Lee explains his history of finding, then deciding to make *4 Little Girls*. After reading an article in the *New York Times* on the thirtieth anniversary of the Birmingham bombings he suddenly felt he had to make the documentary. He visited the families off and on for many years until he finally got their permission to be interviewed for the documentary.

the crowd of agendas we have to deal with every day. He has created a new documentary form that features his curious, opinionated, on-camera everyman persona, who ambushes leaders and followers alike. He asks basic questions about important issues, then gives his own answers in a wondering, sometimes comedic style. He is the only documentary maker living who can fill a Cineplex theater every day for a long run. He has used his money to support independent filmmakers, ACLU cases, and other civil rights and liberties causes. He has spawned many new documentary makers who want to address social issues and tell us about them on camera. John Grierson, who was the first socially active documentarian in the 1930s, would enjoy Michael Moore and his work. Grierson saw the art of documentary as a hammer, not a mirror. Michael Moore is a direct descendent. He is a positive, controversial force in today's documentary world.

Most documentary makers today tell their stories using a mixture of both of these styles. There is a freedom of form now that is liberating to the documentary maker. It is possible to use all of the storytelling tools to tell the story. A lot of thought has to go into deciding what style you are going to use. Watching a lot of documentaries will help you decide which style appeals to you. The story and the people are always the most important elements. But how you showcase your story can enhance the documentary a lot.

Use of the Camera

After you have decided on your stylistic approach, the next decision should be how you are going to use the camera. As discussed in chapter 1, there are two basic aesthetic approaches to camera work: traditional and freestyle. Although these approaches are different, there might be some overlap. Here is a more detailed rundown of these two uses of the camera.

In 1989, Michael Moore made a landmark documentary called *Roger and Me*. Using an on-camera, everyman approach, he set out to find Roger Smith, the president of General Motors, to get answers about why companies were closing factories and outsourcing their manufacturing. This participatory vérité style was new and entertaining. He would go on to set box-office records for his documentary films *(Warner Brothers Entertainment, 2003)*.

• **Traditional** • This use of the camera involves a calm, steady camera, either on a tripod, handheld rock steady, or rigged into a steady cam. The rules of framing are observed: the horizon is always horizontal to the top and bottom of the screen/viewfinder. Head shots have the eyes in the upper third of the frame and graphic IDs, if used, are in the lower third of the frame. The 30-degree rule that sets the eye line of the subject vis-à-vis the camera, so the viewer will be able to see both eyes of the subject, is observed. The traditional camera composes shots using the rule of crossed thirds. The items in the frame are balanced. The aesthetic of the traditional camera is to allow the people, objects, and action to unfold within the frame and not draw attention to the camera. All pans, tilts, and zooms are slow, steady and smooth.

• **Freestyle** • This camera is freer. It is not on a tripod. It moves and often floats around its subjects. While it might observe the rules of framing, it also breaks the rules. Dutch angles, snap zooms, whip pans, on-camera focusing/refocusing are all part of the freestyle repertoire. The camera often becomes part of the scene, with subjects reacting and speaking directly to the camera. The frame is alive with movement. MTV/VH1, ESPN, and many other cable networks pioneered this style in the early '80s. Now we accept a moving camera aesthetic.

When a camera is used with thought and imagination, people will accept the results when it breaks the rules.

• **Some Examples of Camera Use** • In *No Direction Home* (2005), the documentary about the folk-rock singer Bob Dylan, the interviews with the people who know and comment about Dylan are shot in familiar environments, and the camera is traditional in framing, always moving slowly and smoothly. The people are calm as they try to articulate who Dylan is. During the interview sequences with Dylan, the traditional camera doesn't move at all as Dylan fidgets and tries to explain who he is. The contrast reinforces the impression many people have that Dylan is not easy to pin down or categorize.

In *Overnight* the freestyle camera is constantly moving, jumping, jerking, and calling attention to itself. The use of the camera adds to the frenzy of the main subject's life.

Size of the Camera: Intrusion

The size of the camera can impact how you use it. If you are using a large film or HD camera, then you will be limited in a few areas. Larger cameras don't move as quickly as smaller ones. If your subject includes fast-moving people and on-the-fly B-roll, maybe a smaller camera is preferable.

A small, digital camera and an FM wireless lavalier microphone that transmits to the camera can be mobile, fast, and unobtrusive. A crew of two can accomplish a lot. *Spellbound*, a documentary that features eight kids who were part of the national spelling bee competition, was shot with a crew of two, except for the national finals sequences. The two-person crew was able to relax the subjects enough to penetrate their natural reserve. When working in the real world with people who have never been part of the media, smaller is usually better.

If you are shooting staged interviews with subjects in studios, hotel rooms, homes, or workplaces, and they are going to be directed, then larger, more expensive cameras can be used. Still, the director must guide the subject into an interview zone where the subject forgets the equipment and focuses on the story.

Filmmaker Keiko Ibi made an Academy Award–winning documentary about older New Yorkers who had decided to act in a community center play about dating. The documentary is called *The Personals* and Ibi shot most of the footage in the old folks' apartments. She chose to use a small, digital camera and a crew of two so the seniors wouldn't be intimidated. Over time they revealed themselves and created a fascinating story.

The Personals was a master's thesis film for Keiko Ibi at NYU. *The Personals* follows a group of senior citizens as they rehearse and perform an original play at a community theater on the Lower East Side of Manhattan. Drawn from the comedy and drama of the seniors' lives, the play features elderly people looking for dates through the personal ads. As the rehearsals progress, the camera turns to the individual members of the group in their homes in an attempt to uncover both the joys and sorrows of growing old in America. With longing for love, sex, and relationships as its theme, *The Personals* creates a surprisingly humorous and compelling portrait of a not-often-seen segment of our society.

As Ibi followed the seniors, she became part of their lives and they opened up to her. Her completed documentary was 78 minutes long. She submitted it blind to HBO's documentary division in 1998. HBO screened the documentary, liked it, and offered to buy the rights for distribution. HBO then asked Ibi to edit the documentary down to under 40 minutes, which she did. HBO provided an editor and an Avid computer. *The Personals* won an Academy Award in 1998 for Best Short Documentary. Ibi's production story is an interesting one. She explained it to me in 2001.

> When I enrolled at NYU, I had no thought of making documentaries. I wanted to be a writer and director of narrative films. During the summer of 1996, I took an acting class just for fun. The teacher was also the director of an acting class for a group of senior citizens on the Lower East Side of New York. When our acting class was over, he invited members of the class to his house for a party and some of the seniors from the senior center were there. That was how I met them. They told me about the play they were in called *The Personals*.
>
> I was intrigued. I didn't see them as old people, or Jewish people, I just saw them as interesting people. I think it was good that I didn't have preconceived ideas about them culturally or generation-wise. For me this was educational. I was able to see them with a fresh eye.
>
> Older people tend to be more open sometimes because they don't care what people think anymore. Also, I wasn't in their community or their generation so what they told me wasn't going to go anywhere in their neighborhood. I was just a girl from Japan who wanted to know about them.
>
> This was in May. I was looking for a project to do over the summer break. That is when I decided to make a documentary on the seniors as my thesis project. They accepted me and liked that I was a[n] NYU student and would be doing a thesis project on them.
>
> The crew was always two people. And sometimes I went alone myself. I liked a small crew. If I had brought a large crew and made it a big production, the seniors would have felt things aren't normal. And I didn't want them to feel that way. I might have sacrificed some in visuals. It could be a lot prettier. It could be lit better. But I felt high production values weren't as important as the seniors feeling relaxed.
>
> You want to see them in their space. See what their lives are like. I asked them what they normally do and I shot B-roll of them. Sometimes I asked them to do it again. I shot the footage of their personal home habits. I shot the details so I could cut the sequences. I made different shots and angles. The documentary cameraman has to know while they are shooting sequences how shots will cut together during editing.
>
> I was polite and not intrusive. I was very respectful. And they loved that. I tried to be a friend and a good listener first. It's important with me to make a better connection with the people first, whether it's going to serve my film or not, to have a good relationship is important.
>
> I had prepared questions for them. I asked them questions that would take them from their first memories right up until now. I asked family histories and details. I asked about their relationships throughout their lives. Daughters, sons, parents, spouses. If things got interesting I just stayed on that subject.
>
> I asked them all basic life-history questions and let them lead me to other personal details. As they remembered things they would go on. I listened to them.
>
> In the beginning I just followed my instincts. I thought they were interesting people and I should do a project with them. Now that I have more confidence, my choices are still what my instincts tell me to do. If you keep following what you want to do, in the end it will come together. You will be rewarded. I am now more sure of myself than I was three years ago.
>
> I like to do documentaries about things

I know nothing about. Most documentary makers like to make pieces on their families or people who are close to them. They like to make pieces about their life's journey. I'm the opposite of that. I find something that interests me and I learn about it, then make a documentary. I'm not interested in who I am and where I come from. I want to learn new things. I'm a gambler.*

A different example is how Deborah Oppenheimer recorded the interviews for the Academy Award–winning documentary *Into the Arms of Strangers*. This historical documentary about German-Jewish children who survived the Nazis in World War II by being adopted by British families featured many older British and American citizens recalling their childhood war experiences. Since they lived in a wide variety of places, Oppenheimer had many of them come to London and shot their interviews in a hotel room. An abstract background was used so no matter where or when the interview was shot, the background looked the same. This staged setting allowed for lights and a larger camera.

Color

Often color can be introduced into your documentary to enhance the visual effect. If you are thinking like this you are probably going to be making a directed documentary. There are many ways to introduce color.

• **Lighting of Faces** • Gelled lights allow the director to add color to the subject. A blue side- or backlight on the subject gives a cold/stark effect, which might fit when your subject is telling a dark story. Sometimes an amber gel can warm up a subject's aura. Darker fleshtones, in particular, can be warmed up with an amber gel.

Colors that distort the "real" look of fleshtones can be effective. In a documentary called *Broken Glass* (2006), which deals with crystal meth addiction, the documentary makers Jennah Trocchia and Jonathan Waller decided to use only a mixture of gelled light on the two addict storytellers. One addict had green, purple, and blue colors mixed on his face and background, while the other had blue, green and red. The interviews were shot with three cameras, two of which were handheld and used Dutch angles. The overall effect was to reinforce the distorted world of meth addiction.

Harsh white light from a lighting instrument on a face and/or background can convey an otherworldly feel, like something is out of control or blinding. In chapter 6, there are more examples of how to use lighting effects during interviews.

• **Backgrounds** • Often a colored gel shined onto the background can give the frame an abstract or stylized feel. The viewer sees a subject lit normally, but the background has been changed to blue, green, red, purple, orange, or yellow. The colors can cover a reality set like a home or workplace, or be used in a studio on a background curtain or textured surface. Matching a color to each subject can help reveal who the person is and where they fit in the story. In a documentary called *Movement X* (2008), the documentary makers Cindy Lewandowski and Susan Meriduena follow a performance artist team through its last season. The interviews were shot in a studio and the backgrounds were created with gelled lighting. There were four members of the team who told their stories, and each had an abstract mixture of yellow, red, and gold colors as his/her background. This created a warm, intense feeling. The fifth subject was the coach, and he was given a blue background. He was the cooler personality

---

*These words were transcribed from an interview I had with Keiko Ibi on June 22, 2001.

who had to remain calm while the team members were more passionate and emotional.

Backgrounds like canvases, walls, bricks, wood, metal, and objects of art can be enhanced with gelled color. The color makes the background have an abstract look and helps project the character of your subject.

Errol Morris often likes to create abstract backgrounds with light to give a disorienting feel to where his subjects are. In *The Fog of War* and his TV series *First Person*, he uses white and blue lights to light an abstract set featuring square glass-like panels. The feeling you get is one of being off balance and disoriented, which contrasts with the hardcore reality of the stories the subjects are telling.

• **Wardrobe** • Sometimes a meaningful color is part of the wardrobe of a subject or subjects. What your storytellers wear also helps tell the story. There is an old rule that you should never wear white or stripes. White can often shut down the camera's iris because of the reflected light back into the lens, and stripes can create what is called the moiré effect. This is when close parallel lines have a vibrating effect. Neckties and striped dresses are the biggest culprits. If you are shooting a series of interviews, there is probably a clothing parameter you want to establish. You probably don't want neckties, suits, and formal dresses mixed in with tie-dyed T-shirts and halter tops.

• **Color Themes** • Often a color will symbolize the theme of the documentary. In the documentary *Leonard Cohen: I'm Your Man* (2005), a camera records the out-of-focus swinging of some hanging red cabaret beads. This image recurs throughout the documentary, sometimes superimposed over another image via post-

production. The soft red evokes a feeling of emotion and passion, which turns out to be what Leonard Cohen's life has been all about. It also functions as a transitional device.

• **Mixing Black and White and Color** • Sometimes juxtaposing color imagery with black-and-white imagery provides an interesting emotional and psychological effect. When doing dramatizations or reenactments, sometimes turning sequences black and white or another color like sepia will achieve a desired effect.

In the documentary *Madonna: Truth or Dare* (1991), the director shot all of the vérité, behind-the-scenes footage in black and white. The performance sequences were shot with multiple cameras in full color. The contrast between Madonna's glamorous on-stage personality, showcased in color, and the black-and-white grind of a small group of musicians, dancers, and make-up artists stuck in the strange world of a long tour works well.

In the documentary *Dogtown and Z-Boys*, director Stacy Peralta tells the history of skateboarding through the prism of eight original skateboarders who belonged to the Zephyr Skate Club in the '80s. The

In the documentary *Madonna: Truth or Dare*, vérité behind-the-scenes sequences are mixed with color performance footage. The effect is to contrast the glamorous performances with the grind of a cast and crew on tour *(Boy Toy, Inc. and Miramax Films, 1991)*.

interviews were shot handheld in 16 mm black-and-white film. They have a grainy, jumpy, archival feel to them. The rest of the documentary is composed of home-movie footage, graphics, and B-roll that are in color. It creates a very effective contrast as we see the interviewees of today in black and white, and footage of them 20 years ago in color. The Zephyr Skate Club was a special group and the black and white footage helps reinforce that idea.

The controversial documentary *Lake of Fire* was shot in 35 mm black-and-white film. The subject matter of abortion is dramatic and emotional. The high-contrast lighting of the black-and-white interviews adds to the dramatic content and impact. The faces are often in half-light. All of the archival and B-roll footage has been changed to black and white, creating a stark look and feel that draws you into the story and the controversy.

Movement

Often establishing a sense of movement throughout your documentary can reinforce a sense of life moving on and things always changing. The documentary *Townes Van Zandt: Be There to Love Me* (2004), is about a singer-songwriter who battles drugs and alcohol while he writes some extraordinary country music. His life is always moving as he travels on the road and moves around constantly. Throughout the documentary, the director shows footage shot out the window of a moving car. The landscape is rural and often desolate. This recurring transition device keeps reminding the viewer of how transient and unstable Van Zandt's life is.

In *Hoop Dreams* many of the interviews were shot in a moving car while the driver talks. Outside the window, the streets of Chicago go by and keep the crowded, urban feeling alive.

In *Jesus Camp*, which unfolds through-

out the rural Midwest and west, sequences of landscapes shot through the windows of a moving car reinforce the feeling of empty spaces. Sometimes a car radio is broadcasting news while the moving shots are of fast-food places within the empty landscape. These moving transitional sequences help to keep the viewer aware of how important religion is to many of these middle–America people.

In the documentary *Food, Inc.*, there is a recurring sequence in which the camera moves quickly toward the horizon. Often the movement is supplied by a camera in an airplane. As it moves, we see fields of crops, farms, and animal ranges. The images reinforce the feeling of immense farms that are in remote places and completely out of our control, but unfortunately under the control of the modern food industry.

Sound Design

Sound is often a forgotten aesthetic element. Often beginning documentary makers don't give sound, in all of its forms, enough thought. Here is a quick overview of the elements that compose sound tracks. Before beginning the documentary journey, everyone should spend time discussing and creating the documentary's sound design.

• **Voices** • Gathering the voices of your storytellers requires a chain of decisions that are related to other aesthetic choices. If you are making a directed documentary in which the subjects will be placed in calm, prearranged settings, and will be seen in composed shots, then you have two options:

➤A small, clip-on lavalier mike that will be either exposed or hidden. The cable for the microphone that runs to the camera or field mixer will be hidden in clothing and always out of sight. If you are using an FM wireless system, then there will be a small transmitter on the subject's body.

➢A shotgun mike that is off camera, positioned within two feet of the subject, that is either handheld or anchored on a boom stand.

Never rely on the camera mike. It is inferior to professional mikes and is not designed for primary sound pick-up.

When making a vérité-style documentary in which the camera is following the action, conversations are captured on the fly, and there is an uncontrolled environment to overcome, many documentary makers like to use FM wireless lavalier mikes. The lavalier mike is hidden under clothing and the cable runs to an FM wireless transmitter about the size of a wallet that is clipped onto the subject's body or put in their pocket. The transmitter broadcasts the sound to a receiving station about the size of a cassette case that is near or taped onto the camera. A cable runs out of the receiving station into the camera then into one of the two audio tracks. The camera mike is run into the other audio track as back up. This system is dependent on batteries in three places: the mike, the FM transmitter, and the receiving station. Bring a LOT of batteries on your shoots.

The cameraperson should always wear a headset so s/he can hear the mike. Crisp and clear should be the goal. If there is any electronic interference due to batteries dying, cables malfunctioning, or switch settings on the camera, the shooter should stop everything immediately and check the audio chain. In general, FM wireless systems are reliable and allow separation of the camera from the subject.

Another system is a shotgun mike, operated by a sound person, that moves with the camera. It is wired directly into either a field mixer or the camera. A variation is outfitting the shotgun with an FM wireless transmitter and broadcasting the sound to a field mixer or a camera. This enables the sound gatherer to be away from the camera.

The goal of all of these systems is to capture clear, crisp sound. Voices are always your main storytellers, so choosing the style of shooting and the proper equipment is primo. Voices can be tweaked in postproduction for sound quality, but if the voice isn't loud, clear, and crisp to begin with, the final quality will suffer.

• **Natural Sound** • This sound is the sound of the environment surrounding the subject. If you are shooting B-roll/cutaway shots that relate to your story, you always want to gather this natural environmental sound that goes with the pictures. Natural sound gives your sound track soul. It allows you to create natural sound montages, and adds a depth to your impression on the viewer.

Always have at least your camera mike activated while shooting B-roll, beauty shots, dramatizations, and any footage that takes place in the real world. Whenever sound will be primary, try to gather it with a top-level mike.

• **Music** • Music is a subjective, sensual element. In almost every case, music can enhance a documentary. Sometimes you know the style and type of music from the beginning. Other times you are searching for the music while going through the phases of production. Either way, it often is productive to start listening to music that relates to your documentary as soon as you get the idea. Music soothes, inspires, stimulates and gets you in the mood for your story.

Sound tracks can be used to establish locale, emphasize action, enhance mood, create pace, and give an aural identity to a story. Voices, natural sound, and music are the main aural colors of your sound-design palette. If you think of your sound track as a series of layers, at any point in your story one of those layers will be dominant, while the others are secondary. Mix them like an artist mixes color.

• Additional Audio Tools You Can Use •
SWEETENING

This is when you add a sound that isn't there. It might be the lapping of waves, birdcalls, traffic, footsteps, a car engine. For whatever reason, sometimes you aren't able to gather the sound while shooting the sequence. Adding the sound from a sound effects library or your own footage from a later shoot might enhance your story/mood/sequence. If the ethics of adding sound that wasn't there originally bother you, then don't do it. But most documentary makers don't mind sweetening their sound tracks if it helps make the story more effective.

FOLEY

Foley is creating/producing sound that wasn't there originally to match action in the scene. If there is a long shot of your subject walking down a corridor and you didn't record the sound of footsteps originally, then you play back the scene and record footsteps to match the action. This technique is used often in narrative films, but not often in documentaries. Still, it is a technique that can be used if you feel the need is there.

SOUND EFFECTS

There might be a psychological/emotional sound that evokes a mood you are looking for, maybe an undertone that helps tie visuals and voice together. You can create these sound effects and use them in the sound track. Since so much music today is electronic, the borders between sound effects and electronic music have almost disappeared.

In the documentary *Jesus Camp*, there is a low, synth-sounding tone that accompanies many of the scenes. The sound is dramatic and reinforces the feeling that re-

ligious fervor is at its roots a mysterious and emotional experience. In Michael Moore's documentaries strange sound effects are used to evoke humor during his B-roll sequences. Sometimes a "whoosh" sound will accompany transitions and/or action sequences in which a specific action like a goal being scored or a special movement take place. Enhancing with sound is a technique that has become popular in recent years.

Green Screen/Rear Projection Backgrounds

Another way to create a visual aesthetic is to shoot your interviews in front of a green background. You light the subject with an awareness that the green background will be filled in with another visual of your choice. It's a good idea to place the green screen background far enough behind the subject so the light on the subject doesn't spill onto the green background. Then you light the green background evenly with other lights.

You now have an opportunity to fill in the green area behind your subject with moving or still imagery. This is a chance to get creative and enhance the theme or subject matter of your story. Green screens come in all sizes. Studios have large, pre-lit green screen walls and backgrounds. But they sell small, portable green screens you can carry to shooting locations and set up behind your subject. You usually have to compose a close-up shot because a wider shot will overshoot the green screen. You can also find a green sheet or paint a wall green to achieve the effect.

In the historical documentary *The U.S. vs. John Lennon* (2006), the director assembles a group of storytellers who are all well known. They are beautifully lit with three-point lighting in front of a green screen background. In editing, still imagery that relates to what they are saying is added to the backgrounds. There is a

Except for one, all the interviews in *The U.S. vs. John Lennon* were shot in front of a green screen that was filled with relevant, abstract imagery during editing *(Lionsgate Films, 2006)*.

color aesthetic that is added to the imagery, creating a pleasing visual that intrigues the viewer. The images reinforce the story and often feature pictures of John Lennon and the Beatles.

Another way to complement your subject in the frame with another image is to position your subject next to a TV monitor. You can feed the monitor either moving or still imagery and create an interesting aesthetic. Hosted television documentary series often use this technique.

Multiple Picture Screens

Often your subject matter will lend itself to filling the screen with multiple images simultaneously. The documentary that pioneered this effect was *Woodstock* (1970). There are many multiple image screen sequences in which one image is of a band performing while another image is of the engrossed listeners. Sometimes there are three pictures on the screen at once. This can be an effective technique if the images complement each other visually and storywise. The multiple images aesthetic is very close to the montage aesthetic. The images are always related and tell their own story within the larger story.

FINAL THOUGHTS

Creating your own design aesthetic is one of the most enjoyable experiences in making a documentary. The various examples cited above just skim the surface of possibility. You are the creator and artist when you are making a documentary. The story is always the primary focus, but finding a design aesthetic that can help you enhance the story is an exhilarating experience. There is always an entertainment element to telling stories. The viewer always appreciates new combinations of familiar and sometimes unfamiliar elements if they fit the overall tone of the story.

In the 1970 classic *Woodstock,* the director used multiple screens to show what was going on simultaneously throughout the large event *(Warner Brothers Entertainment, 2009).*

DOCUMENTARY REFERENCES

Each of these documentary references was chosen because it has a creative element or technique that stands out. Some of the most creative filmmaking has occurred while a documentarian is telling his or her story. It is hoped that the curious reader will be motivated to watch many of these documentaries not only for enjoyment, but also for inspiration.

American Movie. 1999. Chris Smith and Sarah Price. Bluemark Productions. This surprise Sundance winner follows an obsessed Milwaukee filmmaker trying to overcome many obstacles and get his horror film made. Smith and Price were the entire crew as they became friends with the main character. Shot in 16 mm color over the course of two years, this mostly vérité film was made on a shoestring budget, but captures a fascinating story. A must for aspiring filmmakers.

Bowling for Columbine. 2002. Michael Moore. Dog Eat Dog Productions. Using the tragedy at Columbine as a springboard, Moore takes on the issue of gun control and American violence with guns. This documentary was phenomenally successful and has generated millions of words of discussion. Moore's style of playing the inquiring everyman creates a thoughtful collection of vignettes concerning guns.

The Boys of Baraka. 2005. Rachel Grady and Heidi Ewing, Loki Films. Winner of many prestigious film festival awards including Silver Docs, SXSW, and Cine Golden Eagle, this is a hardcore, moving look at a group of inner city kids who travel to a special school in Kenya to find themselves. A digital vérité documentary that also features diary cameras for the kids when they are in Kenya.

Broken Glass. 2006. Jennah Trocchia and Jonathan Waller. Rowan University. This Cine Golden Eagle award winner takes a deep look at crystal meth addiction. A narrative film of a young woman's decline into addiction and recovery is mixed into the interviews and lives of two former addicts.

The Devil Rode on Horseback. 2007. Anne Sundberg and Ricki Stern. Break Thru Films. A first-person account of the genocide going on in Darfur, Sudan, by a former Marine who has been engaged as a photographer to record the atrocities. We follow his awakening as he experiences the tragedy. He decides to return to the United States and become an activist to alert the world of the genocide and advocate for help. This personal journey builds to an emotional climax of realization and is very moving.

Dogtown and Z-Boys. 2001. Stacy Peralta. Vans, Inc. and Sony Entertainment. Double Sundance winner. Sean Penn narrates this fast-paced, creative telling of the origins of skateboarding. Peralta uses his 16 mm skills to add a jumpy, layered look to his B-roll and montages. He mixes black and white interviews with color B-roll and home movie archival footage.

Food, Inc. 2008. Robert Kenner. Perfect Meal LLC. This eye-opening, Academy Award–nominated look at U.S. agribusiness makes the case for more environmentally friendly and health conscious processing of our meat, grain, and vegetables. Interesting on-location interviews, and some clever transitions using graphics and beauty shots.

4 Little Girls. 1998. Spike Lee. Home Box Office. This sensitive, well-researched, historical documentary retells the tragic story of the civil rights church bombing in Birmingham, AL, in 1963. The parents and families of the four slain girls relate the story in intimate interviews.

Gimme Shelter. 1970. The Maysles brothers and Charlotte Zwerin. Maysles Films. This classic vérité documentary shows what can happen when you follow an interesting story and the unexpected happens. Unfortunately, the unexpected was a murder at the Rolling Stones free concert at Altamont freeway in CA in 1969. The story moves fluidly from present to past to present, which was a groundbreaking documentary technique. This film captures the spirit of the sixties and always impresses young people today. A must see for the serious documentarian.

Grey Gardens. 1975. The Maysles brothers. Maysles Films. This film follows the lives of two down at the heels socialites in their crumbling mansion on Long Island. The Maysles brothers spent many months with them and became very involved in their lives. They can often be heard off camera generating questions and actions to the two main subjects. A strange, hypnotic experience.

Hoop Dreams. 1994. Steve James. New Line Home Entertainment, Inc. This three-hour, vérité-style documentary took five years to make (1989–1994) and generated 250 hours of raw footage. It was shot on video using a Betacam video camera. This documentary remains a classic example of dedicated vérité filmmaking.

Into the Arms of Strangers: Tales of the Kindertransport. 2000. Deborah Oppenheimer and Mark Jonathan Harris. This moving, inspirational story of how 10,000 children, mostly Jewish, were sent by their families to England to avoid the Nazis in Germany. Spectacular, pristine archival footage is presented from a child's point of view. Judy Dench narrates this Academy Award winner.

Jesus Camp. 2006. Heidi Ewing and Rachel Grady. Loki Films, Inc. This intense, vérité film about evangelical Pentecostal Christians preparing for religious warfare by running a religious camp every summer is shocking and a cautionary tale. It won many film festivals and was nominated for an Academy Award.

Lake of Fire. 2006. Anonymous Content. Tony Kaye. This beautifully shot black and white documentary deals with the controversial issue of abortion. Both sides are strongly presented and the filmmaker leaves it up to the audience to decide for themselves. It was a labor of love and took 16 years to make.

Leonard Cohen: I'm Your Man. 2005. Lian Lunson. Lionsgate Films. A musical tribute documentary that moves easily between interviews with iconic poet/songwriter/mystic Leonard Cohen and a tribute concert where a variety of singers deliver Cohen's songs in a stripped down, sincere, intense way. Cohen supplied never-before-seen personal archival visuals, and there are some interesting design elements. The song by Antony is an ethereal surprise.

Madonna: Truth or Dare. 1991. Alek Keshishian. Boy Toy and Miramax Films. This is a very interesting film. Madonna's Blonde Ambition world tour provides the background for the gritty black and white, behind-the-scenes, vérité footage and the slick, color performance footage. The camera captures everyone's stress and anxiety. Madonna emerges as an enigmatic, driven, sad, strong woman.

Movement X. 2007. Cindy Lewandowski. Rowan University. This documentary follows a team of color guard performers through their final season. Four members tell their personal stories. The physical and mental toll they pay to perform is eye opening. A fascinating sliver of the performance life.

Murderball. 2005. Henry Alex Rubin and Dana Adam Shapiro. ThinkFilm LLC. The documentary was made by the documentary division at MTV/VH1. This mostly vérité cultural study of the members of a wheelchair rugby team uses sound during the competition sequences in a creative and interesting way. It was a low-budget, digital film that shows if you have the story, production values don't have to be huge. It was nominated for an Academy Award.

No Direction Home. 2005. Spitfire Productions and Grey Water Park Productions. Jeff Rosen and Martin Scorsese. This signature film about Bob Dylan was a ten-year labor of love for Jeff Rosen. Martin Scorsese came on board late (2001) to direct the editing. A brilliant decision to frame the documentary around the coming-of-age years from 1961 to 1966 enabled the documentary makers to explore Dylan's whole life and influences, while still having a narrowly focused story to tell. Dylan's interview setting is subtly creative in a minimalist way, and stands out from the rest of the talkers' settings.

Overnight. 2004. Tony Montana and Mark Brian Smith. DNP Productions. This wild profile of a young director self-destructing in Hollywood took eight years to make. It is a mad mix of film, video, special effects, and home movies. At one point the subject fires the director.

The Personals. 1998. Keiko Ibi. Keiko Films. This touching film won the Oscar for Best Documentary Short Subject. It follows a group of senior citizens on Manhattan's lower east side as they navigate loneliness and friendship. The camera is granted access to intimate moments in their lives, and the result is a seldom seen portrait of aging in America. Originally a low-budget, digital film made for Ibi's MFA degree. HBO liked the 67-minute version so much they agreed to re-edit it to 37 and air it.

Townes Van Zandt: Be Here to Love Me. 2004. Margaret Brown. Rake Films. A creative look at the troubled singer-songwriter Townes Van Zandt. Brown uses a firm but sympathetic approach as she mixes the reminiscences of well-known artists with the nitty-gritty details of his life.

The U.S. vs. John Lennon. 2006. David Leaf and John Scheinfeld. Lionsgate and VH1 Rock Docs. This well-researched, visually interesting documentary follows the transformation of John Lennon from rock star to po-litical activist. The interviews are shot in front of a green screen with creative, layered backgrounds that feature collage-style lettering, photos, and graphic designs. The backgrounds change with each storyteller. By adding this artistic touch to the nuts and bolts interviews, the filmmaker mirrors the art vs. reality conflict Lennon was going through.

The Wonderful, Horrible Life of Leni Riefenstahl. 1993. Ray Müller. Arte and Channel Four Films. Was she making art or propaganda or both? This is the question that drives director Ray Müller to interview Leni Riefenstahl about her life and career. They play cat and mouse with each other until Müller finally loses it off camera. A fascinating study with pristine archival footage of Riefenstahl's classic documentaries: *Triumph of the Will* and *Olympia*.

Woodstock. 1970. Michael Wadleigh. Wadleigh-Maurice. This Oscar winner pioneered the genre of concert films. The use of multiple images on the screen, creative B-roll, excellent sound mix, and shooting with many cameras resulted in an event being captured for entertainment, historical, and cultural purposes. It harks back to Leni Riefenstahl's work and presages Bud Greenspan's Olympic Games documentaries.

4. Researching and Writing a Documentary Proposal

——— Organizing Your Idea ———

The documentary proposal is an organizing task that forces you to think out your idea. Every documentary is grounded in research. It might be the traditional research a historical documentary demands, or it might be nontraditional research that relates to the people and themes in your story. Either way, it is always a good idea to organize your research, think out your resources, try to define a target audience, and have a comprehensive grasp of your idea.

After you have completed your proposal, you can share it with anybody who needs to know your story idea. Often, as the outside world begins to hear about your idea, a buzz develops. People who might impact your documentary want to know about your story and how they might get involved. Having your documentary idea in proposal form gives both you and your idea credibility.

Here is a step-by-step approach to articulating your story idea for both yourself and an interested reader. The proposal can pass through one or more phases as you gather your information and articulate your goals. Outlined below is a three-phase proposal process, but you may be able to combine one or more of the phases.

Phase I

There are a variety of ways you can express your idea as your documentary is being born and before any production begins.

➤A Log Line. This is the essence of the idea for your story in one sentence.

➤The Story: Synopsis. This is a brief, one-paragraph rundown of the highlights of your story.

➤The Story: One Sheet. A distilled version of the idea is called a "one sheet." The one sheet is the essence of your idea and any other significant details, including an estimated budget, reduced to one page. There should be some "sizzle" to the page, if possible. The one sheet will be read by many different types of people. If some of them might be investors, then adding some flare to the description of your idea might help impress them.

➤The Story: Treatment. This is a detailed description of your idea for a documentary. This is called a "treatment" and is similar to the action outline of a narrative film. A treatment is a description of the flow of your story: where you think the story will take you and who the storytellers will be. Compelling characters are a must. Your idea description should include all of the story elements (specific actions, conflicts, locations, themes, social values) that attracted you to the story.

All of these versions of your idea will be used constantly in the documentary production world for various reasons. Each one will enable you to explain your idea to funders, crewmembers, documentary subjects, interested parties, and other people who might be able to help or get involved.

• **Discovery Channel Model** • Connie Bottinelli is a seasoned documentary and film producer. She described to me a production experience she had with the Discovery Channel. Her description is a behind-the-scenes look at how a documentary maker presents an idea to a funding organization.

THE ORIGIN OF THE IDEA

My partner and I were pitching an idea to The Learning Channel [TLC], which is owned by The Discovery Channel. We wanted to do a 13-part series on curses. One of the curse episodes was on King Tutankhamun. The TLC people made a counteroffer: How about a one-hour documentary on King Tutankhamun. They asked us to give them a one sheet on the idea. A one sheet needs to tell the essential story and present a preliminary budget. The one sheet needs to be compelling. In the first two sentences you have to have them by the throat. There is buzz and sizzle in it, but it's got to be grounded in what you can deliver.

We sent them a one sheet and they said, "Wow! Great! We love this. Send us a final budget." We sent them one and got a green light a week later. We signed a contract, with all the terms, all the way down to credits, number of seconds, our logos on the end of the show, rights. The first check comes with the signing of the contract.

PITCHING A SHOW

Pitching a show or a movie usually works like this.

Log Line

First you have a log line. A log line is one sentence that has a beginning, middle and an end. It's a tease. On our proposal for the 13 curses series we had a log line for the King Tut show.

*Pitching Summary
or Synopsis*

If they like the log line, they ask for a pitching summary. A pitching summary is maybe two paragraphs. It's like a longer tease.

One Sheet

If they like the pitching summary, they say, "Do you have a one sheet on that or a leave behind?" They call it both. And, of course, you better say yes because they want you to leave it behind so that they can read it. Depending on the type of program, they might ask for a preliminary budget at this stage.

A Pitch

If they like the one sheet, they'll call you back and ask for a pitch. A pitch is an embellished one sheet—three to four pages. And that pretty much starts telling you who the characters are and who will be in it. Characters in a historical documentary means the experts you're going to use and the other interview subjects. At this point, if you have a proven track record like we do with Discovery, the deal is finalized.

The Treatment

But whether the deal is done or still pending, the next step is the treatment. The treatment is a full-blown document. A treatment can run anywhere from eight pages to 60. It depends. For a one-hour documentary, typically, for me, the length is maybe about 28 pages total. At this point, I have structured the documentary and have the essential story elements in place. At the treatment point, you've already started your research or else you cannot possibly write the story that you have to write. A documentary story line usually runs about 16 pages, maybe 20 pages. All the other pages in there are bios and budget. For you to write 20 pages with turning points and all that, you have to know who your principal players are going to be. You may have already spoken to them on the phone or you may have read a book they wrote, and are able to claim who they were and what they would give you in an interview.

The treatment also includes the bios of your key production people: director of photographer (DP), bookkeeper, unit production manager, editor, director, writer and producer. Since my partner, my company and myself were being contracted, we fulfilled the roles of producer, director and writer.*

Connie was involved with a large cable channel, and her methods of presenting an idea included substantial experience and a track record of success. But she still had to create the beginning of her documentary the same way you should.

• *Behind the Music* **Documentary Series** • Another organizational force impacts your story if you are making your documentary for an ongoing series that has established a content format for every show. VH1's documentary series *Behind the Music* (*BTM*) was the number-one rated prime-time show on VH1 for six years (1997–2003). The production team learned early on that keeping the structure the same worked. Most documentary series use a content format. It harks back to *The March of Time* film series of the 1930s and the television series of the 1950s and '60s. *BTM*'s supervising producer Paul Gallagher explains how the documentaries were created.

> The formula has been there from the beginning. Every episode of *BTM* has a prologue we call a "cold open," then five acts. There are commercial breaks between the acts.

The Cold Open

The cold open is a two-minute teaser of the whole show. You get a sample of what you are about to see. All the hottest bites. A little bit of a peek at the high and low points. You get a sketch of what the show is going to be about. This cold open is very high energy. Quick cuts, lots of music.

Act 1, Part 1: High Energy to the Curve Ball

The top of Act 1 is continued high energy. It sets forth the thesis of what the artist's story is going to be. The thesis comes out of meetings. The producer must know what the show is about. Sometimes I ask the producers to write the thesis down. Sometimes it's obvious before production begins, sometimes it comes out of an interview bite. Anyway, you get to a point after about one and a half minutes into Act 1 when somebody says something that is a curve ball. Not what you would expect to see. It's a left turn after about four minutes of high energy. The viewer says "Oh. Now I'm interested."

Act 1, Part 2: The Backstory

The backstory consists of the nuts and bolts of where the person came from. What formulated them as people. What makes them tick. The pieces we use in the backstory are experiences that will come back in the show. The recurring themes in people's lives. Every act ends with a cliffhanger. A turning point. It could be an accident. A record deal. A bad personality conflict.

Act 2: The Rise

This is where we detail how they became famous. You continue to reveal and reinforce themes. Little things pop up. You foreshadow the future. Act 2 ends on another cliffhanger/turning point.

Act 3: The Challenge

Act 3 is where a person is faced with the biggest challenge of their life, whether it be drug addiction or the death of someone. We see how the fame and money manifests itself. Most of the time the subjects of BTMs are in their early to mid–20s, making millions of dollars, and surrounded by people who have a vested interest in their success. There aren't a lot of people telling you no. It takes a special person to keep it under control. Very few did. Act 3 is either keeping it under control or getting a curveball you never expected. The story is always unresolved.

---

*These words were transcribed from an interview I had with Connie Bottinelli on February 12, 2001.

ACT 4: THE RESOLUTION

In Act 4 the person meets the challenge and moves on with their life or is still struggling. The themes and patterns set in Act 1 have worked themselves out. There is usually a climax in Act 4. By the end of Act 4, just about everything is resolved.

ACT 5: REFLECTIONS

Act 5 is often more of a reflection of where this person is now, the lessons they've learned, the latest album they have out, the music on the album that reflects their journey. Act 5 ties up the lose ends.

The reason the show works is that we look at everybody individually. We figure out what their story is and what it will take to tell that story in a way people can identify with. The formula ends up being the crude mechanical part of how it all goes together. The person's story really dictates how it goes together. Am I comfortable with the formula? Yes. Because it works. We don't blindly follow it. We never pretend to be a comprehensive biography of someone.

What we are, we say: Here's the person's life journey and they happen to be musicians. P.S. They just happen to be like you and me. They may have millions of dollars and be in front of cameras, but they have the same challenges you do. There is something in there you can identify with. That's why I think the show works.*

If you are not making a documentary with a specific time constraint, then you have the freedom to plan an uninterrupted story. But structure is always important. In directed documentaries, the structure comes from the beginning through the director; in vérité documentaries, the structure often doesn't arise until shooting is completed. But good stories always need storytelling structure.

• **The Story: Why You Want to Make the Documentary** • It is always a good idea to write a statement of why you want to make the documentary. This is critical. Your passion for the project needs to be articulated. Documentaries are personal stories of the human condition. It is your passion and personal connection to the subject that will carry you and everyone else through the experience. Readers of your proposal need to feel your passion and be able to read how articulate you are about making the documentary. Don't be afraid to reveal yourself. You are the driving force.

• **Research** • Outline the areas of specific research that your documentary will require. As you discover pertinent information, catalog it all so you can know at a glance what your research resources are. Your research resources will include Web files, hard copies, media (books, still photos, tapes and film), interview outlines, memorabilia, relevant ephemera and artifacts, artwork, and other items. Create storage centers, both electronic and real world, that can hold all of them so your resources aren't scattered everywhere. If you take still photos of people, places, and B-roll items during the preproduction phase, they will help you keep your ideas in front of you.

Research is usually ongoing throughout the entire documentary effort. Having all of the research in one place and at your instant disposal is critical for your production. Google Documents or a similar web location works well. There is a detailed description below of how to use the Web for your production.

• **Storytellers** • Create a list of people and/or types of people who will talk and create story content. In vérité documentaries it is usually obvious who the main characters will be from the beginning. But as the story unfolds, new people are often discovered. Perhaps you can suggest to

---

*These words were transcribed from an interview I had with Paul Gallagher on March 14, 2001, at the VH1 production studios in Santa Monica, CA.

your main subjects someone who would fit into the story. In directed documentaries, besides your central subjects, you might include experts, historians, friends, family, and co-workers of the main subject(s).

Often preinterviews or conversations are a good way to establish a positive rapport with your storytellers and get them on board with your idea. Preinterviews can also be auditions for experts and historians. But sometimes, especially in vérité situations, it is better to begin shooting rather than overtalk the idea and the roles the subjects might play. Vérité documentaries also require preshooting discussions with the main subjects about your plan to capture them and the time frame involved. Everyone needs to be on board with the fact you are making a documentary about them.

Collecting contact information for all of your storytellers is important. Cell phone numbers, e-mail addresses, Facebook and MySpace pages, even Twitter accounts, can all be important. You need to always have this contact information with you, and to update it as necessary. Home and work addresses are also critical. Most producers and directors like to store the important contact information in three places: personal cell phone or BlackBerry, project Web home page (e.g., Google Documents), and a hard-copy weekly planner they carry everywhere.

• **Locations** • Where will the documentary take you? Try to write down all of the places where your subjects and the story will lead you. Think of where you might want to shoot the interviews. The B-roll. Transitions. Montage footage. How much travel will be involved? Is there an art design that might involve special sequences and impact the locations? Recreations and dramatizations might be part of your plan. Where will they unfold? It's hard to know everything at the beginning, but thinking

about the locations needs to begin as soon as you have articulated your story and chosen your storytellers.

• **The Basic Elements** • These are the basic elements discussed in chapter 2. Although you are just at the beginning of your journey, you might have some strong feelings about some of the elements. Here are two key elements again.

STYLE

At this stage of the experience, it is important to decide if you will be making a vérité, directed, or mixed-style documentary. This decision is about control of the documentary. If you are taking the vérité route, then much of your shooting schedule is unknown, because you don't know where your story will take you. Your production timeline will probably be longer than a directed or mixed documentary. If you are making a directed documentary, then you can plan a shooting schedule down to the last detail. A mixed-style documentary will require a lot of thought as you merge the two approaches.

CAMERA AESTHETIC

Next, you should decide how the camera will be used. How free do you want the camera to be? What are the demands of the subject matter? Do you want a calm camera on a tripod or held very steady? Or do you want an active camera that will be moving and at times draw attention to itself?

Will you shoot in film or video? This decision will impact your budget and crew decisions. In chapter 5 there is a comprehensive overview of the equipment that is available for making documentaries. You want to choose your camera and other equipment based on the design elements you want to include in your production. If you feel black-and-white film sequences are vital to your story, then 16 mm film may be part of your plan. If HD is important, then find a camera that will fulfill your needs. Most documentaries these days are shot with digital cameras. In post-production, many "looks" can be achieved, including black and white, colorized, layered, animated, and multiple screens.

To answer these important production questions, you should try to watch a wide variety of documentaries. You will see many different styles and approaches. Part of your research is to familiarize yourself with your documentary peers, then make your own decisions. At the end of this chapter is a recommended viewing list that includes a wide range of styles and subject matter.

The other ten elements of production are covered in detail in chapter 2. But before you can address them, you will need to decide on your style and camera aesthetic.

• **Target Audience** • Try to articulate who you are making your documentary for. Yourself and your friends? A defined group who might pay to see the documentary, either on DVD or in a theater? The general public? A themed cable channel? A public television station? If you are working under a contract or grant, then your target audience has probably been defined. TV stations and networks know who the viewers of your documentary will be. If you are a student or an independent producer, then your target audience needs some thought.

Usually target audiences are described using combinations of age, sex, income, marital status, ethnic background, job, and other, more exclusive categories. There are some very informative Web sites that deal with defining and describing target audiences. The general age classifications as defined by The Nielsen Company, which rates all TV shows, are 2–12 (kids),

13–19 (teens), 18–34 (young adults), 18–55 (adults), 55 and above (older adults/mature adults). These general categories break into smaller groups if the program or film is narrowly targeted. For instance, a college market is 18–24. As you articulate your audience, you will get ideas of who to send the completed proposal to for possible funding and support.*

Phase 2: More Details and a Segment Rundown or Shooting Script

As you continue to add information to your initial proposal, and as you have creative ideas, you will keep adding to and refining your proposal. Documentaries are energy cores and they tend to take on lives of their own. Because you must encounter people as you pass through your preproduction phases, the word gets out and often something happens to steer the documentary in a new direction. There are new storytellers, new locations, new design ideas, new B-roll opportunities. Just keep modifying your original proposal so it always is current.

Director Connie Bottinelli spent a lot of time deciding on her locations for her historical documentary *The Curse of King Tutankhamun* (1998), which she made for the Discovery Channel. She traveled to Egypt and London and wanted to be sure she remembered where she had been and what she had seen. After her location scouts, she was ready to write her shooting script.

> I scouted locations in Egypt and London. I took both video footage and 35 mm still photos on the scouts. Part of the deal with Discovery is to deliver production stills when you are on location. While I was in Egypt, I discovered a complete replica of Tut's tomb and got permission to shoot there. When I got home from my

---

*Target Audiences. A good source for demographic explanation and market breakdowns is http://www.market research.com. The site is free and full of demographic information.

location scouts, I wrote the shooting script right away.

The shooting script will become your schedule for shooting. It will become how much you need to get out of somebody in an interview. It will become your questions for the person. It will become your B-roll. It will address all of the elements of production.

As you write your shooting script, you don't just write words. You write the pictures on the other side, too. When I write a shooting script, the format I use is audio/video columns. The audio is on the right-hand column; the video is on the left. As I write the audio, I see corresponding pictures in my head. That way you learn exactly what you have to get for your pictures. You learn how much archival material you need, where your interviews fit, how much B-roll you need to generate, what the goals of the recreations are. It pretty much gives you a schedule of what you have to shoot where, how much, and when. It tells you what time of day, what the location is. As soon as you finish your shooting script, you are ready to start shooting.

My treatment and the shooting script had to be written in five acts. That's because of the four commercial breaks in the show. And in those five acts, I write a dramatic story using turning points and cliffhangers. Turning points can happen within an act, but cliffhangers always happen before the breaks. Before I go to a break, before I go to Act 2, I've got you hanging by a thread. I do that leading into every single break. In the treatment, I include bites from my preinterviews with my interview subjects. I include recreations and montages.*

Bottinelli was writing for a specific audience and had a time and structure format she had to follow. But she went through all of the steps every documentary maker must address. She calls her guiding outline a shooting script. But a segment rundown is just another name for the same procedure. As Bottinelli emphasizes, the shooting script/segment rundown is a living document and can be altered if a new idea or story element arises.

But the documentary needs structure and organization in order to move forward. Directed documentaries are easier to plan and control. Vérité documentaries can't be so tightly structured, and the crew has to roll with the unknown. But the structure and story usually begin to emerge quickly in vérité documentaries, and eventually you will have all of your footage and the story will be organized into segments before you can edit.

• **Story Organization** • As you approach your first production days, you should expand your treatment into specific segments that have their own role in the larger story. These story segments should be in the projected order and also have time values, so you can see how long your theoretical documentary is going to be. If you are aiming for 58 minutes, which is a PBS hour, or 44 minutes, which is a broadcast or cable TV channel hour, then all of your segments should add up to the expected time. If you are making a feature-film length documentary, then 75 minutes or more will be your goal. If you are making a documentary short, then 30 minutes will be your maximum time. If your documentary falls between 30 and 60 minutes, you will have a harder time selling it or placing it in festivals. But if DVD sales are your objective, then this time length might work.

Phase 3: Ongoing Updates and Segment Revisions

During production, actions and events always happen that impact your original plan. Sometimes the changes are minor and your plan holds up. Sometimes there are major shifts in people, places, and stories. As changes occur you should try to revise your original segment rundown as often as possible. As you begin to digitize footage for editing and organize

*These words were transcribed from an interview I had with Connie Bottinelli on February 12, 2001.

your postproduction tasks, the timelines and bins are going to be labeled according to your revised segment ordering. In chapter 8, there is a detailed description of how to label, manage, and work with your footage, segments, and timelines.

• The Bible: Hard and Electronic • Since the first documentary, producers and directors have had to control a lot of important information during the production phases. Traditionally, there would be a three-ring binder with many hard-copy pages of blank, lined paper and pockets that would hold all of the information pertinent to the documentary. Tabs would label sections in the bible for all of the information: contact list (subjects, crew, and others), location info, the proposal, budget, schedules, transcriptions, logs, rundowns, narration scripts, important research, and various lists. No matter what was happening, the bible was up to date and usually held the answer. The producer/director carried the bible everywhere.

Now, with the computer and the Web, the bible can be electronic and carried around on a computer, flash drive, iPod, BlackBerry, etc. But many documentary makers still like a hard-copy bible that is accessible instantly in a format that is easily readable and changeable in the field.

Google Documents lets you use the Web as your central storage place. Since everyone who is part of the production has access to the Google Documents project pages, and everyone can upload and download, the project pages are priceless. But hard copies are also important both as back up and instantly accessible information in any situation.

Here is a three-ring notebook production bible from an event documentary about creative problem-solving competitions. Inside are tabbed sections for every production task (*Ned Eckhardt, 2010*).

You will decide what works for you. But the reason for having a bible is still the same. All the important project information is easily accessible and in one place.

• **The One Sheet, Again** • Often during your production phases there is a need to inform someone about your idea in a short, quick way. It may be a potential funding source or storyteller or distribution company or presentation outlet. The one sheet has all of the exciting elements, in addition to your story in a nutshell. The one sheet might change as the documentary progresses, but make sure it is current with the bible. One sheets are part of the production industry and often can open a door for you.

• **Using the Proposal** • The proposal is what makes your idea real for other people. No matter how articulate you are in verbally describing your documentary idea, nobody can remember every word you say. If you can hand or e-mail them your idea in proposal form, they can have your idea, refer to it, and refresh their knowledge at any time.

The proposal also gives you credibility. Your idea is no longer just a dream, but a story grounded in research with a purpose, goals, design plans, and real people attached. It has an articulated passion behind it and a game plan for production.

Often opportunity pops up in the strangest places, and the ability to give someone a proposal of your idea can benefit you in many ways.

Although Connie Bottinelli worked with a large budget, her process was the same as yours will be. You may not be shooting in England and Egypt, but your locations need to be visited and planned for.

Arnold Shapiro, who made the classic documentary *Scared Straight!* (1978), went through a different preproduction research phase. He was going to be making a documentary that was based in a prison. His research included listening to many taped hours of conversation between prisoners and teenagers. When he felt he had a handle on who the prisoners were, he returned to the prison to produce and direct the documentary.

I went back to New Jersey and set up my headquarters at the Holiday Inn in Carteret near the prison. With the help of local youth counselors, I found 17 kids and got the releases signed. There were nine prisoners who were going to run the session. I was working by myself. I didn't even have an assistant with me. I was the writer, producer, and director.

It was a nightmare to produce. We had one shot to get the footage. We had 17 kids and they were only going to do it once. We did preinterviews with them two days before, and then whatever happened, happened.

RESEARCH

I sat down with the inmates beforehand and told them that I had watched ten of their previous sessions. The sessions were two and one-half hours each. I had taken notes and I'd noticed things that each of them did that they didn't always do. I had written them all down. I told them we only have one shot at this. And I went down each man and asked him if he could remember to do particular movements when he's talking. They listened and for the most part did.

I was sure a good documentary was there. I was worried if we could capture it on film. My biggest concern was we only had one shot to do it. What if this session doesn't turn out to be as good as others? Live events are scary. All the preparation doesn't guarantee that you will capture the essence or that something might go wrong.

When we were ready to shoot, I brought a cameraman from LA and picked up a second camera in NJ along with two sound people. We also had two assistants to help change film loads.

The afternoon session with these kids was May 1, 1978.*

Below are some examples of proposals for documentaries. Some had funding up front, some didn't. But the proposals were critical in getting the right people to be in the documentary and finding a way to assemble a dedicated crew.

Seabrook Farms Remembered

This historical documentary was completed in 2002. It was made for a museum in southern New Jersey with a grant from the New Jersey Historical Commission. I partnered with the museum in applying for the grant. The product was a 35-minute documentary that told the story of a unique farm in Salem County, New Jersey. After World War II, more than 10,000 displaced immigrants from all over the world traveled to Seabrook Farms and restarted their lives by working together on this fruit and vegetable farm. For 25 years (1945–1969), people from over thirty ethnic groups who spoke 25 different languages lived and worked together. It is a story of sacrifice, redemption, and rebirth.

The primary target audience was middle-school students (male and female 12–14-year-olds), who were the largest group to regularly visit the museum. Because the primary audience was younger, it impacted the design and structure of the documentary. The inspiring story remained, but the target audience influenced the music, narration, graphics, editing pace, and interview settings. The challenge was to create a documentary that pleased the target audience but also appealed to adults.

The documentary was inspired by the book *Growing a Global Village* by Charles Harrison. The author of the book was a friend of mine, and after I read it I knew the story had to be told in documentary form. Charles introduced me to John Fuumi, the director of the Seabrook Educational and Cultural Center, which has been established to preserve the memory of the farm and its workers. When the center decided to be a part of the documentary, it applied to the New Jersey Historical Commission for a $30,000 grant to make the documentary. The grant application called for a three-page outline with a synopsis of the documentary story/narrative, information about the team that would be involved in the production, a budget, and a timeline for the production. It was a miniversion of the deal struck by Connie Bottinelli with Discovery. The grant was awarded in January 2001, and the documentary was completed in the spring of 2002. Here is the proposal one-sheet for the documentary.

Seabrook Farms Remembered
A Proposal

Log Line:

On a farm in southern New Jersey during the mid–twentieth century over 10,000 immigrants from twenty-five countries rebuilt their lives after the unfathomable pain and tragedy of World War II.

Synopsis:

For nearly two decades in the middle of the twentieth century thousands of displaced men and women representing 3 races, 25 ethnic groups, and 30 languages

*These words were transcribed from an interview I had with Arnold Shapiro on March 26, 2001.

worked at Seabrook Farms in the southeastern corner of New Jersey. As they built new lives, they harvested and fed much of the free world during and after World War II.

Most of the 10,000 plus people who lived and worked at Seabrook were Europeans from post–World War II Displaced Persons camps, Japanese-Americans who were relocating after living in internment camps, southern African Americans migrating north, unemployed workers from Appalachia, and Caribbean Islanders. ... all searching for work and a better life. Seabrook Farms became the American Dream for thousands of people.

While they were living and working at Seabrook Farms they created what was probably the first and only rural global village in the history of the United States.

Highlights:
- Incredible stories of hardships and heroism to get to Seabrook
- Japanese Americans tell the story of the internment camps
- Working on the largest vegetable farm on earth
- Living in a village that spoke 25 different languages
- *Life* magazine featured the farm and its workers
- Seabrook had the largest frozen food plant on earth
- Seabrook was the first and only rural global village in the world

Time: 30 minutes
Budget: $30,000 (New Jersey Historical Commission)
Client: Seabrook Educational and Cultural Center
Contact: Ned Eckhardt
eckhardt@rowan.edu
856-256-4415

Next, I needed to create a budget that reflected who the production team would be and how the money would be spent. The Seabrook Educational and Cultural Center completed other parts of the grant that outlined how the museum would use the documentary.

Seabrook Farms Remembered
Budget Breakdown

9 Shooting Days and 25 Editing Days

1. Transportation
   50 miles/day for two vehicles for 9 days: 900 miles
   2 miles/day for 1 vehicle for 8 days: 16 miles
   916 miles @ .20 mile = $183.00

2. Food, Lodging
   Lunches for 4 for 9 days: 36 @ $10.00 = $360.00
   Lunches for 2 for 8 days: 16 @ $10.00 = $160.00
   ($520.00) $520.00

3. Photocopying, Photography
   Production Stills (50 photos and developing/duplication) $50.00

4. Purchase/Rental of Equipment
   Complete field video production package for 9 days
   @ $600/day $5,400.00

5. Salaries/Fringe Benefits
   Field Director (Ned Eckhardt)
   $500/day for 9 days: $4,500.00

Editing Supervisor (Ned Eckhardt)	$1,000.00
Editor (Tom Rosa of Tommy Productions)	
$500/day for 25 days:	$12,500.00
Production Assistant for 9 days	
$75/day for 9 days:	$675.00
Script Consultant (Charles Harrison)	
$500/day for 4 days:	$2,000.00
Technical Consultant (Ned Eckhardt)	
$500/day for 2 days:	$1,000.00
6. Professional Services	
Artist for interview background: $500/day for 1 day:	$500.00
Musician for sound track: $500/day for 2 days:	$1,000.00
Voice Over Narrator	$1,000.00
Total	**$29,328.00**

Movement X

Here is another example of a proposal for a documentary. This low-budget, 40-minute documentary evolved out of Cindy Lewandowski's involvement for many years with a colorguard performance group. The proposal was made in the fall of 2007, and the documentary was made during the spring season of 2008. This proposal is detailed and full of the passion and expertise Cindy was bringing to the project. It is a good example of how a documentarian gathers her idea and translates it into a proposal for others to read and hopefully inspire them to get involved. When she eventually made *Movement X*, it was very close to the way she outlined it in her first segment rundown. This proposal can be a template for anyone who has proceeded far enough to be able to articulate the idea, the storytellers, the locations, and the design details.

Movement X
A Documentary by:
Cindy Lewandowski
21 December 2007

Log Line

After 10 years as a close-knit unit, Apex Winterguard is embarking on the emotional journey of their last season together. *Movement X* will capture all the excitement and drama by following four team members and their coach as they realize what an important impact the activity, and the people involved, have had on their lives.

What It Is

Colorguard is known as the "sport of the arts." It's a demanding activity that requires the performer to have not only grace, but strength and personality as well. To someone in the audience, it may only seem like an interesting blend of color, design, and movement, but to those individuals performing at each show, it is much more than that.

As someone who's been in the colorguard scene for 11 seasons over the course of 7 years, I've been on the inside of the activity and I can tell you truthfully that it is much more than just twirling flags. The winterguard group that I am most closely associated with is called Apex, and it is a group of about twenty individuals, male and female, ranging from the age of 18 to 26. Most of the members are people I've known for years who all have a lot going on in their lives outside of the colorguard world, but still dedicate their entire weekends to an activity that is often draining, both physically and emotionally. For some, it is the first place they've felt a sense of belonging, for others it is their only escape from their problems at home, and still for others it is simply a way to express their artistic and dramatic talents. In the end, no matter what their reason for joining colorguard, this eclectic group of characters must find out how to work closely together for nearly 6 months to put together a show and compete for a chance to make it to the Finals at the World Championships.

Why I want to make it

I'd like the opportunity to delve into the world of colorguard, not only to show what this sport is about on the outside, but also to profile the lives of 3–5 selected members. Through this approach I hope to reveal the personal sacrifices, the emotional roller coasters, the moments of joy, the drama, the physical struggle, and the passion that defines the colorguard activity.

Since this is a sport that I've been involved with for the past 7 years of my life, it is something very close to my heart. I've been there through difficult times and I've been there during fun times. I always wished more people understood why I put so much time, effort, and money into colorguard, but it has always been misrepresented in many forms. I'd like to have the opportunity to tell the story of colorguard through the eyes of my former teammates so that it can open the eyes of people who have no idea what it takes to be involved in an organization like Apex.

By the end of the documentary, I want to not only make the point that being a part of a world class activity requires a lot of sacrifice, but more so that what is most important in life is the people we meet and the experiences we all share. I want to celebrate the individual and show that although no two people are alike, everyone has a story to tell if you take the time to hear it.

Who They Are

• Micah "Desiree," 24, 4 yr Apex veteran. *Description*: Micah is someone who I think would be an interesting character. He is definitely unique. Micah is also 24, and although he's been around Apex for many years this would only mark his 4th year of marching with the group. Micah is a homosexual and enjoys performing in drag shows in his spare time. He works as a make-up artist/stylist in a salon in Philadelphia, but because of his love for couture fashion, he is almost always broke.

• Megan "Wifey," 26, 8 yr veteran. *Description*: Megan is 26 and has been doing colorguard since she was in high school. This will be her 8th season in Apex, but that is not the interesting thing about her. She tends not to talk about her home life too much, but I know that things are rough. Her parents are separated, she has a teaching degree but works at Wawa, and she's never had a boyfriend. Only knowing this about her would lead you to believe she's a miserable, social delinquent, but in reality she's one of the friendliest and upbeat people you will ever meet.

• Jackie "Paper," 24, 6 yr vet. *Description*: Jackie is 24 and will be entering her 6th year in Apex. After high school, Jackie moved from Delaware to New York City to pursue an acting career, but has not found much work aside from a few small plays. She now lives in Philadelphia with her boyfriend Ken who is also a struggling actor. She still tries to get as many acting jobs as she can, but she is also a pre-school teacher with a true passion for the arts.

• Nick "Nicky T," 27, 9 yr vet. *Description*: Nick is outgoing, loud and funny. He usually finds himself the center of attention and wouldn't have it any other way. He is very passionate about colorguard, as he has been performing since high school and is a 9 yr Apex vet, one of the 15 founding members. Nick is always trying to find the right man to date, but despite several long-term boyfriends he is currently single. He has worked as a pre-school teachers for 7 years, and has also been a bartender on weeknights at Bennigan's for several years. Nick is a great character because he is dynamic, but drama always seems to follow him around.

• Steve, 35, Apex Director. *Description*: Steve is also one of the founders of Apex as well as the director of the organization. Steve is very intimidating, and he tends to rub people the wrong way. I think he would be an interesting side character since he is usually the root of a lot of the drama during any given season. I would also like to use him to give the history of colorguard in general as well as additional commentary on the current Apex season.

Locations

• Community Church, Newark, DE. *Description*: The church's recreation area serves as Apex's main practice facility. It is located almost directly behind Steve's house in Newark, DE. I will be using this location to gather B-roll during practices early in the season. I will also conduct some of the vérité interviews here during breaks at practice. There are always great B-roll opportunities here whether it is a very tense and tiring practice or if it is a more relaxed practice where the members are all bonding and having a good laugh.

• University of Dayton Arena, Dayton, OH. *Description*: The arena at the University of Dayton serves as the official site for the Winterguard International (WGI) Championships in April. What I really want to get out of this site is B-roll of the pre-performance hype, especially in the tunnel right before entering the floor in the arena. This will serve as the focus for the opening and ending of my documentary. I would also like to get interviews with my characters in their hotel the night before their pre-lims performance because I know that is always an anxious, but exciting time for all of the members.

• Local Indoor Colorguard Shows. Locations TBD. *Description*: I would like to travel to 2 or 3 shows that Apex is performing at this season. I want to use these show to get good B-roll of the group overall and also supportive B-roll for my specific characters before, during, and after their performance.

• Wawa, Megan's work. *Description*: This will be a main source for B-roll and interviews for Megan's personal story outside of Apex.

• Drag show, Micah's hobby. Location(s) TBD. *Description*: Since Micah has a very unique hobby of performing as "Desiree" in drag queen shows, I would definitely like to tell his personal story through B-roll and interviews at one of his shows.

• Nick's work in Delaware. *Description*: I could use either Bennigan's or this pre-school as the setting for Nick's personal story, including B-roll and interviews. I may decide to use both by following him throughout a day when he works at the pre-school during the day and Bennigan's at night to show that he has two very different jobs and is also very busy.

• Stage show, Jackie's 2nd job. Location TBD. *Descriptions*: Like Nick, I could use one of her acting jobs as B-roll and an interview setting in order to tell her personal story, but I could also include her work during the daytime at the daycare. I chose one of [the] shows for now because I think it would showcase her dramatic and artistic talents better.

What the Elements Are

• **Use of Camera.** For the majority of B-roll I would like to use the vérité style, but in some cases I might want to direct the subjects in order to get a more interesting shot. As for interviews, it would be ideal to me to do these as vérité and on-the-go as possible, but I think I might end up leaning more towards directed ones with a natural feel to them.

• **Opening and Title.** I'd really like to start the doc off with a shot of the pre–Championship huddle and hype with possibly a short, fast-paced montage of video clips and sound bytes rewinding through the season so that it teases you about what the film is going to be like. I also think it would be interesting to "introduce" my characters and Apex in this opening montage by using home videos of old colorguard competitions.

• **Transitions.** I originally thought I'd want to go as traditional as possible and use simply fades to and from black with white text to introduce each segment, but then I thought it might be interesting to separate it into chapters with a short clip of someone catching a good toss and then freezing on the last frame and fading in text overtop to identify the what and when. (For example, Chapter 1 would have 1 person tossing and catching and Chapter 2 would have 2 people tossing and catching, etc.) I'm still not exactly sure how I would like to transition between my segments, but as far as the structure of the piece I would like to gradually introduce my main characters within the first half of my documentary.

• **Storytellers.** I'd like the characters that I'll be following and interviewing to be the main storytellers, but I would also use text to relate any other important information such as location and time in the season. Instead of using written narration to give a background of colorguard and more specifically, Apex, I think it would be more effective to use interviews with Steve since he can give a more personal account.

• **Music.** Music would depend on the mood of the segment. There would probably be very distinct ups and downs in the overall story, and the music would obviously have to be appropriate. At times, there would need to be very fast-paced music to help reinforce the idea that it is a hectic time, but there may be other very emotional times when a less obvious mood track would be used. From what I know, Apex's show music this year is somewhat mellow and melodic. I may want to find someone to score some original music [that] mimics the style and sound of the songs Apex is performing to and then I will fit it appropriately to each segment.

• **Movement.** This is a documentary that has a lot of opportunity for movement since it is following a sport that is known largely for its beautiful movements with dancing and equipment (flags, rifles, sabers). Since there would be a lot of movement within the frame, I would probably not use too much movement with the camera.

• **Shooting Style.** I would use a mixture of traditional and freestyle, but I would lean more towards the freestyle. I don't think I'd like to tripod too many shots, since I'd like to go for a vérité feel, but in some cases I might like to have a more directed/traditional shot.

• **Pace.** The pace of the documentary would reflect the pace of the average colorguard season. It would start off kind of slow after the opening montage, but then start to pick up pace towards the middle of the season since this is often a fast-paced and stressful time.

• **Graphics.** I don't want my graphics to be too flashy because I never like watching documentaries that put a lot of emphasis on graphics. I'd like to use a plain font like Helvetica or something else sans-serif style for all of my lower-thirds and transitions.

• **Montages.** I would like to use several montages for times that might be a little drawn out and dull otherwise. I think this will allow me to fit more into the story than I would be able to do otherwise. I would also like to use montages during each character's personal story to briefly show their colorguard history through home videos and pictures.

Movement X

Segment Rundown

Opening and Title	Location: Dayton Arena; Dayton, OH. Screen is black and the title "Movement X" appears on the screen as the audio fades in with the sounds of a leader giving an inspirational speech about all the time and energy it took to get to this place. The video fades up and we see a team of young people in full costume who are all in a pre-performance huddle. The speaker continues to talk about the journey they all took to get to this point. The video fades into a montage of very short clips from earlier in the season. As the video fades back to the huddle, the speaker finishes his speech by saying something like "So just go out there and leave your hearts out on the floor." The opening finishe[s] with the team putting their hands in for their traditional chant. Fade to black.	1:30	1:30
Segment 1: Introduction to Colorguard Topic 1: Why do you do it?	Location: Studio, Rowan University; Glassboro, NJ. My 4 main characters will introduce the sport of colorguard by answering the question "Why are you involved in colorguard?" These interviews will be conducted individually in the Studio against a very black background. Fade to black.	2:00	3:30
Topic 2: The history of Colorguard (general) and Apex WG	Location: Steve's home; Newark, DE. This will be a parallel edit between interviews with Steve giving a brief history of how colorguard got its start and how it gained popularity over the years. The video of this will be pictures and old movies from the early years of colorguard. Then the two interviewees will transition into how they formed Apex Winterguard and that this is the 10th year of its existence. B-roll will include pictures and memorabilia from past seasons. This will end with them briefly explaining the show for this season.	3:00	6:30
Segment 2: Beginning of the season	Location: Life Community Church; Newark, DE. The beginning of any season is slow and the emotions are light. This mood will be reflected in this segment. It will include a vérité look into the beginning of the season and the B-roll will include people joking at practice and making many mistakes without any repercussions. It will also include a vérité look at a typical beginning of the season outing that the members engage in as sort of a bonding experience. This segment will include several vérité interviews with our 4 characters.	2:30	9:00
In-depth character 1: Nick	Nick's in-depth segment. This will give us a better look into his history with Apex, but will also focus on his life outside colorguard. It will be conducted as a directed interview inside his home, and the B-roll will include both his job as a bartender and	3:00	12:00

	as a child development teacher. Other B-roll may include additional footage of him at practice or a second camera at the interview.		
Segment 3: Learning the show	Location: Life Community Church; Newark, DE. This segment will continue to show the excitement of a new show and a new year, but frustrations will begin to show as learning work becomes difficult.	2:00	14:00
In-depth character 2: Megan	Location: Megan's house; Bensalem, PA. Megan's in-depth segment. It will be conducted at her house. She will talk about her struggles at home with her family as well as her current job situation. She will also mention her history with Apex. B-roll will include footage of her working at Wawa, family photos, and footage of her at practice.	3:00	17:00
Segment 4: Middle of the season	Location: Local shows; NJ, PA, and DE. This segment will be the 4 characters giving brief explanations on how the show [has] been going so far and what has been good and bad. The interviews will be vérité shot before and after shows/practices and the accompanying B-roll will mainly be of various shows highlighting on the important points that happened up to this point.	2:30	19:30
In-depth character 3: Jackie	Location: Jackie's apartment; Philadelphia, PA. Jackie's in-depth segment. Conducted in her apartment, Jackie will talk about her passion for the arts. She will mention both her love for acting and dance and how this influences her colorguard life. She will also go into detail about the financial struggles of being an actor and being involved with Apex. B-roll will include old pictures/footage of her dancing and acting, as well as her going through a pile of bills.	3:00	22:30
Segment 5: Last practice before Ohio	Location: Life Community Church; Newark, DE. This segment will most likely be very stressful and it will be presented as somewhat frantic because they will be trying to tie up all the loose ends from the rest of the season so that they have a fighting chance at finals. It will end with everyone leaving practice and giving thoughts on what they are most worried about.	1:30	24:00
In-depth character 4: Micah	Location: Micah's family house; Wilmington, DE. Micah's in-depth segment. His segment will kind of lighten the mood after the likely tense practice before Ohio. It will be conducted at his home while he is getting ready to go out and perform at a drag show. He will talk about his experiences with being gay and how colorguard helped him be comfortable with who he is. He will discuss financial problems and having an always uncertain future. B-roll will include photos from when he was growing up as well as footage of him interacting with members at practices.	3:00	27:00
Segment 6: Championships Topic 1: The build-up	Location: Practice site and hotel; Dayton, OH. This will show the high level of intensity and determination at the very last practice the night before the performance. There will be vérité interviews with the 4 characters at the hotel getting	2:00	29:00

	any last reactions on how they feel the final show will go.		
Topic 2: The performance	It will begin with Steve's reactions in the stands to how nervous/excited the[y] are for the team. The performance will be a video montage of the actual performance (since it would be too long to show in its entirety). Audio will be a song that reflects the emotion of the ups and downs of the performance itself. It will end with vérité interviews with the 4 characters immediately following their performance commenting on how they think they did.	2:00	31:00
Topic 3: The results	This will simply be a graphic explaining the turnout of Championships because the results aren't really the important thing; it was really about the people and the journey.	0:15	31:15
Segment 7: What do you pay and what are the payoffs?	Location: Studio, Rowan University; Glassboro, NJ. This segment will be like the "Why do you do colorguard?" segment. Each of the 4 main characters will have the chance to answer the question of "in what ways do you pay by doing colorguard" as well as "what are the payoffs and is it worth it?" This will give us a lasting impression of the sport of colorguard in general and on the individual character.	2:00	33:15

—— FUNDING AND PROMOTING THE DOCUMENTARY ——

There are two kinds of documentaries when it comes to production: funded and speculation.

Funded Documentary

A funded documentary has money up front and a budget paid by a company that is interested in the content of the documentary. The company might be an industrial organization, a TV/cable network, or a film company. If this is the case, then there is a real budget and often there are phases to the money flow. There are contracts, insurance policies, unions, and/or other controlling forces. The documentary idea has been presold. There are variations on how complex the ownership and distribution of the documentary is, but the makers of the documentary surrender some/all rights in exchange for funding and distribution.

Speculation Documentary

The documentary made on speculation is funded by the documentary makers and their network of friends, family, and fundraisers. The driving force is the desire and passion of the documentary makers. Often they go into big debt as they progress through the phases of production. The plan is to showcase the finished documentary at film festivals and hope for recognition and a distribution deal. Another avenue is to present it to TV stations and cable networks and hope for a deal.

Often it takes months or years for a completed documentary to find its niche in the media world. While you are waiting and pitching, you can also open up screening and distribution opportunities in your local and regional communities.

Web Promotion

Many first-time documentary makers use the Web and social networking to promote and sell their documentaries. In that case you are pitching your idea to an online community. The proposal facts and content rundown are on the Web page.

Here is an interesting case of a documentary producer using her MySpace page as a presentation place and selling tool for her documentary. In 2006, while she was a senior in college, Andrea Whiting took her lifelong passion for punk music and made a short, 20-minute documentary called *All Grown Up*. Although she was satisfied at the time with her short documentary, she decided to move to England and remake the film into a one-hour documentary that incorporated footage from her short documentary with new footage of the punk scene in Europe. As she was in the preproduction phase of her new documentary in 2007, she created a MySpace page for the documentary and blogged her progress on the remake of *All Grown Up*. She posted her production proposal on her Web site and added trailers and merchandise related to the project.

As she shot footage and made rough cuts, she marketed the remake on MySpace and took orders for the DVD. When she finished the new version of *All Grown Up*, she premiered it in 2007 in her home state of New Jersey and continued to market it on MySpace. She sold hundreds of copies at $15.95. It's a good example of how a documentary with a narrow target audience can hit that target audience and sell copies of the DVD directly to them. The online punk-rock community is large and looking for new media that celebrates its lifestyle.*

FINAL THOUGHTS

Articulating your documentary idea in proposal form enables you to present yourself and your idea to anyone who might get involved in your project. A well-thought-out and organized proposal gives you and your idea credibility. It makes you and the documentary real for others. By creating Web pages, trailers, still photos, podcasts, and related links, you can present yourself and your idea in a way that tells people you are serious and together. With the essence of your proposal in a written document, you can send it to anyone, anywhere, at a moment's notice. Creating the proposal also forces you to organize the details of production and put together important information in one place.

DOCUMENTARY REFERENCES

Each of these documentary references was chosen because it has a creative element or technique that stands out. Some of the most creative filmmaking has occurred while a documentarian is telling his or her story. It is hoped that the curious reader will be motivated to watch many of these documentaries not only for enjoyment, but also for inspiration.

All Grown Up. 2007. Andrea Whiting. Psyko Punk Productions. This one-hour documentary about the punk scene, past and present, grew out of a college film Whiting made on

*The *My Space* page for *All Grown Up* is http://www.myspace.com/allgrownupthemovie.

punk in the 1980s. The director had hundreds of hours of punk performances she had shot herself, and she integrates it well with interviews and hyper-fast editing.

Behind the Music series. 1997–2006. George Moll and Paul Gallagher. VH1 Productions. This legendary, one-hour documentary series has made over 200 documentaries about musical artists and performers. For many Americans now in their thirties and forties, *BTM* was their first exposure to the documentary form. Although the episodes followed a strict formula, they often broke through the barriers many of the artists put up and mined raw emotions. The drama the show uncovered through well researched interviews was always real.

The Curse of King Tutankhamun. 1999. Connie Bottinelli. Discovery Communications. This documentary was made for Discovery Communications and is structured for television. Director Bottinelli re-creates her historical eras in a creative and effective manner. Her color palette in her recreations features a soft golden glow that references the desert, King Tut's tomb, and Egypt.

Movement X. 2008. Cindy Lewandowski. Rowan University. This documentary follows a team of color guard performers through their final season. Four members tell their personal stories. The physical and mental toll they pay to perform is eye opening. A fascinating sliver of the performance life.

Scared Straight! 1978. Arnold Shapiro. Golden West Television. This classic vérité documentary has the lifers in a maximum security prison trying to scare a group of at-risk teenagers into walking the straight and narrow. The Oscar-winning film captures an event that is only going to happen once. Shapiro met with the prisoners ahead of time, demonstrated to them that he had researched their program and won their trust. The raw language and intensity of the lifers creates an atmosphere that is electric. The observational camera captures it all. Beautifully edited.

Seabrook Farms Remembered. 2002. Ned Eckhardt. Seabrook Educational and Cultural Center. When I made this historical documentary that chronicles the extraordinary activities that happened on a farm in southern New Jersey, the primary audience was both adults and middle school students who visit the museum daily and watch the documentary. I used music appropriate to the audiences and added behind-the-scenes production footage to give the film a more modern look.

Part II: Field and Studio Production

5. Production Equipment and Decisions

The universe of production equipment has changed drastically in the past ten years or so. The tools of production and postproduction are now available to everyone. As a result, as you decide on your equipment, you need to first know the answer to two important questions: Who is your target audience and what is your budget?

TARGET AUDIENCES

There are usually three basic audiences for documentaries.

First-Run Theaters, High-End Festivals, Large Distributors, Television and Cable Networks

If these are your targets, then you are making a documentary for general consumption by a mass audience. That means there is a certain production level you must maintain. You need a broadcast-level camera, along with a professional camera operator, professionally gathered sound, and experienced editing that includes both color correction and signal enhancement.

The high-end, Academy Award–eligible level of film festivals includes Sundance, Toronto, Tribeca, Slamdance, Cannes, Banff, Silverdocs and other festivals at which first-run films are premiered and the distributors are there looking to buy.

There are many stories about first-time documentarians striking gold at the large festivals. Especially Sundance. In 1999 Chris Smith and Sarah Price had their low-budget documentary, *American Movie*, about a young, Midwestern filmmaker trying to get his films made and his life together, win the Grand Jury Prize for Documentary at the Sundance Film Festival. Sony bought the distribution rights for $1 million.

When Michael Moore shoots his documentaries, he uses a high-end HD digital camera and a professional sound person. He is all about making folksy, vérité films for the people, but he makes sure his pictures and sound are worthy of big-screen projection, signal distribution, and DVD mastering. If you look at the 25 documentaries nominated for Academy Awards between 2006 and 2011, half were shot on digital cameras and half with film cameras.

Mid-level Film Festivals, Local/Regional Television, and Personal Contacts

This festival audience watches a mix of production levels. The cheap independent films are mixed in with mid- and high-end ones. There are only a few distributors present, and the festival is mostly for networking with other filmmakers and enjoying independent filmmaking.

Local television stations, especially PBS stations, often will air films they see at these festivals. You can submit your documentary to local documentary series programs. These are competitive submissions, and often the themes/subjects of the documentaries must relate directly to their local-market audience. The going rate for purchasing airings at TV stations in mid-to-large markets is $100/minute. Mostly, the TV stations are looking for short documentaries, 10–30 minutes long. Longer formatted documentaries should be 55–58 minutes so they can fill a PBS station hour or 44 minutes if they have to fill a commercial station hour.

In Philadelphia, PA, there is a public TV station, WYBE, Channel 35. This station is smaller in size, scope, and budget than its rival Philadelphia PBS station, WHYY. WYBE offers a documentary series every year called *Philadelphia Stories*. This is a series of locally made documentaries and narrative films that runs in prime time, in rotation, for months. WYBE pays the documentary makers $100/minute. The documentary maker must sign a contract that absolves the station of any responsibility for content that might hurt its application for license renewal. It is the filmmaker's responsibility to guarantee that all major subjects in the documentary have signed releases, and that there is no footage or music that hasn't been released to the documentary maker.*

The Web is another destination and showcase for newly minted documentaries that don't have distribution deals. Vimeo.com has a large inventory of documentaries, an annual film festival for its users, and a total viewing audience in the hundred of thousands. Similarly, hulu.com. posts thousands of documentaries. The sites are interactive and encourage feedback and ratings. If your documentary brings something new and original to the table, you can create a buzz and an audience. The Sundance Channel is a great resource for viewing recent documentaries that have earned Sundance's official approval. Mondays are "docday" and the channel runs uninterrupted blocks of documentaries for 24 hours. There are also on-demand documentaries for free.

Small Festivals, Personal Screenings and DVD Reproduction and Sales

This audience doesn't demand high production values. The subject matter usually defines the audience. Self-created premieres and screenings are how many of the documentaries debut. Many cities have outdoor screenings in public spaces during the summer, while bars/nightclubs often have late-night screenings for invited audiences. Postings on YouTube, Facebook, and MySpace often are part of the rollout. Sales of the DVD usually don't extend beyond family and friends, although Web promotion might garner some sales. But often a buzz can be generated at these small-venue presentations, and films can move on to larger festivals or revenue-generating screenings.

---

*WYBE's website for the TV station and the documentary series: *Philadelphia Stories* is http://www.mindtv.org/styles/mind/www/about2.html.

By being realistic about who your core audience is, you can narrow your focus and make your production and design decisions. If your finished work captures a fascinating story with compelling characters that a wide audience would enjoy, then your documentary could become the next *American Movie, Born into Brothels, Jesus Camp, Anvil, King of Kong,* or *Catfish.*

BUDGET AND PRODUCTION DECISIONS

Shooting on Film

Although shooting in film is limiting in many ways, the image is still special. The colors are rich and deep, lighting can be used to enhance the story, low light levels can be used to generate interesting images and colors. Film captures what is called a "wider dynamic range of color" than digital video.

The documentary *Crumb* (1994), directed by Jerry Zwigoff, was shot in 16 mm color film because Robert Crumb is a comic book artist who often works in bright colors. Film was able to capture these rich colors. Crumb's life is often psychologically and emotionally dark, and the crew, shooting in a vérité style, often worked in low light levels as they followed Crumb through his odd life. In many settings, especially interiors, the film was able to reinforce the contrast between the relative lightness of his art and the darkness of Crumb's personal life.

In another use of film, Stacy Peralta's *Dogtown and Z-Boys* (2001) captures the edgy world of the early skateboarders by shooting the interviews in grainy, 16 mm black-and-white film. Contrast between black and white is better when shot in film than in color video that gets changed to black and white in post. The contrast ratio is greater and the look is more grainy and aesthetically interesting.

The limitations of shooting in film are cost, expertise, and time involved. To buy a 16 mm film camera costs much more than a digital video camera. Renting a film camera is also expensive and includes a lot of specialized production skills regarding lenses, film stock, developing, and transfer to digital for editing. Film stock is expensive compared to the cost of a 60-minute videotape or large P2 card. The operation of a film camera demands more skills than the average digital camera. Mistakes are more drastic when shooting in film. Sound gathering requires a sound person to operate a separate audio recorder at all times. This person needs skills not only in sound gathering, but in clap synching and film loading and changing. The developing step in film is costly and creates a downtime between shooting and waiting for the developed film and then for having it transferred to digital video so it can be edited on a computer.*

Film is a strong option if you are shooting a directed documentary for which you can control most of the shooting. However, if you are making a vérité documentary, then the convenience of long, uninterrupted shooting that digital gives you, along with the short downtime for changing tapes/cards and the ability of the camera to follow the action for long periods of time, make digital video usually the best option.

---

*Costs for film and developing vary widely, but a 400 foot roll that records 11 minutes of footage costs between $90 and $145 to purchase and $60 a roll to develop.

During shooting, most 16 mm cameras can only support 11-minute rolls, so there is a lot of down time connected to changing and storing film reels. Super 16 mm film creates a wider picture. But film forces you to plan and budget your shooting, so there is less wasted footage than with digital video. Not every documentary is best served by film, but it is definitely worth considering. Film provides a "look" that deepens the colors and uses lighting that can provide more of an art overtone.

Digital Video

Most documentaries these days are shot on digital video. There are a lot of digital video cameras and formats. Equipment selection can be very confusing. Here are some organizational guidelines that should help you choose the right equipment for your project.

• **Workflow** • Before you choose your camera and editing software, you need to understand the workflow of the production process. This flow is important. It goes like this:

➤Acquisition: Camera and sound system. Maybe lighting instruments.

  ♦ **Digital tape**: The easiest ways are either to connect a Firewire cable directly from your camera to your project computer or use a separate, dedicated playback machine to digitize the footage.

  ♦ **Memory card**: As you are shooting, your card will fill up and you will need another computer and/or flash card to transfer the footage from the card. Since the card erases data as you transfer the footage, you might want a backup storage system just in case. The next step is to transfer all of the raw digital footage stored in your "holding" computer and/or flash cards to the project computer.

➤Moving files into your editing software. Once you have digitized your footage and transferred it into the project computer, you can move all or some of these digitized files into the editing software program and begin the work of building your project.

➤Editing with your software.

➤Color correcting and enhancing your video during postproduction. After your documentary is completed in a final cut, you want to go back and color correct all the video so it looks matched in every sequence.

➤Exporting the finished product to DVD and other high-resolution storage devices.

Setting up this workflow is complex, even if you are shooting with a prosumer camera and have a low budget. Make sure you have enough hard-drive memory and constantly back up the project files. When in doubt, always ask for a second opinion. It's always good to have a technical advisor connected to the project.

• **Digital Cameras** • There are so many excellent digital cameras on the professional and consumer markets that finding the right one for your needs is a challenge. Before we get into some specifics, here is a piece of advice: Sony, Panasonic, and Canon are generally considered the three best makers of video cameras. They have been doing it for a long time and they stand behind their products. They make cameras for many levels of shooting; spending some time researching them should enable you to find the right camera. Check the Web—camera specifications and prices are all there. You should also try to find local media production shooters who own their own cameras and have an informed opinion on what cameras can and can't do.

After some thought you might want to consider renting a camera package from a local professional rental company. These companies create camera packages that include your choice of camera, a sound system, lights and accessories. If you are sure of your number of shooting days, this may not be a bad way to go. Another way is to hire a shooter who owns his/her own equipment. Shooters have day rates for their services. Figure on between $400 and $1,000 per day, depending on his/her experience and expertise.

But if you and your friends are going to make the documentary, you need a camera good enough to insure your pictures and sound will be worthy of screenings, DVD mastering, and broadcast. Here are some items to think about as you prepare for your production.

➤Framing accuracy involves the camera delivering what you see in real life onto the digital tape or card. Since digital video can lose up to ten percent of the visual information around the edges, you have to shoot and frame in such a way as to allow for this loss. The camera should be run through tests so you know that what you are framing is what you will get, minus the loss around the edges. The area of the frame that will definitely retain information is called the safe area. Many camera eyepieces or screens will have the safe area marked.

➤Color balance is an electronic function in digital video, and the camera operator needs to understand color registration via internal menus and white balance to adjust for different lighting conditions. Failure to understand how the camera makes pictures and adjusts to light will result in poor color reproduction. Sometimes a mistake in white balance can be corrected in postproduction, but most of the time it cannot.

➤Manual zooms, f-stop controls, and focus are three essential responsibilities of a camera operator and are also important for successful capturing of your story. It is never a good idea to put the camera in "automatic" in these three areas and just let

the camera roll. You remove your own personal touch when you turn over the decision making to the camera. Today's cameras are modern miracles of engineering, but you bring the aesthetics to the capturing of reality. And having control over your focus, f-stops, and zooms in order to fill your storytelling needs is important. All members of the crew should practice with all of the equipment prior to starting the documentary. You never know when you might get pressed into duty because someone can't make a critical shoot.

Here is a quick rundown of the camera universe. It is far from complete, but it shows the range and capabilities of cameras.

LOW-END, CHEAPER CAMERAS

➤Flip cameras (standard and HD): $200. Ten minutes of video storage, low-medium quality, difficult to transfer to editing software. Good for quick, raw footage to complement other footage on a better camera. Small and unobtrusive. Can be hidden easily. Getting good audio is a problem. Works well for B-roll if a home-video look is what you want.

➤35 mm still and video cameras (standard and HD): $1,900. These cameras enable you to change lenses, work in the 35 mm aspect ratio, and record still images and 11 minutes of HD video. The quality is excellent and the signal digitizes easily. You must clear the memory every 11 minutes, which means you need a separate storage device to which you can transfer the footage. You can't work as fast as with other systems.

➤Digital Panasonic DVX100 A or B or Sony HVR-V1U or Canon XL2 (standard and HD): $2,500. These cameras are workhorses and field proven. Many feature films have been shot with these cameras. They come in standard and HD, tape or P2 card. These cameras are Firewire ready for digitizing. The audio inputs accept Canon three-pin cables and the menu settings allow for control of the image, if necessary. The documentary *Murderball* (2005), produced by the documentary division at VH1, is notable for having been shot with a very low budget. The main camera used was a Panasonic DVX100. A Sony PD150 was used to shoot some of the early interviews. The crew rigged a Sennheiser shotgun microphone to use as a boom, and relied heavily on lavalier wireless microphones as well. Available lighting was used almost exclusively. Additional light was provided using an inexpensive china ball. In one example of on-the-spot lighting, a flashlight beam was diffused using only a napkin.*

➢DVCProA/B Standard or HD Sony and Canon broadcast cameras: $8,000–10,000. These cameras are the broadcast workhorses. They have three chips, which create a beautiful picture that holds up through the workflow process. They're larger than the DVX100 and weigh 15 lbs. Many high-end narrative and documentary films have been shot with these cameras.

➢Red and blue cameras: $30,000. These are the current standard for high-end shooting. Their memory cards allow direct recording onto a computer. There are many menu controls for optimum pictures in almost every light level situation. The cameras aren't mobile because of the computer connections and size. But the picture is exceptional. The price has been coming down each year.

Sound Systems

Needless to say, capturing clean, crisp sound is always a challenge. An understanding of microphones and their pick-up patterns is essential. Here are some tried-and-true systems. Systems consist of microphone and recording device. Sometimes the recording device is in the cam-

era, and sometimes it is a separate piece of equipment.

• Microphone Choices•
Shotgun Mikes

This is a highly directional microphone that must be pointed directly at the sound source, and be within three to six feet of the subject. Often the shotgun mike is mounted on a handheld fishpole, pistol handgrip, or a larger boom pole. If you use a shotgun mike, there is a need for a sound person to hold and point the mike. If you are shooting a directed interview, then you can mount the shotgun on a boom stand.

The sound person might also have a sound-recording device around his/her neck, so movement and flexibility is limited. If the microphone connects directly to the camera, then the camera operator becomes the sound person and must monitor the sound via headphones and VU meter in the viewfinder.

Shotguns can be FM wireless. That enables the sound person to be freer, but then the sound person must also control a transmitting station. The receiving station will be on the camera or cameraperson. Shotgun mikes are good for B-roll shooting, run-and-gun news-type shooting, and vérité-style shooting if the mike has been accepted by your subjects. Two-person shooting teams need to practice how they will work together before beginning production. It can't be said too many times: there are far more mistakes in sound recording than in video recording.

Lavalier/Clip-on Mikes

These mikes are omnidirectional and pick up sound from all directions equally. If there is ambient sound in the shooting environment, then the lavalier mike will pick it up. For directed interviews, clip-

---

*Special Feature Director Commentary on the DVD of *Murderball*.

These are the three microphone options for documentary shooting. FM wireless systems can make them wireless, but they need batteries for their transmitters and receiving stations. A headset is critical for monitoring sound *(Ned Eckhardt 2010).*

ping on a lavalier mike is quick and efficient. You need to decide if you want an FM wireless version. If so, then the subject will have a transmitting station the size of a pack of cigarettes clipped out of sight. If you are in a controlled situation and your subject is stationary, you might want to use an audio cable that runs directly into either a sound mixer or the camera.

If you are shooting in a vérité style, then often the best miking system is to hide the lavalier mike under the clothing just under the chin. Companies make very small lavalier mikes that can be hidden easily. If you add an FM wireless system to the mike, then your subject is free to move just about anywhere. Sometimes it's easy to place the transmitter on a belt behind the subject, or even hide the transmitter in a pocket or handbag. But because there is clothing around the system, you need to make sure the sound doesn't have any rustling noise in it. Also, both the lavalier

mike and transmitter need batteries, so you need to always have a fresh supply.

HANDHELD MIKES

If you have an on-camera host/subject who is talking to the camera, you might want to consider a handheld mike. This gives the subject a "newsy" look, but maybe that is what you want. Once again, you need to decide if the mike is wireless or not.

The subject can do quick interviews/bites/man-on-the-street features using the handheld mike. The cameraperson can frame tight head-and-shoulder shots and keep the handheld mike out of the frame.

CAMERA MIKES

The biggest mistake rookie documentary makers make is to rely on the camera mike as the primary sound-gathering mike. Camera mikes are made to pick up sound from the general area of shooting. Most of the time the mike is too far away from the subject to deliver clean, crisp sound. It is there for backup and B-roll sound, not for primary sound like an interview or quick bite.

On the other hand, don't deactivate the camera mike. Always have it recording. It is there for backup. Plug your primary sound mike into the other audio channel. If your camera won't accept an external microphone, then you are in trouble and probably want to rethink your choice of camera.

• **Headset** • Someone (camera operator and/or sound person) must listen to the recorded sound during shooting. If a hiss or crackle develops only the headset listener will catch it. The audio signal will still look OK in the viewfinder, but a headset will catch it. If you hear an unwanted sound, like an air conditioner, airplane, buzz, hum, or bothersome ambient noise, always stop production immediately and fix the problem. If you don't, then all of your pictures will have unusable audio.

• **Film Camera Sound Recording Systems** • If you are shooting in film, you will need a separate audio recorder. A digital audio recorder like a Sony, Nagra, or other high-end digital recorder is recommended. It puts a time code on the digital audiotape or hard drive.

"Clap Synch" is a time-tested way to synchronize the audio with the film. Someone stands in front of the camera, then both the film camera and the audio recorder are started. When they are up to speed, the person claps. Both devices see/hear the clap and it is possible to easily match the audio with the picture during editing.

Camera Mounts

• **Tripods** • These are the most-used camera mounts. There are light tripods for the field, and heavier tripods for inside and studio shooting. Tripods are there for camera stability and level horizons. They are most used for interviews and directed B-roll sequences. Your camera aesthetic will tell you if you are going to be using a tripod.

• **Monopods** • These are single-leg camera mounts that allow the camera to move quickly and still have a steady, level shot. On small digital cameras they work well as a flexible accessory. They telescope into an easily portable system when they are not being used.

• **Steady Cam Harness Systems** • Full, big rigs for steady cams are expensive and very heavy. Usually they weigh over 50 lbs. with a mid-level-sized camera. They are a specialized piece of equipment and you usually have to hire a steady cam operator who owns the rig and knows how it operates.

There are smaller, lighter stabilizing systems that are built for small digital cameras. These aren't as heavy and complex. You can buy or rent them and your camera will be stabilized as you move through your shooting. Since movement is an aesthetic element, you need to determine how much freedom your camera will have.

• **Jib Arm** • This is a telescoped pole with a camera-mounting system on the end. The pole extends anywhere from six to 20 feet, depending on the size of the camera and the needs of your production. There is a monitor at the bottom of the pole that enables you to see what the camera is seeing. Large jib arms involve a driving base and a cranelike arm. Smaller jib arms can be operated by one person. Jib arms enable the camera to rise or fall during a shot and deliver a high-angle shot.

Camera Aesthetics

The camera is a flexible and creative tool in creating the "look" and style of your documentary. Although the camera has infinite potential, how you will decide to use it will probably fall into one of two categories.

• **The Traditional Camera** • This camera is steady and calm and doesn't draw attention to itself. The frame is always calm. It is either on a tripod or "rock steady" handheld. It keeps the horizons level and follows the rules of framing. In directed documentaries in which all the elements are decided in advance, the traditional camera is probably what you want. Historical documentaries especially call for calmly filmed experts to tell us the story.

Ken Burns is a master of composing interview shots of his storytellers with a traditional camera on a tripod in a setting that subtly enhances the aura of the talker. In Spike Lee's *4 Little Girls* (1997), he had his cameraperson frame his subjects with standard framing and lighting in home settings. Everything is calm and still as the parents tell their tragic stories of the deaths of their daughters. In the documentary *Enron: The Smartest Guys in the Room* (2005), the director composed the shots with his interview subjects in upscale conference and boardrooms, using a tripod camera and beautifully composed shots that obey the rules of traditional framing. These settings evoke a feeling of order and power that contrasts with the chaos the subjects' decisions are wreaking on the financial world. Errol Morris often likes to compose long shots of his storytellers with another large object in the frame with them. In his documentary *Gates of Heaven* (1978), sometimes it is a tree or a building or a landscape. The camera is traditional and observes level horizons. These long shots are so artistically composed they are like paintings and make us appreciate how insignificant we sometimes are in relationship to our surroundings.

Director Errol Morris sometimes frames his storyteller with a composed long shot that includes an external object to balance the image *(Independent Film Channel and Fourth Floor Productions, 1978).*

• **Freestyle Camera** • This camera is not confined to a camera mount. It is always handheld. In vérité-style documentaries it is always moving. The frame is always alive. If the subject is still, the camera floats while it shoots. If the subject is moving, it moves with the subject. Sometimes quick snap zooms and whip pans are part of the camera aesthetic. The content of the documentary should lead to a decision on using a freestyle camera. Dutch angles, low- and high-angle shots can also add to the look.

The director of *Dogtown and Z-Boys* used the handheld, freestyle aesthetic as he shot interviews in the field in the settings where the story unfolded. The subjects are rebels and the moving camera gives the viewer a sense of excitement. *Overnight* (2003) was shot over a number of years with a variety of film and video cameras. The story is a chaotic one and the jerky, handheld camera work reflects the instability of the life of Troy Duffy, the main subject. *The Cove* (2009) is a social-issue documentary that reveals the horror of an annual dolphin slaughter in Japan. The camera often gathered footage that was controversial or unwanted by the subjects. The handheld feel reflects the urgency of the story. In *Madonna: Truth or Dare* (1991) director Alek Keshishian mixed his tripod performance cameras with his handheld vérité cameras. These behind-the-scenes cameras moved, floated, whip panned, snap zoomed, and adjusted focus to create an edgy, constant movement aesthetic that is just like Madonna.

In the documentary *Madonna: Truth or Dare,* the director mixed steady, color footage of the performance sequences with grainy, handheld, behind-the-scenes footage *(Boy Toy, Inc. and Miramax Productions, 1991).*

• **A Mixed Style** • Sometimes it is possible to mix traditional and freestyle looks. Maybe there are vérité sequences in which the camera is freestyle, then interview sequences in which the camera is traditional.

The documentary *American Hardcore* (2006) is a look at the world of punk rock from 1980 to 1986. The production values are low and the stylized interviews feature a mix of tripod and handheld camera work. The settings are a wide variety of streets, homes, workplaces, and stores. The interview setups are a mix of lit and available light. The overall aesthetic is one of raw reminiscence by the punk rockers who

were there. The mixed style doesn't intrude on the story; these are rule-breaking folks to begin with, so the style breaks rules too.

The documentary *Murderball* explores the world of wheelchair rugby and the disabled men who play it. It is mostly vérité documentary that has a mixed shooting style for the interviews. Some are handheld with mild movement and some are traditionally shot on a tripod. The calm interviews contrast with the wild mayhem of the competitions, and reinforce the courage of the players.

The documentary *Buena Vista Social Club* (1999) uses a mix of handheld and tripod interviews. Because the story is about Cuban musicians remembering their younger days while they are still playing and recording their own special brand of music, the director added an interesting visual aesthetic. He had his camera constantly moving during the musical performance B-roll and the many storyteller walks through Havana. Some of the interviews have the camera circling the subjects while they talk. This aesthetic of the moving and circling camera adds a feeling of being surrounded by the musical ethos of Havana. The camera was on a steady cam apparatus and the constant movement infuses the viewer with a sense of how the music makes people want to move and dance.

The documentary *King of Kong: A Fistful of Quarters* (2007) uses both handheld footage and tripod footage to present the world of old-school video gaming. Well-lit, composed-shot interviews are mixed in with arcade and B-roll footage that is handheld, rough and real.

FINAL THOUGHTS

Your equipment choices will impact your entire production process. Decide on

how you plan to use the camera, then research the types of cameras available to you. As part of your research, watch documentaries that have used a variety of cameras and shooting styles. Make your equipment selections, then practice with the camera, sound system, and lighting instruments, if necessary.

DOCUMENTARY REFERENCES

Each of these documentary references was chosen because it has a creative element or technique that stands out. Some of the most creative filmmaking has occurred while a documentarian is telling his or her story. It is hoped that the curious reader will be motivated to watch many of these documentaries not only for enjoyment, but also for inspiration.

American Hardcore. 2006. Paul Rachman. Envision Films. This film focuses on six years of punk rock music and culture (1980–1986). The music clips are wild and the interviews are a crazy mix of handheld and tri-pod cameras in lots of different settings. The production values are low, but the feeling of rule-breaking adds to the effectiveness of the film.

American Movie. 1999. Chris Smith and Sarah Price. Bluemark Productions. This surprise Sundance winner follows an obsessed Milwaukee filmmaker trying to overcome many obstacles and get his horror film made. Smith and Price were the crew as they became friends with the main character, Mark Borchardt. Shot in 16 mm color film over the course of two years, this mostly vérité film was made on a shoestring budget but captures a fascinating story. A must for aspiring filmmakers.

Anvil! 2008. Sacha Gervasi. This charming story of two guys in their fifties who have been playing heavy metal music in bands since they were 14 was shot in digital video with a minimum of production values. The story, although surrounded by music, is really about the deep, complex friendship of the two main subjects. This is a good example of how sticking with interesting subjects will often lead to a compelling story. It shares a lot of the elements of *American Movie*.

Born into Brothels. 2004. Zana Briski and Ross Kauffman. Red Light Films. This is a personal story of how a woman with a camera can make a difference to neglected kids being raised in the red light district of Calcutta. This Oscar winner was shot with a small digital camera and a lot of love.

Buena Vista Social Club. 1999. Wim Wenders. Road Movies Film Produktion. This film captures the beauty of both the older jazz musicians and Havana, as director Wenders documents the making of a jazz album and subsequent concerts by the jazz immortals who created the music. Many interesting interview settings and often the camera work is surprising. The sound track is phenomenal if you like classic jazz.

Crumb. 1994. Terry Zwigoff. Crumb Partners. This Sundance winner was shot in 16mm color film and has a vibrant, dark aesthetic, not unlike the subject, Robert Crumb. Its vérité style captures the strange, intense life of an iconic artist.

Dogtown and Z-Boys. 2001. Stacy Peralta. Vans, Inc., and Sony Entertainment. Double Sundance winner. Sean Penn narrates this fast-paced, creative telling of the origins of skateboarding. Peralta uses his 16mm skills to add a jumpy, layered look to his B-roll and montages. He mixes black and white interviews with color B-roll and home movie archival footage.

4 Little Girls. 1998. Spike Lee. Home Box Office. This sensitive, well-researched, historical documentary retells the tragic story of the civil rights church bombing in Birmingham, AL, in 1963. The parents and families of the four slain girls relate the story in intimate interviews. As the story progresses the framing of the parents begins to subtly break the rules and adds an intensive feel to the story.

Jesus Camp. 2006. Heidi Ewing and Rachel Grady. Loki Films, Inc. This intense, vérité film about evangelical Pentecostal Christians preparing for religious warfare by running a religious camp every summer is shocking and a cautionary tale. It won many film festivals and was nominated for an Academy Award.

King of Kong: A Fistful of Quarters. 2007. Seth Gordon. LargeLab. This low-budget, digital documentary explores the world of arcade gaming by following the top two scoring gamers as they compete for the highest score. Production values are low but the story is compelling.

Madonna: Truth or Dare. 1991. Alek Keshishian. Boy Toy and Miramax Films. This is a very interesting film. Madonna's Blonde Ambition world tour provides the background for the gritty black and white, behind-the-scenes, vérité footage and the slick, color performance footage. The camera captures everyone's stress and anxiety. Madonna emerges as an enigmatic, driven, sad, strong woman.

Murderball. 2005. Henry Alex Rubin and Dana Adam Shapiro. ThinkFilm LLC. The film was made by the documentary division at MTV/VH1. This mostly vérité cultural study of the members of a wheelchair rugby team uses sound during the competition sequences in a creative and interesting way. It was a low-budget, digital film that shows if you have the story, production values don't have to be huge. It was nominated for an Academy Award.

Roger and Me (1989) and other films of Michael Moore. Dog Eat Dog Films. Michael Moore has done more to raise the national interest in documentaries than any other individual ever. Since he made *Roger and Me* in 1989 he has made four feature length documentaries: *Bowling for Columbine* (2002), *Fahrenheit 9/11* (2004), *Sicko* (2007), and *Capitalism: A Love Story* (2009). He is in the tradition of John Grierson, who used the documentary form in the 1930s–1960s to reveal problems in society that needed immediate attention. Michael Moore is controversial. He is an on-camera everyman who wants answers to tough questions. He is a spokesperson for the Americans who don't have a voice. He has won Academy Awards and Cannes Film Festivals, his documentaries have been seen by more people than any others, and he has grossed millions of dollars. If you want to find out what he does with the money, visit his web page http://www.michaelmoore.com/. I feel he has brought the documentary form to the people. He is one reason there are now so many documentaries that demand honest behavior from individuals, corporations, and institutions. Before you pass judgment on him, watch his documentaries.

6. Your Storytellers: Interviews and Conversations

DECISIONS FOR PRODUCERS, DIRECTORS AND PRODUCTION DESIGNERS

If you are creating directed interview sequences in your documentary, then all of the design and composition decisions are under your control. Matching the "look" of your storytellers with the "tone and feel" of your documentary subject matter takes a lot of thought. If you are shooting in the vérité style, then very little is within your control. But there are some suggestions you can make to your subjects that might enhance your story.

There are many ways to present your storytelling subjects. All of the possible settings fit into two categories: reality environments or stylized environments. What follows are analyses and many examples of both standard and nontraditional interview setups. There are many references to documentaries that were shot from 2000 to 2010. If you would like to see the way the referenced setups look, the documentaries should be available for free on the Web or inexpensively via Netflix. If you would like to purchase the DVD, it should be available on Amazon. Here are a wide array of approaches to shooting your storytellers' interviews or conversations.

Reality Settings

• Outside: Natural Light, Sunny Day •
Sunny days generate high contrast between the direct sunlight areas and the shadowed areas. Most digital cameras have at least a 40:1 contrast ratio tolerance before the iris starts to shut down. The average sunny day exceeds the 40:1 ratio. Here are some ways to deal with the sunny-day environment.

USE THE SUN AS A BACKLIGHT

You position the subject with his/her back to the sun. This creates a halo effect around the hair and shoulders. The face is evenly lit in shadow. You can either use a reflective material (bounce board or flexfill) to create a keylike effect from the front or just shoot the shadowed face. These types of interviews are usually most effective if the shot is a relatively tight one. Stand-up interviews shot outside are hard to sustain because of the awkwardness of everyone standing. But sitting someone on a chair/bench/rock/wall can be very effective, especially if there is an object or vista in the frame with the subject that enhances the interview.

USE THE SUN AS A KEY OR SIDE LIGHT

This requires the sun to strike the subject directly. If the subject has fair fleshtones, the light reflection usually causes hot spots on the face that exceed the 40:1 contrast ratio—ok if you're breaking the rules for effect. You can also close the iris and correct for hot spots. If the subject has darker fleshtones, this lighting often works better because dark skin absorbs more of the light.

SHOOT IN THE SHADE

This creates a darker, even lighting of the face. If you want a tight shot of the face, you may want to open the iris a stop or use the ultra light/sun gun on the camera. Beware of the sunlight in the background of the shot. This could cause too great a contrast ratio and "blow out" the picture with a white-bloom effect—although sometimes this blown-out white effect works for your design aesthetic.

In Andrew Jarecki's documentary *Capturing the Friedmans* (2003), there is an interview with one of the adult sons of a convicted sex abuser. The son is sitting on the steps that lead to his suburban house. The camera is 15 feet away and frames a wide shot of the son and the entryway to

Capturing the Friedmans is a study of a family and town trying to deal with a horrific crime. This interview with the son of a convicted sex offender on the steps of his home gives a sense of the neighborhood and economic status of the family *(Hit the Ground Running LLC and HBO, Inc., 2003).*

his home. The son is miked with an FM wireless mike because the wide shot eliminates a boom mike. There are two other tighter-framed shots during the interview that create visual interest. The interview was shot with the sun behind him and the sunlight changes as the interview goes on. Because the negative attitudes of many of his neighbors are part of the aftermath of the crime, the impact of the long shot with his home and neighborhood in the background is powerful.

Capturing the Friedmans was nominated for an Academy Award in 2003. Director Andrew Jarecki tells the story of a family torn apart by charges and convictions of sexual abuse of local children by a father and son. As the story unfolds, you realize there are really two stories: the main one of the family dealing with the shock of the charges of sexual abuse and a secondary one of how the local community (Great Neck, Long Island) deals with the notoriety of the case. *Capturing the Friedmans* is a directed documentary that reveals during its interview sequences the inside and outside of a typical, middle-class home in the community.

Capturing the Friedmans presented a dilemma of objectivity for Jarecki. As he transitioned from the research phase to the shooting phase, he formed the conclusion that the father and son were innocent of the crime of sexual abuse. This was in direct opposition to the courts that had found the two guilty. Rather than infuse his documentary with his point of view, he tried to walk the line of objectivity. The documentary was praised by audiences and critics as an objective study of the strange crimes. Then Jarecki admitted that he felt the father and son were innocent. That threw his objectivity into dispute and raised the question yet again of whether the documentarian has a responsibility to present truth as s/he sees it or whether s/he should try to remain objective and let the audience decide. This fascinating conundrum is still playing out in the documentary world.*

• **Outside: Natural Light, Cloudy Day** • On a gray-sky day, although it appears dull, the sky is really generating a lot of light. Even with today's digital cameras that have a contrast ratio of at least 40:1, too much sky in the picture can shut a camera iris down and result in the foreground turning dark. A good idea is to purposely shoot the sky out of the shot as much as you can. The cloudy sky will evenly light your subject if you position him/her so there is no sky in the shot. You can use buildings, gardens, or natural or human-made settings as backgrounds.

Some modern documentaries that effectively use outdoor interviews are *My Architect* and *The Weather Underground*. If you are shooting a vérité documentary like *Hoop Dreams* and *Jesus Camp*, you want to try to always be aware of where the sunlight source is in relation to your subjects. As your subjects talk to the people in their worlds and/or talk to the camera, try to always know where the sun is and use it for either key, back, or side lighting. Often the camera operator can adjust the angle of the camera to utilize the sunlight best. The same would apply if you are using natural sunlight inside. You would try to not shoot out the window, because the sunlight might shut down your iris. Rather, you would try to position yourself so the camera has its back to the window and the sunlight is falling on your subject.

• **Sound Outside** • Natural or ambient sound ("nat sound" is the universal production reference) is great for B-roll but tough on interviews. If you don't want the audience to see a microphone, then you will probably use a shotgun mike that is positioned just out of the frame. Because shotgun mikes are usually high-quality mikes, they pick up all the ambient sound within the pick-up range. If you want the shotgun mike close to the sound source, then frame a tight shot rather than a wide shot.

A better system might be a lavalier or small clip-on mike positioned close to the subject's mouth, with or without a wind screen on it. *Whether or not you are going to reveal mikes is an important decision.* You might want to hide a small FM wireless lavalier mike on your subject so you will always have good sound. The FM transmitter must also be on the subject, but it can be clipped onto a belt or put into a pocket.

If you are going to be shooting in outdoor environments that generate a lot of ambient sound, try to get a microphone as close to the sound source (mouth) as possible. Sometimes sound quality can impact a lot of the pictorial elements in interview setups that occur outside of studios, workplaces, and homes. Some modern documentaries that have an "immediate" feel to them actually mix sound systems: shotguns out of the frame for some footage, hidden lavaliers for others. If you have an oncamera host/narrator, you need to decide if a handheld mike or lavalier works best, or if a shotgun mike outside the frame is best.

FM wireless mikes allow subjects a lot of freedom, but add more technology to the shoot. Also, a *field mixer* is recommended whenever possible. But often shooting outdoors adds a "run-and-gun" overtone to things, and simplified mike systems work best.

---

*Special Features on the DVD included a commentary by Andrew Jarecki on the making of the documentary. Roger Ebert wrote a perceptive review of this film. http://rogerebert.suntimes.com/apps/pbcs.dll/article?AID=/20030606/REVIEWS/306060302/1023.

There are always a lot of decisions to be made concerning sound systems and the production team needs to spend a lot of time thinking out the sound design. Chapter 5 goes into more detail about all the sound systems that are available and when to use them.

• Outside: Quick Stand-up Interviews/ Bites/Man on the Street (MOS) • Most of the time, people are uncomfortable being interviewed at length standing up. Short interviews and/or shorter MOS bites and/ or quick statements are all you can usually achieve with a subject standing up. Still, your shots of subjects might include quick bites, so be prepared.

Design decisions might include whether everyone is standing in the same environment, or all/some are in different environments. Also, is the camera hand-held or steady? Will you alternate eye direction or have everyone look in the same direction? Will the subjects look into the camera lens or slightly off-camera at the unseen listener/producer? If the statements are short, looking directly into the lens is very effective, and the subjects can usually sustain direct eye contact with the camera. Documentaries that have a lot of subjects in real-world settings need to have a plan for these short bites. Watching *Lake of Fire*, *Boys of Baraka*, or *Hoop Dreams* can help you see how others have solved this problem.

• Outside Location Selection •
DYNAMIC BACKGROUND

It's often useful when the background helps tell the story. So try to put the subject in an environment that relates to the documentary. Then frame the subject so we see story-related objects in the frame with him/her.

In Stacy Peralta's 2009 directed documentary *Crips and the Bloods*, he shot all of the interviews in front of colorful, graffiti-covered walls. The graffiti helps keep the idea in the viewer's head that this is a hard core, urban story. In the two-

Director Stacy Peralta told a grim but inspiring tale when he created his documentary *Crips and Bloods*. To keep the urban aesthetic in the front of the viewer's mind, he shot all of his interviews in front of a long wall that was covered in multicolored graffiti (*Gang Documentary, 2009*).

continent story of *The Boys of Baraka*, urban Baltimore and rural Africa provide radically opposed backgrounds, and reinforce the contrast of the two worlds during the outdoor, vérité-style interviews and conversations.

Neutral Background

Sometimes the objective is to just get a bite that will add to your story. A neutral background like a wall, building, or tree might help throw the emphasis on what is being said and who is saying it.

Moving Interview and Beanbag Trick

Sometimes shooting an interview with a subject while s/he is walking/riding/jogging can be effective. You might have to track him/her by having your camera and sound person walk/track with the subject or use a dolly or a car/truck. These moving interviews require a lot of logistical thought, but can be very effective. One way to get a steady camera while shooting out of a moving truck or car is to set the camera on a big beanbag or pillow and have the

shooter sit or lie down while shooting. The beanbag stabilizes the camera and absorbs most of the movement of the vehicle.

Driving Interview

Here the subject is driving and talking to the camera, which is located in the passenger's seat. We also see what is going on outside the vehicle, which helps tell the story. The TV show *COPS* pioneered this shot and uses it all the time. It can be very effective, especially if the subject is commenting on what the car is going by. The camera is usually either on the shoulder or in the lap of the shooter. If in the lap, flip the eyepiece/screen so you can see what the camera is shooting. Almost all of the time, the shooter is in the front seat, but sometimes it works if the shooter is in the backseat.

The position of the sun in relation to the driver's side windows is important. Try to shoot the interview when the sun will be shining on or near your subject. At night, you can light the subject with the car's overhead light, a sun gun/Omni-light on the camera, or a flashlight/LED light on the subject.

In the documentary *American Movie*, which profiles an obsessed, Midwestern independent filmmaker struggling to get his independent film made, there are many revealing sequences that were filmed with the subject driving through his Wisconsin neighborhood and commenting on his situation. Driving sequences take place both day and night. At night, the filmmakers used a small light to illuminate the driver's face. Because driving interviews provide a constantly changing background,

In the documentary *American Movie,* there are many driving conversations with the main subject, Mark Borchardt. We see his Milwaukee neighborhoods go by as he gives his wild reveries about filmmaking *(Sony Pictures Classic, 1999).*

there isn't as great a need for cutaway B-roll shots.

Hoop Dreams also uses the driving conversation to reveal how a middle-school scout for basketball talent has to move through the city of Chicago to find the latest budding superstar. Later in the film, after one of the two featured boys has become a star, the scout and the star have a conversation in the car to bookend the journey of the boy. Outside the window the setting is always the hard streets of Chicago, and the street scene that flows by keeps reminding us this is an urban story.

Inside: Real-world Settings

• Inside Locations: Homes, Workplaces, Entertainment Settings, Hotel Rooms •
Here is an overview of many different interview setups.

REAL WORLD, REAL BACKGROUND, DIRECTED STYLE

This setup has the subject sitting or standing in a setting that reveals a part of his/her world. The background has been selected to help tell the viewer more about the subject. Items in the background are composed along with the subject in the frame. Framed photos, awards, related objects, and desktop items like lamps and flowers are all typical parts of an interview setup. The camera is on a tripod and at eye level, the lens has a great depth of field, and everything is in focus. Lighting is standard two- or three-point lighting.

A variation is to create a shallow depth of field and have the background in soft focus, which gets softer as you zoom in. To achieve this you need to place the camera a distance from the subject. When the camera zooms into a close-up, the depth of field becomes shallower and the

background goes out of focus. Closing the iris a stop can also help reduce the depth of field.

VH1's documentary series *Behind the Music*'s supervising producer, Paul Gallagher, shot hundreds of interviews over the six-year life of the show. His design plan was clear.

> We never shot interviews in a studio or hotel room, if possible. We had five clubs around LA we could shoot in if we needed to, but we liked to shoot in the subject's everyday environments if we could. We liked to compose the head shots with a shallow depth of field. This softens the background and throws all of the attention on the person.
> It takes about one and one-half hours for our shooters to set up, mike and light an interview. We used freelance camera people, and each had his/her own way of lighting and composing interview shots. We tried to match these styles with the person we were featuring.*

4 Little Girls, Spike Lee's directed documentary on the 1963 civil rights bombing in Birmingham, AL, used composed interview setups in the homes of the bombing victims' parents. He positioned framed photos of the deceased children in the frame with the parents. As the documentary progresses, Lee subtly breaks the rules of framing to emphasize how horrendous and life altering the tragedy was.

In Alex Gibney's directed documentary *Enron: The Smartest Guys in the Room*, he tells the complicated story of the fall of investment giant Enron. There are many talkers and the interview setups all took place in upscale hotels, boardrooms, workplaces and homes. The subjects were lit beautifully and the elements in the frame were composed. He used a clever device of positioning a reflective surface in front of many of his interviewees. The reflections of the storytellers' faces reinforce the idea that there are two sides to

---

*These words were transcribed from an interview I had with Paul Gallagher on March 14, 2001, at the VH1 production studios in Santa Monica, CA.

Director Alex Gibney wanted to visually reinforce how two-faced and surreal the corporate crooks at Enron were, so he positioned reflective surfaces to be part of the interview framing *(2005 Magnolia Home Entertainment).*

every story and that the world of the Enron disaster was surreal in many ways. A recurring visual in the film is a wide shot of the shiny, reflective surface of the twin Enron buildings. The reflective images in the interviews reference the reflective image of the buildings.

In Alex Gibney's next documentary, *Taxi to the Dark Side*, for which he won an Academy Award in 2007, he created a different aesthetic for many of his interview settings. The documentary is an exploration into the U.S. government's abuse of human rights during military interrogations in Iraq and Afghanistan. For most of the military storytellers who were in the war zones, he established an abstract, dark set-ting by using one key light and occasionally a back light. The rest of the frame is either limbo black or extremely dark with a dim light on a dark, heavy curtain. In these settings, the emphasis is on the subject who is trying to understand and explain why the interrogations got out of control. For various lawyers, politicians, high-ranking military personnel, book authors, and experts, he returned to the beautifully composed and lit shots in upscale settings he used in his Enron documentary. The two contradictory worlds are reinforced by the radically different interview settings.*

Director Connie Bottinelli likes to direct the technical aspects of her inter-

Taxi to the Dark Side. This interview with director Alex Gibney shows how choosing an aesthetic for interviews can impact and enhance the story. http://www.filmmakermagazine.com/issues/winter2008/taxi.php.

"We had to dive in, find our way, and then slowly put together some kind of visual plan. We didn't know exactly what we were going to find along the way—what photographs, what images. And when I found the Dilawar story that, for my purposes, was important, because it weaves through the whole system, from Afghanistan through Abu Ghraib to Guantanamo. And only then did I begin to think of the film's imagery. For the Bagram [sequences in this film], we had precious few images [to work with], and you have a very complicated series of relationships there with the military intelligence, the military police and the prisoners. I wanted [viewers] to feel like they were in Bagram, so we came up with a plan of how to shoot the interviews. The Bagram [subjects] would be shot in a completely different way than all of the other interviews. We made a backdrop, a canvas *(continued on page 112)*

views. In her documentary *The Curse of King Tutankhamun*, she knew what she wanted for her "look," but she always allows for a change in the direction of the interview.

> I listen to the way potential subjects sound during a preinterview phone call. How they sound is crucial. I also look for their storytelling skills, and if they are passionate about their lives. I look for a sense of humor. These preinterviews also give me the basic information for my shooting script. Before the actual interview I reassure my subjects by telling them we will discuss the same things we talked about on the phone.
>
> I tell my shooter to get the wide, establishing setup shot first. I always have the camera positioned far away because I want to sit close to them and engage them in a conversation. So the camera is behind me. I sit back with the lens right over my shoulder and I talk to my subject just for a minute. A little bit of a warm-up while the camera is rolling, getting established, a couple of nods, you know, things like that. If I feel it's going to be a real compelling interview, I tell my shooter, don't go to sleep behind that camera. Listen to them. Watch for emotion. When it comes, do a very slow, gentle push to him/her when s/he starts telling something heartfelt. Shooters have to listen.
>
> As the interview progresses, and if the story is getting compelling, I will actually move closer to the subject. When we start, the lens is right over my shoulder. When I move closer, the lens moves out of their sight line. So they do not see that lens, they see me. I work hard to keep them engaged. And what we do is we have a conversation. I have questions here, and never look at them. We have an absolute conversation back and forth, and I just have to be very careful I don't step on their answers. And that's what I do.*

In vérité-style interviews and conversations, you are using just available light. This brings sunlit windows and fluorescent and incandescent household lighting into play. If you are using a digital camera, then you need to continually white-balance the camera as you move through different light-source settings.

In the documentary *The Weather Underground* (2002), which is a mix of vérité and directed interviews and conversations, the outdoor and indoor settings were all shot using available light. The storytellers are all in settings that relate to their current lives.

American Movie is a mostly vérité documentary that uses the main subject's home, jobs, car rides, film-production sets, and recreational settings for all of the interviews and conversations. As the filmmakers followed their subject for a year, they needed to be creative and opportunistic within these settings as they captured their story.

The vérité documentary *Crumb* uses his daily world as the settings for conversations with the artist Crumb and his dysfunctional family and friends. Occasionally Terry Zwigoff, the documentary maker, would use a lighting instrument in situations where the light levels were low. Because the documentary was shot in film, the camera was able to capture most of the low-light environments well.

Sometimes in vérité documentaries there is more than one conversation going on at the same time. At this point the producer/director must make a decision on who the camera person should follow. Because everything is unfolding so quickly, the decision is usually a gut call. This very situation happened to director Arnold

---

(continued from page 111)   painted with dark browns and grays, and carried it with us wherever we went, whether it was London, Ohio, Washington, whatever. We shot all the people who were at Bagram against that background. So every time you see one of those interviews shot against that backdrop, you get a visceral feeling. All of the people who were shot against it become united in some way. Even if you can't follow who is the M.P., who is the M.I. and who is the prisoner, you know they're from Bagram. Also, the [Bagram interviews] are lit very harshly with one side of the face in light and one side in darkness. They have kind of a prison feeling."

*These words were transcribed from an interview I had with Connie Bottinelli on February 12, 2001.

Shapiro while he was shooting his classic vérité documentary *Scared Straight!* inside of Rahway State Prison in New Jersey. He was following a group of at-risk teens as they made their way through the prison to meet a group of lifers in the auditorium. There came a moment during the shooting when he was pulled in two directions.

> There was an amazing moment I had as the director. Marlene, one of the girls, gets thrown off of the stage for moving her arm. She picks up her shoes and she goes off of the stage. Ordinarily, when they throw someone off the stage, they keep them off. An inmate goes to the back of the auditorium and they talk one-on-one. Marlene started to hysterically cry after fifteen seconds of being thrown off. She broke down. The pressure of it all had gotten to her. I had to make an instant decision: Do I break away one of the cameras and shoot her crying or not risk taking a camera away from the session which was still going on and respect her privacy and leave her alone? I made a mistake. I didn't shoot her. She looked in agony and I figured I'm not going to do this. That was wrong. Five minutes later she was fine. I could have kicked myself. That could have been a very powerful moment.*

REAL WORLD, STYLIZED SETTING

In this style the subject is lit for effect—maybe just a front key light or maybe a gelled light (blue, amber, yellow) on the face. The camera might have a low angle or high angle. The background might be out of focus. Framing might break the framing rules.

In the documentary *No Direction Home* (2005), the director shot the interviews with Bob Dylan using one key light on Dylan's face. The light falls off behind him into darkness and, depending on the camera angle, there is either total darkness or a soft darkness with some room items visible. In some of the sequences, there is a soft backlight on Dylan's leather jacket.

The camera moves subtly during the interview from high angle through eye level to low angle. The fact that Dylan is surrounded by darkness as he narrates his life story helps to reinforce his mysterious persona. In contrast to the Dylan interviews, in which the camera is still, in most of the interviews with the other storytellers, the camera is moving, either physically or zooming. The lighting on the people is much brighter than in the Dylan interview sequences. This provides an aesthetic that reinforces the documentary's goal of trying to capture the always-moving Dylan and shed light on his mysterious personality. The story centers on five years in Dylan's life and the other storytellers are seated in composed settings that relate to west Greenwich Village in NYC during the mid–1960s. Martin Scorsese is credited with directing the documentary, but he didn't come on board until after the interviews were shot in 2000. The documentary began in 1995 and was completed in 2005.†

Background Enhancement

Lighting effects might include streaks, colored backgrounds, patterns and/or combinations of all three. Perhaps an important element in the background is highlighted.

Canvas/Paper/Textured Material

Sometimes you can bring an appropriate background with you. A favorite is an eight-by-12-foot canvas that has been painted with a color or colors to give it an industrial/artistic/textured look. You can further enhance it with lighting effects.

MULTIPLE INTERVIEWS, ONE LOCATION

Sometimes documentaries that have a lot of subjects from many areas beyond the travel budget of the project will invite a group of subjects to one location for a

---

*These words were transcribed from an interview I had with Arnold Shapiro on March 26, 2001.
†DVD Special Feature director's commentary by the filmmaker on the DVD *No Direction Home*.

day of shooting. If the location is a *hotel room*, place the camera in the center of the room and move the chair for the interviews around the room. This creates different angles and different background looks for each interview. If the location is a home/workplace, then create different looks within the location, always remembering that the backgrounds are different for each interview.

The 2000 Oscar Award–winning documentary *Into the Arms of Strangers* used this approach. The filmmakers created an abstract background by lighting a large piece of material with gelled lights at various angles. The background traveled to a variety of locations, but always created a slightly different but uniform look in the background of all the interviews.

DEPTH OF FIELD AND BACKGROUNDS

Whether the background is in or out of focus depends on how far the camera is zoomed in and where it is positioned in relation to the interviewee. If you position the camera far from the subject and zoom in, you create a shallow depth-of-field and the background will be out of focus. If the camera is close to the subject and zoomed out, you create a great depth of field and everything will be in focus. You need a lot of space to achieve the out-of-focus-background look.

The MTV/VH1 documentary series *Behind the Music* (1997–2003) often used three clubs around the LA area to shoot interviews with various band members. The space provided by the clubs allowed for the interview setups to include gelled lights placed far behind the interviewee and to have them in soft focus, creating an onstage look that fit with the performance aesthetic of the series.*

• **Sound Inside** • You have to develop your sense of hearing *indoor sounds* that

are so familiar to us that we no longer hear them. These sounds are heating and air conditioning circulation, mechanical noise, media playback, and *outside sounds* that can be heard inside, like industrial noise, traffic, airplanes, and people noises. It's best to scout locations for sound as well as visual information. Stand in the middle of the location and listen for the ambient sound. If it is too loud, try to improve it by shutting down heating/air conditioning, closing windows, and/or asking people to move or be quiet. After the interview ask everyone to be quiet and shoot one minute of *room tone* that matches your interview ambience. You might need this sound for editing.

Studio Settings

Bringing the interview subjects into a studio to shoot interviews can generate a lot of different looks. Here are some standard studio setups and looks.

• **Limbo Black** • Here the background is a deep, rich black. This can be achieved two ways. The first is by using a black curtain. The subject is positioned far enough in front of the black curtain so no light spills on the backdrop. The second way works if you don't have the black curtain but do have a lot of space. Position the camera a distance away from the subject and zoom in to a tight shot. This results in a shallow depth of field, and the light in the background falls off into darkness/blackness. During editing, you can use some of the colorizing tools to enrich the blackness.

From a design perspective, this black background puts all of the focus on the talker. The white light that lights the subject from the front creates a high-contrast ratio with the black background and results in a

---

*These words were transcribed from an interview I had with Paul Gallagher on March 14, 2001, at the VH1 production studios in Santa Monica, CA.

nice visual effect. You need to remember that subjects with dark/black hair and fleshtones need to be backlit so they don't fade into the limbo black background. And ask your subjects not to wear black. This is a dramatic look, so the content of the interview should be relatively serious.

• **Symbolic/Abstract Backgrounds** • The background is created by textured material and/or lighting effects like pools, streaks, gels, patterns. Color is used for mood and tone. Sometimes objects that relate to the subject are positioned stylistically between the subject and the background to create a composition. These objects can be highlighted.

In Samantha Cressen's documentary *Tonal Colors* (2005), jazz artists are interviewed in a studio setting. Each of the four musicians has his own gelled color on the background curtain, and his instrument is on a pedestal within the frame, top lit with white light between the storyteller and the curtain. The effect is one of connection between the subject and his instrument in an abstract world of color, and reinforces the relationship between jazz and the tonal colors the instruments create.

• **Chroma Key Background/Green Screen/ Rear Projection** • The subject sits in front of a solid-color, evenly lit background. The color is usually green or blue if working in a linear-recording production studio. If the color is going to be replaced later via software chroma keying in a computer, gray and beige can also work for the background. The subject can't wear any clothing that is in the color range of the chroma key color. The subject should have both front and back lighting so the subject will separate well from the background. The background should be evenly lit for best results.

The goal of chroma key interview setups is to key in images and/or footage that will enhance what the subject is saying. Once again, the images can be real or abstract. If *tape playback* is being used, sometimes the footage is B-roll of the subject or related to what is being discussed. Sometimes *home movies* work nicely in this effect. If you are going to be shooting *special footage for chroma keying*, make sure you remember to shoot the most important elements in the frame either screen left or screen right. The subject's head will be taking up almost one half of the screen space. The chroma key footage will only be distinguishable on the screen in the side opposite the head.

The documentary *The U.S. vs. John Lennon* (2006) uses many green screen interview setups. The footage in the green screen background is archival stills from the 1960s and freeze-frames layered and

In the historical documentary *The U.S. vs. John Lennon,* Yoko Ono, John Lennon's wife, is the only storyteller to appear in front of a limbo black background. The black background sets her apart and gives her an unusual presence *(Lionsgate Films, 2006).*

collaged into graphic designs that relate to what the subjects are saying. John Lennon's wife Yoko Ono is the only storyteller who appears with a limbo black background. This aesthetic decision sets her apart and gives her a more powerful screen personality.

Alex Gibney's documentary *Gonzo* (2008) is about the rogue journalist and media maverick Hunter Thompson. Gibney used a wide variety of settings for the storytellers. There are beautifully composed wide shots that incorporate both home and work settings. There is always a great depth of field, so everything in the background is in sharp focus. For contrast, Thompson's wife is in front of a green screen to which archival and abstract images were added that relate to what she is saying. Thompson was always unpredictable, and the calm, artistically composed and lit interview settings create a sharp contrast with the wild archival footage and the chaos of Thompson's life.

CREATING IMAGINATIVE BACKGROUNDS FOR GREEN SCREEN

If the imagery behind the subject is going to be abstract, the possibilities are endless. If you are looking for mood-enhancing images, one way to achieve moving colors is by shooting food coloring in a Petri dish or teacup. You add the food coloring to water, then shoot the swirling colors with a video camera for ten minutes or so. Often the dreamy effect is enhanced by shooting slightly out of focus. This blends the colors together. You can edit together the ten-minute sequence into a 30-minute tape, and play back the swirling colors into the chroma key background live during the interview or add it during editing.

Another way to create interesting images is to play back a video that has lots of movement in it into a TV monitor. You shoot the playback of the footage in a TV monitor while the camera lens is way out

of focus. The blurred movement is just a mass of indistinguishable movement. But it can look cool as a background.

DIGITAL BACKGROUNDS VIA GREEN SCREEN

There is a new trend that begins by using a green screen as a background for interviews. After the interview is shot, during editing you replace the green background with a premade digital visual. There is a company called Digital Juice that provides for a fee hundreds of these moving, colorful, layered backgrounds. You can preview these backgrounds on the Web by going to the company's Web site. Photoshop can help you layer still imagery into interesting backgrounds.

Framing the Subject

How the subject will look in the frame requires a lot of careful thought. Designing the look of the interviews will impact the documentary in many ways. Here are the rules to follow to create a traditional-looking interview.

• **Eye Direction** • There are two ways to do it. The most common is to have the subject look *slightly off-camera* at an unseen listener/questioner, or to have the subject look *directly into the camera*. It's easier for the subject to look at someone, rather than at a camera. But talking to the camera is more intimate and breaks down the fourth wall. *Think this choice out carefully*.

The legendary documentary maker Errol Morris solved the problem of maintaining storyteller eye contact with the questioning director and the camera/viewer by inventing the Interatron. This teleprompter-type camera has a live picture of Morris on a monitor in front of the lens. A camera shooting Morris live feeds the monitor. The interviewee can carry on a conversation with Morris's image in the monitor. *The Fog of War* (2003) star and host Robert McNamara used the Interatron to maintain constant eye contact with the viewer, as did the storytellers in his documentary *Standard Operating Procedure* (2008).

• **30-degree Rule** •If you choose the slightly off-camera look, then the subject should not be turned more than 30 degrees. *This enables both of the subject's eyes to be in the frame.*

• **Nose/Lead Room** • If you are using the slightly off-camera look, then frame the head with some additional space in the frame in the direction the subject is looking.

• **Eyes in the Upper Third** • The subject's eyes are in the upper third of the frame. This is the space that makes us comfortable listening to people talk.

• **Head Room** • You need to decide if the subject's head will have any space between the top of the head and the top of the frame. Tight shots might cut off some of the hair. Looser shots will include all of the hair. If you aren't sure just remember, eyes are more important than hair, so big hair or a hat should not force the eyes below the upper-third line.

• **Graphic Inclusion in the Lower Third** • Are you framing the head with a graphic ID in mind? If so, and if the graphic will be placed in the lower third of the frame, then provide enough room for the graphic not to touch the lips.

Probably the best examples of sustained, rule-driven interview-subject shot composition are found in the documentaries of Ken Burns. He is a historical documentarian, and his storytellers are critical to the flow of his story. He frames his storytellers following all of the rules of framing. Watch a Ken Burns documentary to see how carefully he composes his frame during interviews.

• **Breaking the Rules** • It's not a good idea to break the rules unless you have thought everything out and understand the consequences of doing so. Rule breaking brings attention to what you are doing. Have a good reason for doing it. Here are some rule-breaking examples:

RADICAL FRAMING

The storytellers are framed looking off of the short side of the frame and/or with too much/too little head room. Sometimes the framing goes beyond the 30-degree rule, so the subject is in profile.

STROBING

During the editing of the interview a special effect called strobing is used, giving the picture a jerky look. The audio stays synched, but the video looks stylized.

UNORTHODOX CAMERA ANGLES

This style would include Dutch-angle shots or extreme low-/high-angle shots. Errol Morris used this technique in *The Fog of War*. A floating camera that keeps the frame alive is popular. Vérité documentaries like *Jesus Camp* and *Hoop Dreams* use this style. A jerky camera like the ones used in *Overnight* and *King of Kong* is more radical, but can work in the right situation.

TWO-CAMERA INTERVIEWS

One shoots in a traditional style, one shoots in a handheld freestyle, or one is set at a different angle than the other. During editing you mix the two cameras. Maybe one camera is changed to black and white or colorized.

BEHIND-THE-SCENES SHOOTING

This is done with two cameras. One shoots the interview subject, the other shoots the camera and crew shooting the interview. This revealing of the production process is a popular technique.

SHOOTING THE MONITOR

The interview is played back into a monitor and a camera shoots the monitor, or a second camera shoots the monitor live. This provides an interesting effect.

SHOOTING THE EDITING COMPUTER

This is a camera shooting the interview in postproduction. This includes shooting the editing computer, the timeline, video windows, and anything else interesting in the computer.

In my documentary *Seabrook Farms Remembered,* the target audience was young. Since most of my storytellers were older, I used the "process" of making the documentary as part of the design elements *(Seabrook Educational and Cultural Museum, 2002).*

Shooting in Steps

This is a very important area to consider. By *shooting in steps* you create interviews that have two or three different shots of the subject. By varying the shots of the subject, you can provide variety during the on-camera portions of the interview. Different shots of the subject also allow you to edit the interview without using B-roll to cover up the jump-cut edit points.

In the documentary *Gonzo* the cast of talkers is large. Many of the subjects appear many times during the documentary. By shooting in steps, the subject sur-prises us each time we return with a fresh shot.

Although the *jump-cut editing* of interviews is accepted now as a legitimate technique, you need to decide how you want to use the interview after it's shot. Another legitimate technique is to record only *one shot during the interview.* In the documentary *Into the Arms of Strangers,* the storytellers are framed in only one shot. Because their stories are emotional and the archival B-roll is so well matched to what they are saying, the decision was made to respect the storytellers and let them calmly tell their stories and not use stylistic techniques. The director, Mark Jonathan Harris, and producer, Deborah Oppenheimer, had an interesting challenge when it came to interviews.

> We knew that we did not have the money to go to each of the subject's houses. These were older people who were not necessarily affluent. We had people who lived in nursing homes, some people were going to meet us in a hotel in England, some people didn't have houses with high enough ceilings for our equipment to come into. We were worried that varying backgrounds would be distracting to the viewer. So we brainstormed a stylized look. It was an abstract design with colors on a canvas background. We standardized the look and brought it with us.*

Below are the most commonly used step sequences.

• **Two-Step Shooting** • Two shots are selected. Usually a close-up and a medium shot, or a medium close-up and an extreme close-up. You begin the interview with one of the shots, then change to the next shot after the first answer, while the producer is asking question two. You alternate these two shots throughout the interview. If there is a progression to the questions that will lead to an emotional climax, make sure you are on the close-up for those moments.

*These words were transcribed from an interview I had with Deborah Oppenheimer on March 10, 2001.

• **Three-Step Shooting** • Three shots are selected. Usually a wide shot, medium shot and close-up or extreme close-up. You mix these three shots as needed.

• **Dramatic Zoom** • During the interview, if the storyteller gets emotional or dramatic, then the camera zooms to the next step or a close-up. The director needs to rehearse the camera operator on the visual reference points for these steps, and go over whether dramatic zooms are part of the plan.

• **No Steps** • This is also a legitimate technique. You frame a shot, then hold it for the entire interview. In this style the emphasis is on what is being said and the camera doesn't intrude on the story. You need a lot of B-roll if you use this technique.

Multiple-Person Interviews

Sometimes it can be effective and surprising if you group some or all of your storytellers together for a group conversation. Finding a location where everyone feels comfortable and the surroundings relate to the documentary story is challenging. Sometimes it's obvious: a team in its participation space, students in a classroom, lifeguards on the beach, musicians in a rehearsal hall, lawyers in a courtroom. But sometimes it's not so obvious and you can get creative. In the punk-rock vérité documentary *Bucket Flush* (2010), director Ivan Kowalenko and producer Dana Frack shot four sequences with the band informally grouped together talking to the camera in a rundown park in Philadelphia. These improvised conversations were framed by the chaos and unpredictability of the rest of their lives. The sequences enabled the punkers to relax and have some fun, and also allowed the viewer to catch their breath from the wild ride of the rest of the story.

Using two cameras can help capture the stories better. One camera keeps a wide shot while the other continually finds the talker. Other times you may find yourself in a home wanting to interview two people together. The corner of a couch usually works best. You want to eliminate space between the two as much as possible. Once again, two cameras can make it easier to capture everything.

Role of the Director: Two Choices

• **Unseen and Unheard Listener** • This is the traditional role of the director, who asks questions off-camera. The subject answers while looking at the director. The result is a series of sequences in which the storyteller is seen by the viewer as looking slightly off-screen, either screen left or screen right.

• **Participating Listener** • A variation on this traditional approach is for the director to be heard asking the questions. This makes the director a presence in the documentary and removes the distance the fourth wall creates. In the documentary *Brother's Keeper*, directors Joe Berlinger and Bruce Sinofsky take it one step further by including not only off-camera questions, but commentary as well. In *The Wonderful, Horrible Life of Leni Riefenstahl*, the director Ray Müller is heard off-camera responding to many of Riefenstahl's statements, and at one point gets into an argument with her.

In vérité documentaries in which you are eavesdropping on life while following your storytellers, you might ask a question and capture the response. You will have to decide if your subjects will address the camera if/when they talk to you. If you are eliminating yourself from the story, then often you can ask your subject to explain something to either you or the camera. In *The Boys of Baraka*, the young urban African American kids often talk to the camera as they try to explain their lives and what is happening to them.

FINAL THOUGHTS

The core of any documentary is the people who are living and telling the story. The settings of the interviews and conversations are important because they can help tell the story. Try to watch a diverse group of documentaries to see how wide a range of choices you have.

DOCUMENTARY REFERENCES

Each of these documentary references was chosen because it has a creative element or technique that stands out. Some of the most creative filmmaking has occurred while a documentarian is telling his or her story. It is hoped that the curious reader will be motivated to watch many of these documentaries not only for enjoyment, but also for inspiration.

American Movie. 1999. Chris Smith and Sarah Price. Bluemark Productions. This surprise Sundance winner follows an obsessed Milwaukee filmmaker trying to overcome many obstacles and get his horror film made. Smith and Price were the entire crew as they became friends with the main character. Shot in 16mm color over the course of two years, this mostly vérité film was made on a shoestring budget but captures a fascinating story. A must for aspiring filmmakers.

Behind the Music series. 1997–2006. George Moll and Paul Gallagher. VH1 Productions. This legendary, one-hour documentary series

In the vérité documentary *The Boys of Baraka,* directors Heidi Ewing and Rachel Grady often had their young subjects address the camera as they expressed their thoughts. Their urban setting is always in the background to reinforce the feeling of an inner-city neighborhood *(Loki Films, 2005).*

has made over 200 documentaries about musical artists and performers. For many Americans now in their thirties and forties, *BTM* was their first exposure to the documentary form. Although the episodes followed a strict formula, they often broke through the barriers many of the artists put up and mined raw emotions. The drama the show uncovered through well researched interviews was always real.

The Boys of Baraka. 2005. Rachel Grady and Heidi Ewing, Loki Films. Winner of many prestigious film festival awards including Silver Docs, SXSW, and Cine Golden Eagle. A moving look at a group of inner city kids who travel to a special school in Kenya to find themselves. A digital vérité documentary that also features diary cameras for the kids when they are in Kenya.

Capturing the Friedmans. 2003. Andrew Jarecki. Gang Documentary. This film was nominated for an Academy Award in 2003. Director Andrew Jarecki tells the story of a family torn apart by charges and convictions of sexual abuse of local children by a father and son. As the story unfolds you realize there are really two stories: the main one of the family dealing with the shock of the charges of sexual abuse, and a secondary one of how the local community (Great Neck, Long Island) deals with the notoriety of the case. *Capturing the Friedmans* is a directed documentary that reveals during its interview sequences the inside and outside of typical, middle class homes in the community.

Crips and Bloods. 2009. Stacy Peralta.

Gang Documentary. In this 2009 directed documentary director Peralta shot all of the interviews in front of a colorful, graffiti-covered wall. The graffiti helps keep the idea in the viewer's mind that this is a hardcore, urban story. The multi-colored background provides an aura of hope as the subjects tell their grim stories.

Crumb. 1994. Terry Zwigoff. Crumb Partners. This Sundance winner was shot in 16mm color film and has a vibrant, dark aesthetic, not unlike the subject, Robert Crumb. Its vérité style captures the strange, intense life of an iconic artist. The director's comments are interesting as Zwigoff explains how odd it is to make a documentary about a friend and iconic cultural figure.

4 Little Girls. 1998. Spike Lee. Home Box Office. This sensitive, well-researched, historical documentary retells the tragic story of the civil rights church bombing in Birmingham, AL, in 1963. The parents and families of the four slain girls relate the story in intimate interviews.

Gonzo. 2008. Alex Gibney. HDNet Films LLC. An artistic, gritty study of rogue journalist Hunter Thompson. Director Gibney uses a green screen in his recreations that is creative and effective. How time is presented is also interesting. He chose to not tell Thompson's story chronologically.

Hoop Dreams. 1994. Steve James. New Line Home Entertainment, Inc. This three-hour, vérité-style documentary took five years to make (1989–1994) and generated 250 hours of raw footage. It was shot on video using a Betacam video camera. This documentary remains a classic example of dedicated vérité filmmaking. It captures the lives of its two subjects as well as the inner city life of Chicago.

Jesus Camp. 2006. Heidi Ewing and Rachel Grady. Loki Films, Inc. This intense, vérité film about evangelical Pentecostal Christians preparing for religious warfare by running a religious camp every summer is shocking and a cautionary tale. It was shot on digital video over a seven-month period. It won many film festivals and was nominated for an Academy Award.

My Architect. 2003. Nathaniel Kahn. Louis Kahn Project LLD. This vérité documentary follows illegitimate son Louis Kahn as he searches for clues to the mystery of his world famous architect father. Featuring some creative on-camera hosting sequences, this personal journey documentary was nominated for an Academy Award.

No Direction Home: Bob Dylan. 2005. Spitfire Productions and Grey Water Park Productions. Jeff Rosen and Martin Scorsese. This signature film about Bob Dylan was a ten-year labor of love for Jeff Rosen. Martin Scorsese came on board late (2001) to direct the editing. A brilliant decision to frame the documentary around the coming-of-age years from 1961 to 1966 enable the documentary makers to explore Dylan's whole life and influences, while still having a narrowly focused story to tell. Dylan's interview setting is subtly creative in a minimalist way, and stands out from the rest of the talkers' settings.

Tonal Colors. 2005. Samantha Cressen. Rowan University. This story of young jazz musicians discovering themselves and their music is designed like a jazz riff. Artwork, graphics, abstract studio interview settings, creative B-roll, and a jazz music track give the feeling of the improvisation of jazz and life.

The U.S. vs. John Lennon. 2006. David Leaf and John Scheinfeld. Lionsgate and VH1 Rock Docs. This well-researched, visually interesting documentary follows the transformation of John Lennon from rock star to political activist. The interviews are shot in front of a green screen with creative, layered backgrounds that feature collage-style lettering, photos, and graphic designs. The backgrounds change with each storyteller. By adding this artistic touch to the nuts and bolts interviews, the filmmaker mirrors the art vs. reality conflict Lennon was going through.

The Weather Underground. 2002. Sam Green and Bill Siegel. The Free History Project. This in-depth look at the people who made up the radical 1970s group, the Weathermen, uses a handheld, immediate approach to the interview sequences. They are shot outside and inside in settings relevant to what people are saying. This film was nominated for an Academy Award in 2004.

The Wonderful, Horrible Life of Leni Riefenstahl. 1993. Ray Müller. Arte and Channel Four Films. Was she making art or propaganda or both? This is the question that drives director Ray Müller to interview Leni Riefenstahl about her life and career. They play cat and mouse with each other until Müller finally loses it off camera. A fascinating study with pristine archival footage of Riefenstahl's classic documentaries: *Triumph of the Will* and *Olympia*.

7. Shooting Creative and Effective B-Roll

"B-roll" is the term given to the pictures and sound that support the on-camera interviews and narration sequences. B-roll footage is critical for reinforcing and explaining what people are saying and for helping the documentary maker craft his/her story. There are many ways to create effective B-roll. It enables you to be creative with visuals and sound.

There is an old saying storytellers respect: there is never enough good B-roll.

VÉRITÉ AND DIRECTED B-ROLL NEEDS

Directed Documentaries

Try to shoot the interviews first so you know what the storyteller has said and the outline of your overarching story is clear. In the interviews are cues for B-roll shots and sequences. Narrated sequences also carry cues for supporting visuals and sound.

Vérité Documentaries

As you follow your subjects, try to take advantage of the times when you can break away from the story and shoot footage that will support your story line. Constantly transcribe the footage when your subjects talk. Having these transcriptions handy helps you form the story and guide the production.

AREAS WHERE B-ROLL CAN BE GENERATED

Cutaway Footage Shot by the Documentary Crew

This includes footage that supports the story being told and relates directly to the people and places you've been shooting. For instance, if you have interviewed a puppet maker, then natural B-roll would be footage of the puppet maker making his puppets, his workshop, tools, fabrics, strings, etc. Additional B-roll would include exterior shots of his building, places he buys his materials, and many shots of his puppets and other puppet masters at work during practice and performances. Include whatever you can think of to make his story more visual and interesting, yet which still relates to the main story. A montage sequence using B-roll footage with natural sound and/or music is one of the most creative and effective ways of enhancing your story.

In Werner Herzog's visually stunning documentary *Encounters at the End of the World* (2007), he shot many interviews with the scientists and workers who live in Spartan conditions in a remote scientific study camp at the South Pole. The interviews were shot on the fly in the workplaces of the subjects. We see them either doing what they do every day or at their computers working with numbers, research sequences, or underwater footage. Herzog shot footage of all of them engrossed in their work, then used it as B-roll as they talked to him in these same work spaces. Seeing welders, scientists, heavy-machinery drivers, and underwater divers all living and working in these tight spaces reinforces the feeling that these are special people dedicated to advancing science in a place very removed from civilization. Herzog often used the images on the state-of-the-art computer screens as B-

roll to help explain what people do. Cutaway footage matches what they are talking about. Herzog's eclectic curiosity, always present, led him to document this remote outpost on the fringe of civilization. The footage was shot over a two-week visit and Herzog crafted the story into an Academy Award–nominated documentary in 2008. This documentary is a good study of how to use a dynamic interview environment as a source of cutaway B-roll.

Personal Archival Visuals

This includes old photos, memorabilia, ephemera, artifacts, clothing, and whatever you can find in the subject's world that visually supports the story. You can shoot these items after your interview. You can shoot them one at a time or arrange them into composed groupings or displays.

Documentarian Connie Bottinelli

Director Werner Herzog went to the South Pole to find a story of dedication and strange beauty when he made *Encounters at the End of the World*. Often he used freeze frames on his storytellers' computers to add interesting B-roll to his story *(Discovery Communications LLC, 2007)*.

made an award-winning documentary, *Intimate Portrait: Jessica Savitch* (1999), about the life of the pioneering broadcaster who died tragically in an automobile accident. Savitch's parents had stored all of the photos and memorabilia connected to their daughter's life in their attic. When Bottinelli saw this, she arranged all of the items on the floor of the attic and creatively lit them with white and gelled lights. She then shot hours of footage from every angle, framing newspapers, headlines, high-school yearbooks, flowers, diaries, photos, clothing, hats.... When she was done, she had almost all of the personal B-roll needed for the documentary.*

Often people have old footage of themselves. The best plan is to ask to borrow the tape/film, then convert it to a format you can digitize and transfer to your computer. If the subjects refuse to give you the tape/film, there are ways to still acquire the footage. In Jason Kitchen and Cheryl Kurn's documentary *Fatal Mistakes* (2005), which retells the story of the murder of a woman by her husband, the surviving sons had only one copy of a videotape of their mother early in her marriage. The sons were reluctant to part with the VHS tape, so director Kurn played the tape back into the family TV set and shot the screen. The images have not only a home-movie look, but also reinforce the family feeling by being shown on the family TV.

National Archives

If you are making a documentary that could be enhanced with footage from the United States National Archives and Records Administration, and you have the time to visit the Archives in College Park, MD, you should definitely do it. However, there are a few procedural steps you need to know.

The video and film archive is on one floor of the National Archives. Still photos are on another floor. Many of the still photos are online and you can preview them, and in some cases download them for use. A series called "Picturing the Century" has thousands of still photos that relate to thousands of subject areas.

Begin at http://www.archives.gov/ research/start/. Next, you need to spend time on the Web to see if video exists in your subject area. You can check the various databases online. http://www.archives. gov/research/order/film-sound-video-dc. html.

As of 2009 only about ten percent of the archive's film and video holdings were listed on the Web site. To access the remaining 90 percent, you need to visit the archive and find the tapes/films yourself. After you make your appointment following the instructions on the Web site, you should plan on spending at least two days at the archive. Searching the archives and recording your footage takes time, and the archive moves slowly. There are reasonable hotels nearby.

• **Two Ways to Use the National Archives to Obtain Footage for Your Documentary** •

Do it Yourself—It's Free

You can bring your own video camera and capture the footage yourself. This involves bringing your camera, tape/card, audio and video cables, and tripod and passing through a rigorous checkpoint. The archive doesn't allow visitors to bring in any pens, pencils, or other items that could harm the contents of the holdings. You are given a rolling cart that you can put your camera gear on.

When you arrive on the film and video floor you check in with one of the archivists who explains the cataloging sys-

---

*Director Connie Bottinelli explained this creative B-roll situation in a documentary production class she taught as a visiting artist in April 2006 at Rowan University.

tem. It involves a learning curve because the system is complex and often confusing.

You then wheel your gear to a computer, sit down, and begin to check the listings for possible clip candidates for your film. As you compile your list, the clips will either be on film or three-quarter-inch SP videotape, which is a format used in the 1980s and '90s. The archive is slowly creating DVDs of its holdings, but as of the summer of 2009 only 10 percent of all the 150,000 film reels and 20,000 videotapes had been converted to DVD. If your clips are on DVD, then the archive will make you a free DVD copy. If you want to pull one of the three-quarter-inch SP video tapes, you go to the sliding videotape shelves and find your tape. You can then sit at a preview station with a three-quarter-inch SP playback machine and find your footage. Sometimes the tape box contains a time-code log of the footage, and sometimes it doesn't. When you find your footage, you can connect audio and video cables from the three-fourths-inch player to your camera and dub your clip. Some of the footage looks very good on the three-fourths-inch tapes and makes a high-end dub. Other footage looks substandard and may not be up to your technical standards.

If you want a clip that only exists on film, you give your clip choices to an archivist. Twice a day (late morning, mid-afternoon), the staff pulls 16 mm films and makes them available for taping. When they notify you that your films have been pulled, you pick up the film in its canister and accompany an archival specialist into the dub room, which consists of a series of old-style, flatbed Moviolas. The archivist gives you a quick lesson in threading and running the Moviola, then leaves you on your own. You set up your video camera and frame the eight-inch screen on the Moviola. You play back the film and record it on your camera. There is an audio

output to use if there is sound on the film and you want to input it into your camera. All of this takes a lot of time. You have to use the Moviola to find your clip and preview it. Then recording the clip onto your camera requires a lot of tripod-horizon set up, focusing, framing, audio-level setting, and using the camera viewfinder for reference. It can be a frustrating and time-consuming process. But almost all of the 16 mm film footage looks sharp and crisp, especially the black-and-white footage. It is possible to capture excellent images.

BUY A PROFESSIONAL DUPLICATION OF YOUR CLIP SELECTIONS

If you decide you would like to buy your clips, the Archives contracts with professional companies to reproduce "broadcast quality" copies of its film and video holdings. These companies charge substantial fees and take a long time to fill orders. The archives' Web site leads you through the complicated process of finding and contacting these vendors. If you choose to go this route, you will probably still have to visit the Archives to find your clips and compile your list.

Even though it can be frustrating, it is exhilarating and fun to visit the film and video archives and be surrounded by so much media history. If you have a good digital camera and your clips are in good original shape, you can capture excellent archival visuals yourself to enhance your documentary.

One other important area to address is whether the footage can be used without copyright infringement. Each film and/or video source tells you whether the footage is restricted in any way. Sometimes it isn't clear who owns the rights. Many of the films/video were gifts to the Archives and the donors put restrictions on their use. You need to check with the archivists if you have any questions.

Photomation and/or Animotion

Photomation and animotion are the names given to the technique of creating motion with still photos. The motion is provided by the camera through pans, tilts or zooms over the surface of the photo. This technique can be done in the real world by mounting the photo on a smooth surface and shooting the photo, or done in your editing software using a motion effect. Because he uses the technique so much and so well, historical documentarian Ken Burns has been honored by having this technique named the Ken Burns Effect.

When you know you will be shooting still photos, there are a number of ways to approach your design aspects. Remember, the TV screen has an aspect ratio of 4:3 or 16:9. This is a horizontal rectangle. If the photo is square or in a vertical aspect ratio, you won't be able to frame the entire photo.

> **Tip:** Log the time code of the photo shooting session as you shoot. Mark the best sequences. This will save time during digitizing and editing.

Here is a brief rundown of your motion options.

• **Mounted or Single Photos** • The photos are pinned to a corkboard, put on a music stand, taped to a wall, or laid on the floor or in an album. The camera is on a tripod or held rock steady. Sometimes a floating camera can be effective. You want to think of the photos as part of the art of your story. There are ways to creatively present them that will enhance your visual elements and emphasize the spoken words and music.

Here are some shooting techniques:

➤Full-frame shots. Frame the photo and record it for ten seconds.

➤Zoom within the frame to a preselected finishing point. You can create surprise, drama, or humor if you think out how you will zoom. Zooms should be slow and smooth unless snap zooming and whip panning will work within a design plan.

➤Two-multiple-step shots. Frame the photo full frame and record it, then shoot a close-up of one element of the photo. For example, shoot a group photo, then do a close-up of one person. You can edit from the close-up to the wide shot or vice versa.

As mentioned above, documentarian Ken Burns is a master of this technique. He understands that within one photo there are often many stories. In his classic nine-part series *The Civil War* (1990), there are many examples of how cutting from a close-up shot within a photo to a full frame shot of the whole photo can surprise and make an emotional connection with the viewer.

• **Overshooting the Photo and Photo Displays** • In this style of photomation, the photo exists in a larger world that relates to what is in the photo and what the story is about, or the photo enhances the design of the sequence. The surrounding surface is part of the design. The displays can be abstract, imaginative, or manipulated with lighting. The items should add an emotional element to the shot.

Here are some examples:

➤Photo displays. A World War II photo arranged in a display with a war medal, a flag, and/or uniform. A team photo arranged with a ball and a letter jacket. A performance photo arranged with a violin and a sheet of music. These composed, display-photo arrangements can be creative and fun to put together. Using lighting effects with gels, streaks, and shadows can enhance the look. These photo displays connect the photo with the world of the documentary and the storyteller and add a warm feeling to the sequences.

➤Real-world settings. The photos are

shot where they exist in real life. In frames. On tables, desks, walls.

➢Glass glare. Most framed photos are behind glass. You need to watch how you light the photo and the angle of the camera in relation to the photo. If you tilt the photo on a slightly downward angle, the light will reflect below the camera and won't be seen in reflection. Sometimes it is better to remove the photo from the frame and work with it that way.

In the documentary *Crazy Love* (2007), which tells the story of a tragic,

In my documentary *Seabrook Farms Remembered*, which was about a unique farming experience that involved thousands of World War II refugees, I often placed eight-by-ten still photos in display settings to keep the farming relationship in the frame with the people *(Seabrook Educational and Cultural Museum, 2002)*.

dysfunctional love affair between two people, the filmmakers used the technique of over-shooting single photos, with the surrounding space black. The director often added a pan or zoom to the move and we see the surrounding black at either the beginning or end. The story is a dark, sad one and the limbo black surroundings of the photos help reinforce the dark psychological overtone of the story.

• **Postproduction Movement** • Most editing software has a variety of special motion effects built into it. Panning, tilting, and zooming over the surface of a photo is usually called "picture-on-picture" or "pan and scan." To use these effects you need to scan and/or digitize from the tape/card the full frame photo. You can then edit the photo into your project timeline and add your camera movement via the special effect, or you can create a special sequence with your photomation move and use it later in your timeline. Software photomation is very precise. Zooming works well. But if you need to pan, tilt, and zoom all

in one move, it's not always easy to plot your movement on the X, Y, and Z axes. There is also a robotic feel to the moves that some documentarians don't like. Think over beforehand how you want your photomation to look. Maybe you can mix live shooting moves with postproduction editing moves.

• **Posters** • Posters are usually in a vertical format, so you end up shooting sections of the poster. This can result in a montage of the various visual elements within the poster, which can add interesting design aspects to your visuals.

• **Shooting Newspapers** • Newspaper articles are a common source of B-roll, especially in documentaries that are dealing with historical facts and events. However, newsprint doesn't always look as good as a photocopy of the article. Try both, if possible. Here are some tips on shooting newspaper B-roll.

➢Step-shooting. Shoot the headline and/or the full article. Then shoot key phrases and lines from the story. Panning the headline can work. You can cut from a close-up of a word or two to a wider shot of the headline or whole newspaper.

➤Studio shooting or post. If you are shooting in a studio, you can highlight words and phrases with a wipe effect. If you are doing the effect in post, use a highlight effect.

➤Layering. Often newspaper shots can be layered in postproduction to give an "immediate" feeling. We see many headlines and articles layered on top of each other.

➤Mixing. If you have a lot of newspaper/magazine articles about your subject, you might want to mix them together on a flat surface, then shoot various parts of the bunch and use them as they fit into the story.

In the documentary *Fatal Mistakes*, a small crew set out to revisit the sensational murder of a mother in Toms River, New Jersey, and the subsequent trial and sentencing. They interviewed all of the major players in the case. They knew they would be constantly referencing newspaper and magazine articles of the case for B-roll. While they were interviewing one of the detectives, he mentioned that the official police file had copies of all of the newspaper articles written about the crime over a four-year period. The director asked if she could record the articles and he agreed, as long as she didn't take the file from the station. She found a large tabletop and spread all of the newspaper and magazine articles out on the surface in a random way. She shot the articles and headlines in close-ups, medium shots, and wide shots. She panned, tilted, and zoomed over the articles and headlines. By the time they were finished shooting, she had a wide variety of B-roll to draw from. They added a layered effect in editing that provided visual appeal and enabled them to cover the same information and/or event from more than one paper at the same time.

Recreations, Reenactments, Dramatizations, and Reimaginings

Often the best way to support someone telling a story about the past is to recreate the story. This requires a lot of thought. A cheesy recreation can damage the credibility of your story. A factually inaccurate dramatization can mislead your audience. Here are some approaches that should help you decide if you need to create a recreation, reenactment, dramatization, or reimagining.

In general, the terms recreation, reenactment, and dramatization are interchangeable. Recreations and reenactments tend to apply to historical sequences, while dramatizations refer to more stylized retellings of everyday stories.

• Reenactments and Recreations: Historically Accurate • Historically accurate reenactments often are used in historical documentaries and involve reenactment groups that specialize in historically accurate details. Revolutionary War and Civil War groups can often be utilized on the very sites where the battles happened. These groups are usually very cooperative with filmmakers.

Ethnic groups that have preserved the clothing, instruments, music, and food of their ancestors can also enhance a documentary that has an ethnic overtone. These groups are usually based in churches, libraries, or historical societies.

The historical documentarian Ken Burns often uses historical elements of these groups, like a cannon or weapon or flag, as B-roll visuals.

Paintings of your subject matter from the same era can provide beautiful visuals for your story. If you want to use a well-known painting or artist, there might be a copyright problem if you shoot a reproduction photo in an art book or poster. You can usually find the answers to ownership of rights on the Web. If the painting was created prior to 1923 and is hanging in someone's home or your local library or historical society, then it should be fine to record the content.

Crime reenactments are another story. It is very difficult to achieve believability with actors and sets if you are trying for full-scale historical accuracy. It can sometimes be done with a big budget and film-directing skills, but be wary of falling short and hurting your credibility. If you do go this route, make sure you do enough research so your details are accurate: clothes, furniture, vehicles, hairstyles, time of day, and locations. *Rescue 911* and *America's Most Wanted* use recreations all of the time, and rarely do they ring true. But they are more concerned with giving the viewer a sense of what happened rather than a full-scale recreation. In the case of *America's Most Wanted*, the main objective is to trigger a viewer memory that will hopefully result in capturing the criminal.

The Academy Award–winning documentary *Man on Wire* (2009) uses realistic recreations well. Most of the dramatization scenes were shot with a lot of close-ups of parts of the scenes (hands, wheels, gear, feet), and all of the footage was changed to black and white in post. The viewer never sees a full-face shot. The reenactment action is keyed to interview descriptions. The black-and-white aesthetic lends a surreal overtone to the reenactments and allows our imagination to fill in many of the details.

• **Stylized Reimaginings** • These dramatizations tend to be subjective and emotion filled. They exist to make a point more than be historically accurate.

Errol Morris pioneered these artistic dramatizations in his classic documentary *The Thin Blue Line* (1988). At the heart of the story was a murder of a police officer. Everyone who was at the scene had a dif-

Director James Marsh used a stylized approach when he filmed his recreation of the Twin Tower wire walk by Philippe Petit. As the team entered the towers, made their way to the tops of the buildings, and prepared to set the wires, he never showed any faces, just parts of people. He shot it in black and white to contrast with the color interviews and give a feeling of the past *(Magnolia Home Entertainment, 2008)*.

Because everyone who was there had a different story, documentary maker Errol Morris stylized his reimaginations of the murder of a police officer. Each time he showed the crime details were different *(Independent Film Channel and Fourth Floor Productions, 1988)*.

ferent account of what happened. One of the themes of the documentary is what is truth? As a result, the reenactments are stylized in their visual composition, sound track, action, and point of view. They play with our perceptions and draw the viewer into the story.

• **Dramatizations** • Ken Burns likes to create a mood with his dramatizations. In the series *The Civil War*, he created tableaus that combined with music and/or narration to establish the mood he was after. For instance, after describing a bloody battle, he placed an authentic Civil War–era cannon on a hill at sunset. The camera composed a beautiful shot while sad, mournful music played underneath and a narrator completed the scene. In another example, he used a dramatically lit table-top filled with a map, inkwell, oil lamp, a pair of glasses, and some handwritten letters to show how the politicians and generals were limited in their firsthand knowledge of the war.

As one of his historians is describing the death of a general, we see a recreation

In his classic documentary series *The Civil War* Ken Burns uses a recreation of the items on a politician's table to reinforce the point that communication was slow and difficult between the battlefields and the command centers *(1990 Ken Burns).*

of the room with authentic bed, chair, and table. No people. There is a bowl with a sponge in it and vials of medications on the table. It is a stark environment. This is an authentic recreation of the room the general died in and as the story unfolds the camera shoots a wide shot; then close-ups of various elements in the room; then shots of the window, outside the window, and the horizon and the trees; and finally a soft-focus shot of the trees as the narrated story of the general's death comes to an end.

In another part of *The Civil War*, the narrator speaks about Fort Pulaski in Georgia. We see bits and pieces of the fort with no people: cannons, walls, battered windows, no people. The music and people-less shots give a haunting feeling to the sequence.

In Laura Cava and William Donald Kaufman's documentary *Blowing Smoke* (2007), which is a cautionary tale about the dangers of marijuana addiction, one of the addicts is telling on camera how he got arrested for stealing a car. As he tells the story, two more moving-picture areas appear on the screen with him. As he explains the action, we see pieces of the action in the two other screen areas. The reenactment has been broken up into fragments just like the addict's life.

In Carolyn Scharf and Rasheed Daniel's documentary *Wasted Youth* (2000), a woman describes how another woman was raped after a night of binge drinking. The reenactment is in black and white and only shows extreme close-ups of key moments of the action: a male hand grabbing a female arm, an empty bed with rumpled sheets, a ceiling fan turning slowly, a showerhead spraying water, the water going down the drain. The reenactment ends up in the viewer's mind because all of the missing details must be filled in by the viewer. It can often be effective to recreate the emotion rather than the actual events.

When director Connie Bottinelli was making her documentary *The Curse of King Tutankhamun*, she knew she would have to create three dramatizations of key moments in her story. In an interview in 2001, she explained how she did it:

> A recreation is supposed to be an impression of what may have happened, an impression to give you a visual image. I mean, you don't have to see somebody stabbed to get the picture that somebody has just been stabbed. All you have to see is the blood going down the drain, you know, like in *Psycho*. So you just see the images. Sometimes abstract designs that just give you an idea.
>
> We didn't use any dialogue in the recreations. That's one of the mandates of the Discovery Channel production department. And I agree with that stylistically, too.
>
> There are certain important parts of the story that I wanted to see. I didn't want to hear somebody telling about them. One of these dramatic moments was going into the tomb and finding the gold. The only reason I could do that is because in Cairo there exists an actual replica of Tut's tomb.
>
> Now what I could have done was tell the dramatic story of breaking into the tomb by using archival photographs, which I had. But I didn't have the exact moment of them breaking into the tomb, only shots of the search party working through the tomb to get the treasure out. I could have done it that way with still photos and my narrator. But I wanted to recreate it.
>
> So, when we returned home after shooting in Egypt and London, I knew I would have to stage three additional recreations: Carter breaking into the tomb and finding Tut and the gold, the death of Carter, and the inside of the tomb that included actors playing King Tut and his young bride. I chose a Masonic temple in

Cherry Hill, New Jersey, to shoot all of the recreations. It had high ceilings and lots of open space. I had a picture in my mind of how I wanted the scenes to look. It's interesting, while I was in Egypt I found Carter's actual house on the edge of the Valley of the Kings. I knew I wanted to shoot there and that I could write to that moment, but when we were shooting in his house I realized the scene would be better as a reenactment.

> The day before the reenactment shoot in the Masonic temple in Cherry Hill, NJ, I met with my gaffer and director of photography. We walked through the hall and I went through every scene with storyboards. They had ideas and I used many of them. It was collaborative. They made my dream real.
>
> In two of the recreations, we shot footage of people against a green screen. During editing, I put the Egypt shots of the inside of the tomb into the green part of the screen.*

Artistic Sequences

Often adding art to your documentary can enhance your storytelling and provide enjoyment to the viewer. Art sets you free. You can explore your imagination and creativity. But this freedom comes with a price. How you use art needs to be thought out. You don't want to overwhelm your story or confuse the viewer or just get artsy because it's fun.

Sometimes you can help tell your story by creating an artistic sequence that illustrates the emotions you are trying to make the viewer feel. In *Lake of Fire* (2006), which is a two-sided study of the issue of abortion, the documentary begins with a series of close-ups of candles burning. The emotional and contradictory symbolism the candles bring—religion, fire, pain, peace—draws us in. The accompanying symphonic music establishes a serious mood and prepares the viewer for an emotional journey through this controversial issue.

In *Dogtown and Z-Boys* (2001), Stacy Peralta establishes a fast pace and an aes-

*These words were transcribed from an interview I had with Connie Bottinelli on February 12, 2001.

thetic of layered and moving visual elements to complement his story of the pioneering skateboarders of Southern California. He uses animated graphics, grainy 16 mm footage, layering, special effects, fast editing, and a creative use of archival photos to match his visuals to the fast-paced, hectic, rebellious lives the skateboarders lived. To Peralta, skateboarding is an art form, and his visual aesthetic reinforces this feeling.

The black and white documentary *Lake of Fire* deals with the controversial issue of abortion. In the opening sequence director Tony Kaye uses a soft focus group of burning, melting candles to show how religion and faith are being tested by both sides of the abortion issue *(2006 Above the Sea)*.

In Morgan Spurlock's *Supersize Me* (2004), he uses clever animated sequences to reinforce his points. There are maps, animated characters, songs, statistics, all created in bright colors and a simplified form. The production values aren't super high, but his story focuses on waking the viewer up to a societal problem of obesity. In this context, his B-roll works.

Meeting David Wilson (2008) is a personal-journey documentary by directors David A. Wilson and Daniel J. Woolsey about an African American man who returns to his southern roots. While the subject struggles to deal with the racism of the past, there are recurring sequences in which the camera is underwater, shooting a person struggling in the water. The mood is dreamy and the action symbolizes the struggles the main character and his race have gone through. The documentary is mostly shot in a vérité style and these artistic sequences take you out of reality for a moment and help make the documentarian's point.

• **Original Art** • In the documentary *Tonal Colors* (2005), which is a study of young jazz musicians learning the art and craft of playing jazz, producer Samantha Cressen created a visual transitional device using a large, original, abstract painting of jazz musicians playing their instruments. During each of six segment transitions, the camera floats over a different section of the painting while special-effects boxes with frame-grab pictures in them and moving graphics are also on screen. The jazz sound track supports the improvised feeling of the visuals.

Using paintings, especially abstract, impressionistic ones that have imagery related to the emotional and psychological themes in your documentary, can add a creative dimension to your story. Finding a local artist and working with him/her is exciting and fulfilling for both you and the artist. Historical documentaries that deal with tragic deaths, such as those of holocaust victims and other violent massacres, can often be enhanced by artwork as well as archival footage.

In the documentary *Red Darkness Before Dawn* (2005), which tells the story of how a generation of Romanian intellectuals was systematically jailed and tortured, director Diana Nicolae used original artwork painted by an artist friend that captures the emotions of torture and pain to complement her story. Throughout the film

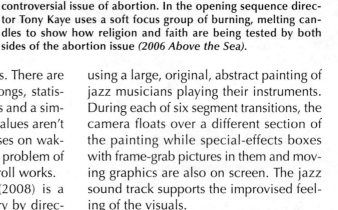

shots of the artwork help remind the viewer how much suffering went unnoticed and unpunished.

In the documentary *Crumb* (1994), which is a vérité look at the artist Robert Crumb, the artist's own artwork is shot as the artist looks at it and explains why and how he created it.

Sometimes you can create a symbolic image that recurs throughout the documentary and reinforces your emotional and psychological story. In the documentary *Finding the Light*, which is an exploration of the Quaker religion made by Ziporah Paskman and Lauren McGarry, they used light as their recurring image. Quakers use the term "inner light" a lot when speaking of their spiritual life. Throughout the documentary there are visual sequences that use images of light: light shining through windows, candles burning at protest rallies and in peoples houses, light reflecting off of water, the sun forming starbursts when the camera shoots directly into it.

• **Montages** • A montage is a series of images and/or sounds that tell a story. The montage story almost always reinforces a larger story or theme. All of the images in the montage are related to each other. One of the most creative tools for storytelling is creating a montage that enhances your story/themes. Montage can be created using different elements. The most common montages are visuals with music.

Montages can be used as B-roll for an interview or a narration sequence, as a transitional device, or as a stand-alone sequence to advance the story. Montages allow you to work creatively with music and sound. Montages bring art to your story and affect the viewer in an emotional way. Natural sound and picture montages put the focus on the sounds as well as the images.

In the documentary *Movement X* (2008), which follows a colorguard team

through its final season, producer Cindy Lewandowski uses montages of the team performing its routines throughout the documentary. Original music and natural sound accompany the montages until we get to the final performance, which is an emotional ending for the team. The montages help to build to the final crescendo of the final sequence, and help draw us into the emotions the team is feeling.

Nature

Often using the elements of nature can help you tell your story in a creative way. No one uses nature better than Ken Burns. Matching nature shots to mood and story can appeal to both the emotions and our minds. Shooting artistically composed nature shots of environments where the action of your story unfolded can give the viewer a chance to fill in the missing pieces.

Shooting natural settings at night with the moon or sunset/sunrise in the frame generates mood connected to the music and/or narration. Composing natural elements of water, forest, farm, industrial, and suburban settings can add emotional elements to your story. Moods like inspiration, sadness, anger, and exhilaration can all be represented by nature shots. In the documentary *Food, Inc.* (2008), which is a scathing indictment of the food industry, director Robert Kenner frames wide shots of beautiful, colorful, vast landscapes. It is only after we get closer to the farming and cattle ranching that we see the ugly underbelly of the way our food is processed.

Slow-Motion Sequences

Often using a series of images in slow motion can create a mood that works for your story. When image flow is slow and coupled with music, the effect always triggers an emotional response.

In the documentary *Capturing the Friedmans* (2003), which is a study of a sex crime and the effect it has on a family and its hometown of Great Neck, Long Island, NY, there is a B-roll sequence of three shots. The first is a fast-motion shot of the town's clock and the passing traffic; then there is a shot in slow motion of a commuter train slowly pulling into a station. Finally, there is a slow dissolve to a slow-motion shot of young boys swimming in a pool. The music is dramatic, slow, and sad. The sequence reinforces the two intertwined stories: child abuse and the effects it can have on a town.

In the documentary *Food, Inc.,* director Robert Kenner composes many beautiful landscape shots to ironically dramatize how the food industry is putting profit, abuse of nature, and convenience over nutrition and health *(2008 Perfect Meal LLC).*

FINAL THOUGHTS

Creating B-roll that enhances your story and brings art and surprise to your aesthetic is one of the most satisfying experiences a documentary maker can have. All documentaries are emotional in one way or another. Each story is personal and the viewer appreciates creative framing of the story. Letting your mind go as you visualize B-roll sequences can help you enjoy the production experience and connect you to your audience in deep and profound ways.

DOCUMENTARY REFERENCES

Each of these documentary references was chosen because it has a creative element or technique that stands out. Some of the most creative filmmaking has occurred while a documentarian is telling his or her story. It is hoped that the curious reader will be motivated to watch many of these documentaries not only for enjoyment, but also for inspiration.

Blowing Smoke. 2006. Laura Cava and William Donald Kaufman. WDK Films LLC. This Cine Golden Eagle winner used creative special effects to enhance reenactments of a young man's descent into addiction. Kaufman divided the screen into thirds, with two of the frames showing different aspects of the reenactments and the last third holding the face of the subject telling the story.

Capturing the Friedmans. 2003. Andrew Jarecki. Gang Documentary. This film was nominated for an Academy Award in 2003. Director Andrew Jarecki tells the story of a family torn apart by charges and convictions of sexual abuse of local children by a father and son. As the story unfolds you realize there are really two stories. The main one of the family dealing with the shock of the charges of sexual abuse, and a secondary one of how the local community (Great Neck, Long Island) deals with the notoriety of the case. This is a directed documentary that reveals during its interview sequences the insides and outsides of typical, middle class homes in the community.

The Civil War: TV Series. 1990. Ken Burns. PBS.

In this ten-hour, nine-episode series created for PBS Burns often creates tableaus that combine with music and/or narration to establish the mood he is after. For instance, after describing a bloody battle he will place an authentic civil war era canon on a hill at sunset. The camera composes a beautiful shot while sad, mournful music plays underneath and a narrator completes the scene. In another example he will use a dramatically lit tabletop filled with a map, ink well, oil lamp, a pair of glasses, and some handwritten letters to show how the politicians and generals were limited in their first hand knowledge of the war and rarely up-to-date with critical information. This series is still the most watched series in the history of PBS. Every aspiring documentarian should watch this film because many of the techniques now considered part of the grammar of documentary storytelling were pioneered in this amazing series.

Crazy Love. 2007. Dan Klores and Fisher Stevens. Shoot the Moon Productions. This film tells the story of a tragic, dysfunctional love affair between two people. The directors use the technique of over-shooting single photos, with the surrounding space black. Often a pan or zoom is added, and we see the surrounding black either in the beginning or end of the move. The story is a dark, sad one and the limbo black surroundings of the photos help reinforce the dark psychological overtone to the story.

Crumb. 1994. Terry Zwigoff. Crumb Partners. This Sundance winner was shot in 16mm color film and has a vibrant, dark aesthetic, not unlike the subject, Robert Crumb. Its vérité style captures the strange, intense life of an iconic artist. The director's comments are interesting as Zwigoff explains how odd it is to make a documentary about a friend and iconic cultural figure.

The Curse of King Tutankhamun. 1999. Connie Bottinelli. Discovery Communications. This documentary was made for Discovery Communications and is structured for television. Director Bottinelli re-creates her historical eras in a creative and effective manner. Her color palette in her recreations features a soft golden glow that references the desert, King Tut's tomb, and Egypt.

Dogtown and Z-Boys. 2001. Stacy Peralta. Vans, Inc., and Sony Entertainment. Double Sundance winner. Sean Penn narrates this fast-paced, creative telling of the origins of skateboarding. Peralta uses his 16mm skills to add a jumpy, layered look to his B-roll and mon-

tages. He mixes black and white interviews with color B-roll and home movie archival footage.

Encounters at the End of the World. 2007. Werner Herzog. Discovery Communications LLC. Director Herzog went to the South Pole to find a story of dedication and strange beauty when he made this film. Often he used freeze frames on his storyteller's computers to add interesting B-roll to his story.

Fatal Mistakes. 2005. Jason Kitchen and Cheryl Kurn. Rowan University. This film retells the story of the murder of a woman by her husband. The surviving sons had only one copy of a videotape of their mother early in her marriage. The sons were reluctant to part with the VHS tape, so director Cheryl Kurn played the tape back into the family TV set and shot the screen. The images have not only a home movie look, but also reinforce the family feeling by being shown on the family TV.

Finding the Light. 2004. Ziporah Paskman and Lauren McGarry. Rowan University. This film is an exploration of the Quaker religion. Directors Paskman and McGarry used light as their recurring image. Quakers use the term "inner light" a lot when speaking of their spiritual life. Throughout the documentary there are visual sequences that use images of light. Light shining through windows, candles burning at protest rallies and in peoples houses, light reflecting off of water, the sun forming sunbursts when the camera shoots directly into it. Merging the real and the spiritual in the light images helped explain the uniqueness of Quakerism.

Intimate Portrait: Jessica Savitch. 1993. Connie Bottinelli. Lifetime. This film is about the life of pioneering broadcaster Jessica Savitch who died tragically in an automobile accident. Jessica's parents had stored all of the photos and memorabilia connected to their daughter's life in their attic. When Connie Bottinelli saw this she arranged all of the items on the floor of the attic, creatively lit them with white and gelled lights, then shot hours of footage from every angle, framing newspapers, headlines, high school yearbooks, flowers, diaries, photos, clothing, hats, ... when she was done she had almost all of the personal B-roll needed for the documentary.

Lake of Fire. 2006. Tony Kaye. Anonymous Content. This beautifully shot black and white documentary deals with the controversial issue of abortion. Both sides are strongly presented and the filmmaker leaves it up to the audience to decide for themselves. It was a labor of love and took 16 years to make.

Man on Wire. 2008. James Marsh. Magnolia Home Entertainment. Director Marsh used a stylized approach when he filmed his recreations of the twin tower wire walk by Philippe Petit. As the team entered the towers, made their way to the top of the building, hid from the guards, and prepared to set the wires he never showed any faces, just parts of people and rear shots. The recreations are in black and white to contrast with the color interviews and give a feeling of the past.

Meeting David Wilson. 2008. David A. Wilson and Daniel J. Woolsey. MSNBC and Official Pics LLC. This film is a personal journey documentary by director David Wilson, who returns to his southern roots after he finds out that a white man with the same name as his still lives near the slave farm of David's ancestors. While he struggles to deal with the racism of the past, there are recurring sequences where the camera is underwater shooting a person struggling in the water. The mood is dreamy and the action symbolizes the struggles the main character and his race have gone through. The documentary is mostly shot in a vérité style and these artistic sequences take you out of reality for a moment and help make his point.

Movement X. 2007. Cindy Lewandowski. Rowan University. This documentary follows a team of color guard performers through their final season. Four members tell their personal stories. The physical and mental toll they pay to perform is eye opening. A fascinating sliver of the performance life.

Red Darkness Before Dawn. Diana Nicolae. 2005. Cineluci. This historical film tells the story of how a generation of Romanian intellectuals was systematically jailed and tor-

tured. Director Nicolai used original artwork painted by an artist friend that captures the emotions of torture and pain to compliment her story. Throughout the film shots of the pain the artwork depicts helps remind the viewer how much suffering went unnoticed and unpunished.

Seabrook Farms Remembered. 2002. Ned Eckhardt. Seabrook Educational and Cultural Museum and New Jersey Historical Commission. This film tells the story of a unique farming experience in southern New Jersey that involved thousands of World War II refugees. I often placed 8 x 10 still black and white photos in outdoor and indoor display settings to keep the farming relationship in the frame with the people.

Supersize Me. 2004. Morgan Spurlock. Kathbur Pictures. Morgan Spurlock channels Michael Moore and takes on the obesity epidemic in the United States. He lives on McDonald's food for 30 days and lets the viewer keep him company.

The Thin Blue Line. 1988. Errol Morris. Third Floor Productions. Perhaps the most influential and groundbreaking documentary of the last 22 years. Morris tells the story of the murder of a police officer in Dallas and reveals that the wrong man is serving a life sentence. Morris brings art to the film by using a score by Philip Glass and using stylized recreations to make the point that the truth is often hard to find.

Wasted Youth. 2000. Carolyn Scharf and Rasheed Daniel. Rowan University. Binge drinking and its tragic consequences are the subject of this social issue documentary that has been viewed by tens of thousands high school and college students. Creative use of a recurring surreal party reenactment enhances the message.

Part III: Postproduction

8. Editing and Postproduction

The final phase of your project is the postproduction phase. This is when you begin to shape your footage and creative elements into a crafted story. Organization is the key. Here is a list of essential tasks that you will have to address. Some are creative, some are technical, and some are organizational. All are important.

LABELING TAPES/FILM ROLLS/CARDS

Tapes

As you shoot footage and fill up tapes, it becomes critical that you label each one on its front and its spine and label the front and spine of the cassette box. Because the tapes are small, you need to develop a shorthand that tells you what number the tape is and what is on the tape. Usually, footage can be classified by "Interview" or "B-roll," so labels might look like this:

Tape #3 John Doe—Interview
#4 John Doe—Interview
#5 B-roll JD work
#6 B-roll sunset, car
#7 B-roll JD photos

Sometimes using color-coded circle stickers on the cassette boxes works for quick reference, e.g., red stickers mean interviews, green stickers mean B-roll. Yellow stickers might mean something else, like home movies or archival footage or special footage or narration or music.

Cards

If you are shooting with P2 or other cards, when the card is filled you will transfer all the footage to a computer or portable hard drive for storage. Once again, you need to label the footage in the computer or drive so you know what was on the card. Since the P2 card will be erased after you transfer the footage, you need to always double-check that the footage was captured correctly on your computer or drive. A lot of producers like to transfer the footage off of the card onto two storage devices so there is a backup system.

Cards are the future, but until they develop further, if you are going to be shooting on the move and for long periods of time, you might want to consider using tape. Stopping production while you transfer footage from a card to a computer or portable hard drive might negatively affect your production rhythm.

Film

If you are shooting in film, you will probably be using a 16 mm camera that shoots 11-minute rolls. Once again, there is downtime as you unload and reload a new roll. Labeling the film rolls is just as important as labeling tapes. At some point, you will have the film footage transferred to a video format for digitizing. These tapes or cards must also be labeled correctly. All media labeling must match.

STORING MEDIA OUTSIDE THE EDITING COMPUTER

Controlling the flow and storage of footage is a big responsibility. The tapes or films should always be stored in a safe, dry, temperature-controlled environment. One person, usually the producer, editor, or director, should be responsible for the footage storage. Shelves next to a computer are the best place to store tapes/films. It is critical to create a central place, that everyone on the crew knows, where tapes can be found and digitizing can be done.

At some point, production and postproduction will overlap. This usually happens after the first interview.

On the DVD for Stacy Peralta's documentary *Crips and Bloods* (2009), there is a special feature in which Peralta explains how the project went through postproduction. You can see how he created a room with computers and keyboards. These systems were used for previewing footage, digitizing clips and bites, and creating ed-

In this photo are all of the sources for preparing for editing: carefully labeled tapes, interview transcriptions, music CDs, project computer, and segment rundown *(2010 Eckhardt)*.

iting stations. It is all organized and doesn't take up a lot of space. More than one person can work at the same time because everyone is using headsets.*

QUICK PREVIEWING

As footage is shot, it should be screened immediately for sound and picture quality. On site is preferable, but do it back at your home base for sure. If you are on the road, checking footage after the shoot is a must. Similarly, interviews should be checked to see if there are any doubts about content. Reshooting might be possible if you catch a mistake or omission right away.

TRANSCRIBING INTERVIEWS, BITES, AND CONVERSATIONS

A key element in the postproduction process is typing out the words that your subjects say. This requires playing back the interviews and/or vérité statements and typing the spoken words into a written document. There are a few ways to do this. This is not a fun activity. It is tedious and time consuming. But it is vital to organizing your story for final editing. Here are some transcribing systems:

➤Digitize the whole interview and put it on a computer. Play it back, stopping and starting, until you have typed it all into a document.

➤Play back the videotape in the camera, while it is sitting next to your computer. Use headphones that are jacked into the camera's audio output. Using the function buttons on the camera, stop and start the tape and type out the interview.

➤Burn a DVD of the footage and play it back on your computer as you type.

➤Record the audio from the tape onto a CD. Use CD playback to type the transcription. This is sometimes called a "radio track."

➤If you are shooting in film, have the film transferred to a video-tape format that you can easily digitize.

The reason transcribing is so important is that most or all of the story line of the documentary is in the subjects' conversations. The producer and director need to have this content at their disposal as they craft the story. Editors also use the transcriptions for reference and decision making. Tape numbers and time codes should be noted frequently as you transcribe. Most people single-space the subjects' words and double-space between questions. Leave a lot of white space on the sides of the page to allow room for comments and thinking out loud. Here is a typical transcription format. The documentary is a social-issue story focusing on prescription-drug addictions.

Generation RX

April 7, 2008
Interviewed by: *Paul*
Interviewee: *Mary* (Part 1)
Transcribed by: *Paul*

Crips and Bloods DVD. Special Feature of director's commentary by Stacy Peralta.

Tape 14

11:26:24:00–11:26:33:00
Paul: Can you tell me your name and how old you are?
Mary: Mary, 29 years old.

11:26:34:07—11:27:31:15
Paul: What was your life like when you were growing up?
Mary: Ah, I'm a product of two addicts. My mother and father both used. Um. My dad was an alcoholic. My mother was a prescription-pill user. Ah, so it was a pretty sad household. My dad was always beating up my mom. Uh, always with babysitters, never any family time, ya know, it was basically my brother and I always fending for ourselves, taking care of each other. We really didn't have parental figures. Ya know, I look at families today and I see what I wished my family would have been like, but it was the complete opposite, there was no love, there was no, ya know, I know my mother and my father loved me, but I don't think that they loved themselves enough to be able to give love to anybody else, so that's—

11:27:31:15–11:28:31:28
Paul: Are there any stories that stand out that, um, ya know, my father was an alcoholic so I remember all kinds of crazy chaos going on. Anything stand out?
Mary: Um, I remember a specific time, it was my birthday and my mom had arranged for me to have a sleepover and, ah, my dad came home drunk and, uh, he beat my mother up in the kitchen in front of all my friends an', uh, he hurt her real bad that time, she had to go to the hospital. Not only did I see it, but all of my friends saw it as well and my secret was out like everyone knew, what my home life was like and that was an everyday occurrence for me, was to actually come in and see that, ya know, it was pretty traumatic not only for me but for them too, so.

11:28:31:29–11:29:48:28
Paul: When did you realize that your mother had a prescription-drug-abuse problem?
Mary: Uh, from the time I was little like, when I was on vacation, my grandparents, I remember my mom telling me to take my grandmother's pills and put them in my sock and bring them home to her in New Jersey. Um, I always remember her taking pills out of her containers when I was little, we would go into the bathroom or the kitchen or wherever, she was always taking something from her. So, I always knew something was up with my mother, ya know, I didn't really know the extent of it until I got older, but she was always, ya know, she used me to help her get high a lot of the times, so she would take pills, from my aunt, she would take pills it was something I would remember constantly, seeing her going through people's cabinets and looking through their medicine bottles that they had an'. Yeah.

Tip: The average person speaks three words per second. Count the number of words per line of the transcription, then find an average word count per line. Divide the average line number of words by three and you have the time each line takes. Now you can add up the lines and know how long the bite/statement takes. This is a quick way you can estimate the time of your statement. TV stations use the "line time" rule to time their news stories.

Highlighting

Whoever transcribes the interviews should read them afterwards, add some thoughts about the content of each one, and maybe even use a highlighter to indicate important statements. This helps in the final decision making about what will be in the documentary. If your word processing program has a color highlighting tool, use it to indicate the comments you think are relevant to your story. If multiple people will be reading the transcript, then it helps if each reader uses a different color highlighter. The color overlaps will probably mark the important statements.

Google Documents (docs.google.com)

Google now offers free Web storage of documents and projects at its Google Docs Web site. You can create your own secure documents/project Web site and upload all of your transcriptions, logs, treatments, narrations, and other relevant written information. The site can be accessed by all members of the production team simply by sharing the password. You can also use it to create spreadsheets, share photos, and communicate with each other. Google Docs is accessible from any smart phone or computer with an Internet connection. There is a highlighting tool on the Web site that all members of the production team can access. You can also create templates for all of your needs: logging, transcribing, tape lists, segment lists, digitizing lists, edit decision lists, etc. Google Docs is a great, centralized location for the paperwork of the project. Because you can upload all of your files, it is also a secure backup storage location for all of the project's paperwork. And maybe best of all: it is FREE.

There is another Web site called Review Basics (reviewbasics.com) that allows you upload low-resolution video for project sharing. You can create a group, then password protect the group. Although the video isn't top grade, Review Basics allows for video sharing so people can stay updated on the progress of the project.

Logging B-roll

Another important element in the postproduction process is logging B-roll footage. This is essentially all of the non-speaking footage. Someone has to review all of the B-roll and decide which shots are worthy of digitizing and are candidates for final inclusion. When logging B-roll, it is good to have a template that enables you to evaluate and describe the footage. Most templates look something like this:

Tape#	Time Code	Shot Description	Rating
3	03:22:10–03:42:10	John Doe playing w/daughter	***
3	04:14:12–04:22:08	Daughter CU big smile	****
3	04:45:10–04:58:04	Daughter hugs JD funny	****

Just like transcribing, logging is hard, tedious work. You screen and log your footage either in the camera before digitizing, or after the footage has all been digitized. But when you are finished, you have described all of the footage and found the usable shots. These can now be digitized and transferred into the project. Meanwhile, your written logs are there for future reference if needed. Logging is a study in reduction. You separate what works from what doesn't. And, most importantly, you remove all of the technical mistakes and unusable footage.

If your editing computer has enough memory storage, you can digitize all of the B-roll footage and pick the worthy clips for your B-roll bins. But the most useful way to handle B-roll footage is to log it and only use what is realistic for the project. Maybe late in the editing phase you might desperately need a B-roll shot. You can reread your logs and hopefully find the shot.

ORGANIZING YOUR PROJECT COMPUTER: EDITING SOFTWARE

There are three editing software programs that are readily available and affordable for everyone. They are Final Cut, Adobe Premiere, and Avid. All three come in various levels of capacity and complexity. Whether you are a Mac or PC person might determine which one you will use. However, now all three programs have versions for both Mac and PC.

Final Cut is popular with beginning "big" project users because it is the most user-friendly of the three. It began as Mac software. It is also the cheapest. If your documentary is going to be simple in its flow—a small amount of tapes/cards, just cut/dissolve edits, no special effects, a simplified sound track—then Final Cut is a good choice. Final Cut is emerging as a competitor with Avid as the industry standard.

Adobe Premiere is the company's mid-range program and includes the Adobe Creative Suite (Photoshop, After Effects, and Audition). It began as PC software. It is user-friendly and relatively inexpensive.

Avid is used the most often in the professional world of high-end film and television. It is known for its organizational capability and ability to manage large projects. Avid has its own platform that has versions for either PC or Mac computers. It's the most expensive.

You can't go wrong with any of them. They all function on the same organizational principles.

Creating and Opening Your Project

Make sure your computer has enough memory and storage capacity to hold all of the media for your project. Then, open your project and protect it with a password.

Backup Drives

In order to protect the project, you should back up both the files and the media on portable hard drives and/or additional computer hard drives.

DIGITIZING FOOTAGE INTO BINS

You begin your editing journey by digitizing footage, integrating it into your project, and then organizing it into bins. First you create and label the bins, then add labeled clips taken from interview/conversation transcriptions and B-roll footage logs to the proper bin. After you have filled your bins with the appropriate B-roll footage and subject statements, you can begin to edit. Eventually, there will be bins for elements like music, narration, archival footage, animations, graphics, and special creations, but once you have the B-roll and interviews/conversations into their bins, you can usually begin editing some parts of the documentary.

EDITING FLOW

Timelines: Segments and Master

Documentaries are edited by segments, which are sometimes called "scenes" or "chapters." As you organize your story, you break it into chapters or segments. Each segment is a complete part of the larger whole. A segment can be an interview or sustained conversation with B-roll, a musical montage, a narration with B-roll sequence, a transition, the opening/title sequence, or whatever other story elements you might want to edit by themselves. You should create a timeline for each segment. That way, you can work out of sequential order if you want. Eventually, you may have ten to 30 segment timelines. When you feel the time is right, you create a master timeline and begin putting the segment timelines together.

Rough Cuts

When you first combine all of your segments into a master timeline, you have created a rough cut. This is your first attempt to tell your whole story with all of the segments in the proper order.

After you review the rough cut, you can begin to get a feeling for how the entire story plays out. Perhaps you will create different versions of the master timeline by combining the segments differently. Perhaps you will shorten or lengthen a segment in its own timeline, then replace it in the master timeline. Every editor and director has his/her own way of managing the story segments. But the key to the process is initially working in segment timelines, then combining them near the end.

When director Arnold Shapiro was editing his classic vérité documentary *Scared Straight!* (1978), he gave his editor a lot of creative freedom. The process of a director collaborating with an editor is often a matter of trust and letting go. In this excerpt from an interview I had with Shapiro in 2002, he explains this simpatico relationship.

> I've done over 150 documentaries and I give at least 50 percent of the credit to the editors. I gave my *Scared Straight!* editor, Vaughn Neemack, many notes and a structure. A rundown scene by scene and turned him lose.
>
> We had 30 hours of footage. He cut it down to 56 minutes.
>
> We edited on a Moviola. No video transfers for previewing and logging. We put the whole thing together segment by segment. We showed it to management and they were astounded.
>
> I remember one dilemma we had. There was a moment in the beginning of the documentary before the kids go deep inside the prison to the auditorium. They were lined up in a hallway. One of the kids mouths off to a guard and they are about to fight. It was a very tense, dramatic moment. During editing I argued for weeks with Vaughn whether we should use that scene. He thought it was too much too early. Let's let the piece build. I thought it was too powerful to leave out. Until two days before the final transfer to video that scene was in. But Vaughn and others finally convinced me to take it out. To this day I think *Scared Straight!* could have been greater with the hallway sequence in.
>
> I remember when we were doing the film-to-tape transfer at the lab, people from all over the lab started to hear this language. Everybody stopped doing what

they were doing and gathered in that telecine room to watch the transfer. That was my first inkling that we had something very special.*

Fine Cut

As you near the end of the editing, you will make your final content decisions; these versions are called fine cuts. At this point you are down to tweaking and polishing.

Picture Lock

Picture lock means you have finalized all video and visuals.

Final Cut

This means the sound has been finalized and the documentary is completed.

Sound Tracks

The sound in your documentary deserves as much attention as your visuals. A good way to approach sound is to think of it in layers. Walter Murch, who has been a guru of sound for feature films for generations, has a theory that sounds are like colors. There are warm and cold sounds. In order to create a sound design that uses these opposites, you need to think out the sound the way an artist combines colors for maximum effect. Because you have an infinite number of audio tracks in your timeline, it is easy to craft a mixture of sounds.† There are

three main sound sources: voices, natural sound, and music.

• **Voices** • These are the storytellers. Clean, crisp audio is required. In sit-down interviews, this is the standard. In vérité documentaries, it is often harder to achieve the clarity and crispness you need. But the audio programs in the editing software enable you to overcome a lot of unwanted, ambient audio. Sound quality must be checked often as you are recording, so you know what is usable. Good sound editors can save a lot of poor-quality audio by playing with the frequency levels of the sound.

As you create your segment timelines, if there is a storyteller voice in a segment, always put it on the first audio track in your edit timeline. If you recorded the voice on two tracks, you might want to use both tracks. If you have your primary mike on one track and the camera mike on the other, you may want to use just the pri-

Choosing your sound system is critical to the success of your sound gathering. The three choices are shotgun mike, lavalier mike, and handheld mike. All three can be wireless by using an FM wireless transmitter-receiver unit *(Eckhardt 2010)*.

---

*These words were transcribed from an interview I had with Arnold Shapiro on March 26, 2001.

†Walter Murch is generally considered one of the great editors of the present era. He edits feature films and many soundtracks. He has written extensively about his technical and philosophical approach to gathering and editing all sorts of sounds and music. A web site that introduces his ideas and techniques is http://transom.org/?p=6992.

mary mike. Listen to the voice bites with and without the camera mike. Sometimes the camera mike adds an interesting quality to the primary mike.

In a vérité sound bite, the camera mike usually has too much ambient noise in it. So remember to not use that audio track. Instead, use the primary mike.

• **Natural Sound** • These are the sounds of the environments that are in your documentary. If you are editing B-roll, you want to use natural sound if it enhances the footage and helps tell the story. If you have footage of a train going by, people want to hear that familiar sound. Sometimes you can use the natural sound of shots to edit a montage of pictures and natural sounds. A parade, athletic event, or industrial setting usually has a lot of distinct natural sounds that would allow for a natural-sound montage.

Music can be mixed with natural sound to create a layered sound effect that is pleasing to hear and adds emotion to your story.

As you make your B-roll edits, always include the natural sound if it is there. You will often be mixing the natural sound under your storytellers' voices. This is exciting because your natural sound is helping your storyteller tell the story.

B-roll footage without natural sound doesn't have the immediacy and impact of B-roll with sound, although it is possible to break this natural-sound rule and be effective. In the documentary *Murderball*, which is a study of wheelchair rugby athletes, there are some montages of the rugby action with full-on natural sound. In other montages of rugby action in which the natural sound has not been used, the video has been slowed down and stylized, and music is used on the sound track. The lack of the natural sound gives the sequence a dreamy, unreal overtone compared to the natural-sound sequences. It is very effective because it allows you to

watch the action while you think about the strange, courageous world of wheelchair rugby.

• **Music** • Almost every story can be enhanced with music. The music you select and how you use it will be two of the biggest decisions you will make. Deciding where and how you use and mix your music will come at the end of the editing journey. But the segments that you plan to use music in will often undergo many versions as you experiment with your music.

Decisions like whether to use music under all or part of your interviews will take some thought. Many documentary makers don't like to use music under interviews because it is distracting. Others like to add the emotion that music brings to the interviews. Errol Morris, Werner Herzog, and the Maysles Brothers use it often during interview and conversational segments. In the Maysles' classic vérité documentary *Gimme Shelter* (1969), which follows the Rolling Stones, during a 1969 summer tour in the United States, many times the Rolling Stones' music is heard under the conversations.

In the historical documentary *Unforgivable Blackness*, which is a character study of the turn-of-the-century black heavyweight fighter Jack Johnson and examination of the racism he encountered during his life, director Ken Burns uses period music under most of the interviews and B-roll sequences. His archival stills and moving pictures are sweetened with natural sound that he has created. At one point he recreates with actors' voices some dialogue from a court trial, and matches the dialogue with appropriate pictures. This documentary is a fine study in the mixing of sound elements for story enhancement and added emotion.

In the vérité, personal-journey documentary *Meeting David Wilson*, director David A. Wilson revisits the southern farm where his ancestors had been enslaved.

The story begins in the urban streets of Newark, New Jersey, travels to rural Virginia, moves on to Ghana, Africa, then ends in New York City. There were many moods established and David wanted a diverse musical sound track that followed the action. After searching for a composer for many months, he decided to use his brother, who was a prodigy in electronic music composition. He found and created the score David was looking for.

• **Sweetening** • This is the term given to adding sound to the sound track that wasn't there on the original footage. If you have some beautiful shots of the ocean and waves, but your sound isn't up to your standards, you can sweeten your sound track with ocean sounds from a sound effects library or record the ocean sounds at another time and use it with the footage. Similarly, if you are using still photos as B-roll and the content of a photo shows a prison jail cell, you can add the sound of a cell door closing for dramatic effect.

Michael Moore enjoys sweetening his B-roll sequences with comic sounds that help him maintain interest and make his points. In *Bowling for Columbine* (2002), his anti-gun documentary that explores our obsession with guns in light of the Columbine High School tragedy, he sweetens his archival footage with random gunshot sounds and bowling-pin noise.

• **Narration (Voice Over)** • If you are using a narrator to help tell your story, you don't need to secure your actual talent until near the end of the editing phase. Most documentarians follow this model:

➤*Narration (first draft)* written before shooting begins. A rough guide for telling the main story, it is used as a production reference. It emerges out of the treatment of the idea.

➤*Narration (second draft)* written after shooting is over, footage has been screened, and additional research has

been factored in. This draft is created before editing begins.

➤*Narration (third draft)* is recorded by a production team member as a reference audio or scratch track. This narration will be edited into the documentary as editing passes through segment and master timeline editing. There may be additional reference narration writing and recording during editing.

➤*Narration (fourth draft/final draft)* is recorded by the voice that has been selected to narrate the documentary. At this point, the picture is locked, so all narration sequences must be timed out to fit the spaces allotted for them.

How many generations the narration passes through is different for each documentary. But the important aspect to remember is that the narration is a fluid element and can change as new ideas generate new directions. That's why you save recording your narrator until the end of the editing phase.

In the documentary *The Curse of Tutankhamun*, director Connie Bottinelli knew the story she was about to tell. She wrote a reference narrative line to go with her segment rundown before any shooting. This served as a guide for her as she found her storytellers and crafted which parts of the story of King Tut they would tell. Choosing her narrator's voice was a familiar process.

I needed a storytelling voice. I heard a man. I heard a man because the story involved mostly males, and it was historic. So, a man's voice felt right for it. But I've used women before. I tend to use women who have deep voices. They seem to be more "storytelling sounding" for me.

I contacted a talent agency I use a lot and asked them to send me a CD with samples of their long-form talent. I picked a couple of voices and I sent them to Discovery for approval. By chance, my writer said he knew of another voice that was easy to work with and direct. He sent me a show he had narrated which couldn't have been a better idea. He sent me a whole show on video where I saw the show and heard the guy's voice. He was fantastic. I got approval from Discovery and we used him.

He did all of the narration in two hours. I have had other people spend eight full hours recording an hour show. This guy came in and he did it in two. He was a real pro. They have to read to the picture. I scratch track it, but they read to the picture, and so when they're reading, they have a monitor up there with the time codes running, because I have their in-points written on the script. The thing that's really nice about having an hour is that it is not wall-to-wall narration.

That's a typical problem you have with half hours. If you have something that's good enough to be on TV, a half hour is not usually enough time to tell all the good stuff. So it ends up being wall-to-wall narration. In an hour, you have a chance to let the story breathe. You can use natural sounds, the music can take you away, can do things. So, it's easier for them to read-to-picture in an hour program.*

• **Final Sound Mixing** • As you approach the end of editing your documentary, you will probably finish your visuals first. This is called a "picture lock." Picture locks include all visuals including interviews, B-roll, montages, transitions, and graphics. At this point, you have the time/length of your documentary. Now you must finalize and mix the sound tracks. Narration sequences must be finalized, recorded, and added. Special sound effects sequences must be added. Finally, music is mixed throughout the documentary.

Final Feedback

By the time you have a detailed rough cut or a first version of your fine cut, you have been immersed in your documentary for a long time and may be losing some perspective. This might be a good time to ask for some feedback from people whose judgments you trust. Although there may be production colleagues whose opinions you trust, it might be more productive to show the documentary to someone outside the production team. This is a tough call. At this point, you don't want friendly affirmation, you want critical feedback. How you and your production team evaluate the criticism is often difficult and conflicting, but it can unlock some new perspectives.

On the other hand, the vision of the producer/director may never waver, and the documentary may not need review from outside the production team.

Premieres, Festivals, Copying, Distribution

After you have completed your documentary, what happens next? The answer to this question depends on who you made the documentary for, and what the expectations are if you were contracted to make it. In chapter 10, there is a more detailed analysis of how to repurpose your documentary.

Premieres

Everyone who worked on the documentary, including all of the subjects, technicians, musicians, support people, crew, and their friends deserve to see the finished documentary in a setting that showcases the film and allows for a celebration of the experience. Depending on finances these showcase venues can be anywhere from a large screen in someone's home, to

*These words were transcribed from an interview I had with Connie Bottinelli on February 12, 2001.

a rented theater or auditorium, to a venue provided by someone connected to the documentary. This premiere is a celebration of the project, and food and drink are often part of the event. Speeches by various members of the team are important. This is the first heartfelt recognition of all of the work and emotion that have driven the documentary from its inception. No matter where the documentary goes and what it accomplishes, this initial premiere will get the warmest and most sincere reception. It's a good idea to have many DVD copies of the documentary to give away and/or sell at the premiere.

FINAL THOUGHTS

Postproduction always takes the most out of the creative team. It is a long journey of creativity, technology, decision making, and stress. But when the documentary is completed and it is ready for showcasing and screening, you will feel the joy that comes with taking on a large, meaningful project and meeting the challenge.

DOCUMENTARY REFERENCES

Each of these documentary references was chosen because it has a creative element or technique that stands out. Some of the most creative filmmaking has occurred while a documentarian is telling his or her story. It is hoped that the curious reader will be motivated to watch many of these documentaries not only for enjoyment, but also for inspiration.

Bowling for Columbine. 2002. Michael Moore. Dog Eat Dog Productions. This anti-gun documentary explores our obsession with guns in the light of the Columbine High School tragedy. Moore often sweetens his archival footage with random gunshot sounds and bowling pin noise. The mixing of comic sequences with serious footage throughout the film helps relieve tension while still keeping the message in front of the viewer.

Crips and Bloods. 2009. Stacy Peralta. Gang Documentary. In this 2009 directed documentary director Peralta shot all of the interviews in front of a colorful, graffiti-covered wall. The graffiti helps keep the idea in the viewer's mind that this is a hardcore, urban story. The multi-colored background provides an aura of hope as the subjects tell their grim stories.

The Curse of King Tutankhamun. 1999. Connie Bottinelli. Discovery Communications. This documentary was made for Discovery Communications and is structured for television. Director Bottinelli re-creates her historical eras in a creative and effective manner. Her color palette in her recreations features a soft golden glow that references the desert, King Tut's tomb, and Egypt.

Generation Rx: Prescription for Pain. 2008. Harry T. Fleckenstein III, Steven A. Klink, and Missy Stankowski. Rowan University. This exploration of the tragic world of prescription drug abuse features four former addicts telling their frightening stories. The interviews are shot in a studio with a limbo black background and three cameras. An interesting use of camera angles, faces, hands, and movement.

Gimme Shelter. 1970. The Maysles brothers and Charlotte Zwerin. Maysles Films. This classic vérité documentary shows what can happen when you follow an interesting story and the unexpected happens. Unfortunately, the unexpected was a murder at the Rolling Stones free concert at Altamont freeway in CA in 1969. The story moves fluidly from present to past to present, which was a groundbreaking documentary technique. This film captures the spirit of the sixties and always impresses young people today. A must see for the serious documentarian.

Murderball. 2005. Henry Alex Rubin and Dana

Adam Shapiro. ThinkFilm LLC. The film was made by the documentary division at MTV/VH1. This mostly vérité cultural study of the members of a wheelchair rugby team uses sound during the competition sequences in a creative and interesting way. It was a low-budget, digital film that shows if you have the story, production values don't have to be huge. It was nominated for an Academy Award.

Unforgivable Blackness. 2004. Ken Burns. Florentine Productions and WETA-TV. This is a character study of the turn-of-the-century black heavyweight fighter, Jack Johnson, and the racism he encountered during his life. Director Ken Burns uses period music under most of the interviews and B-roll sequences. His archival stills and moving pictures are sweetened with natural sound that he has created. At one point he recreates with actors' voices some dialogue from a court trial, and matches the dialogue with appropriate pictures. This documentary is a fine study in the mixing of sound elements for story enhancement and emotion.

9. Ethics, Fair Use, and the Law

In the rush and heightened activity to prepare your documentary for production, it's easy to overlook the not-so-obvious questions that will also impact the work. This chapter is an attempt to help you ask yourself how far will you go to capture your story. The chapter also explains the laws that are in place in terms of acquiring footage, using copyrighted/trademarked visuals, and obtaining releases.

ETHICS

Decisions that involve ethics usually follow your own moral barometer. There is a lot of gray area surrounding ethical decisions as they relate to documentary making. Here are some examples that might help you to decide where you stand on certain issues.

Point of View

One of the oldest and most discussed issues in documentary making involves whether the documentary maker can be completely objective. This discussion involves two attitudes: one philosophical and one emotional.

The philosophical addresses whether it is possible to remain objective when it is passion for the subject that created the documentary experience in the first place. News reporters can remain objective because they are trained to put themselves out of the story. But making a documentary means you are personally connected to your story and storytellers just by the fact that you care enough to make the documentary in the first place. The answer to the question "Can I be completely objective?" for most documentary makers is "no." You can't be totally objective through all of the decision making and production experiences. You try to be fair and honest, but the documentary is your story as much as the subjects', and you must find your point of view as the experience unfolds.

The emotional aspect addresses whether the presence of a camera and crew will alter the behavior and attitudes of your subjects. This point has been debated since Robert Flaherty asked Nanook to do something over again because the camera jammed. Jean Rouch, a French documentarian who applied the term "cinéma vérité" to making documentaries in the 1960s, felt that the camera always distorted reality. As a result he recommended the documentary maker become part of the documentary and roll with whatever happens. It's even OK to be in the documentary and influence what is going on. Other documentarians believe the detached observer approach is possible. People can forget the camera and truly reveal themselves if they trust the documentary crew and director.

You will have to decide where you stand on these two ethical aspects of production. In today's world, where cameras and electronic recording devices are everywhere, it is easier for people to feel comfortable in front of a camera. Your choice will be one of three styles: a directed documentary in which you control everything except the content of the interviews, a vérité documentary in which you never know what will happen when you arrive to shoot, or a mixed style documentary that includes elements from both styles.

Time

Sometimes, because of scheduling conflicts or unforeseen problems, you find yourself needing footage after a certain action has ended. Because your subjects have been going through the larger story you have been capturing, you might feel you have missed something you know they experienced but that you missed shooting. You might want to have them reenact the action you missed since they have already experienced it. After capturing this reenactment, do you present the edited footage as if it happened for the first time, or do you acknowledge via a graphic that the action is a reenactment? Most documentary makers will allow the footage to appear as if it is happening in real time. The reasoning is that the subjects lived the action in the first place, and recreated it themselves. However, an argument can be made that

this is falsifying reality. This dilemma is common for documentary makers. It actually happened in two well-known documentaries.

In the event documentary *Spellbound* (2002), which is a mix of vérité and directed styles, the crew was following eight young spellers. When they got to the national spelling bee in Washington, DC, because of the large scale of the event, the makers were unable to capture all of the emotional reactions of the families exactly as they happened. They filmed some reactions later in time, but presented them as if they were happening at the moment they originally did. There was debate about whether these unlabeled recreations were ethical. The majority of critics and lay audience felt it was fine. Asking excited people to revisit their excitement is still presenting reality, but you will always have to decide for yourself.*

The second example is in the seminal classic *Nanook of the North*, which was made by Robert Flaherty and is generally agreed to be the first feature-length documentary. It was originally shot in 1913. But the film was destroyed in a fire and Robert Flaherty reshot the documentary in 1921. The film tells the story of Nanook and his family, who were Inuit Indians living in extremely harsh conditions in northern Canada. Flaherty shot the film himself and often risked his own life to capture his footage. Flaherty was concerned with preserving the way of life of a vanishing group of people. He often told Nanook what to do, and would ask him to repeat an action so Flaherty could film it better. Nanook's own family wasn't interested in the film, so Flaherty rounded up a "wife" and "children" to be presented as Nanook's. When Nanook was building an igloo, Flaherty recorded all of the action, but when he

---

*The *Spellbound* debate over shooting out of event order spurred a lot of discussion. I belong to a Documentary Working Group in the University Film and Video Association and we had an e-discussion about the issue. The majority of participants backed the makers.

took the camera inside the igloo, it was too dark to record on film. So Flaherty asked Nanook to build another igloo that was missing most of the roof and some of the outer wall. Now there was plenty of light to shoot the family in the igloo, and Flaherty presented the footage as if the camera was inside the first, complete igloo. Flaherty also had Nanook hunting with a spear, although the Inuits had converted to guns years before. Still, Flaherty was a good friend of Nanook's and the Inuits. Sometimes Nanook was doing activities that were common for modern Inuits, and other times he was reenacting what once was.

Nanook of the North was very successful in the theaters of the day and Flaherty is considered the father of the documentary form. Because he directed many of the scenes himself, critics and film historians have argued down through the decades about the ethics of Flaherty presenting Nanook and the Inuits the way he did. When you watch *Nanook of the North*, you see that Flaherty was trying not only to capture a disappearing way of life, but to showcase a charismatic Inuit who represented all that is good and noble in this vanishing population. It also hits you that Flaherty shot alone in subzero conditions. Often he had to build a fire under the camera to warm it up enough so the mechanical parts would work. Flaherty was out there on the ice floes with Nanook, living in igloos himself. His only assistants were Inuit friends he taught how to do basic production jobs. Ironically, Nanook died in a seal-hunting accident before the documentary was completed.

On the Criterion Collection DVD of *Nanook of the North*, there are special features that address Flaherty's documenting of Nanook and the Inuits. His sister gives an eloquent defense of Flaherty's production methods and sincerity. The remastered film looks terrific. The documentary has a story arc and is filled with interesting sequences in which we see life in this harsh environment through the eyes of Nanook, his "family," and friends. At this point in film production history, no one had ever attempted to tell a long-form story in documentary form. Flaherty was the first. Flaherty called himself a social anthropologist who documented obscure people in their battles with nature and encroaching civilization. After *Nanook of the North* played in theaters in 1922, a Scot named John Grierson coined the term "documentary," and nonfiction films that tell stories have been called documentaries ever since.*

Nanook of the North is considered the first full-length documentary with a story arc and compelling characters. After Nanook's real family showed no interest in the film, Director Robert Flaherty decided he needed a family and created one for him. A reality dilemma *(1998 The Criterion Collection)*.

How far can a director go before reality ceases to exist or his/her

*There are many books and articles that study Robert Flaherty's life and impact on the documentary form. A great place to start is this thoughtful, scholarly web site: Senses of Cinema. http://archive.sensesofcinema.com/contents/directors/02/flaherty.html.

footage becomes a reenactment? This question is more philosophical than technical, and you will need to decide how will you handle capturing the reality you are presenting.

B-roll

In making the character study documentary *Crumb* (1994), which is primarily a vérité-style documentary, director Terry Zwigoff felt there was footage he needed that his subject, the artist Robert Crumb, didn't provide during certain vérité segments of the filming. Since the director was a friend of his subject, he felt comfortable asking Crumb to shoot a sequence in the Zwigoffs' home, which would be presented as Crumb's home. To create this illusion, the director used a lamp from Crumb's house that had been seen earlier in action in Crumb's studio.*

There will always be times when you might have to shoot a pick-up cutaway shot, or record a subject statement after you have wrapped shooting. My approach is that the story is the determining factor. If your subjects have been honest and willingly presented themselves to the camera, they won't mind if you ask them to reshoot some B-roll or reanswer a question. Where the line can be crossed is if they are unwilling to do what you would like them to do, or say what they aren't comfortable saying. Don't force them to do anything they don't want to. Similarly, you can't use other story elements to make it appear that your subjects support an idea or conclusion that they don't.

In the documentary *Crumb* director Terry Zwigoff replaced the music Robert Crumb was actually playing on the piano with other music he felt better represented the mood of the scene. Another reality dilemma *(1995 Crumb Partners)*.

Sound Track

In another scene in *Crumb*, Robert Crumb is seen playing the piano. On the sound track we hear piano music and assume Crumb is playing the tune. But in reality, Zwigoff used previously recorded piano music by another piano player. His reason for doing this was because the mood of the piece Crumb was playing didn't fit the mood the director was trying to create in the scene in the edited version. The director describes this "faked" sequence and the B-roll sequence at this home and the reasons why he created them during the director's comments extra feature on the DVD.

The reason why the directors of these award-winning documentaries don't have any problem with these out-of-sequence insertions is because what is important is the story. Since the subjects are willingly recreating action, it is OK to move some shots, sound, or action.

---

*On the *Crumb* DVD there is a director's commentary special feature where Terry Zwigoff reveals that he intentionally staged this scene so the audience would think it was Crumb's house because the crew didn't have time to revisit Crumb in his own house. Since Crumb is in the footage Zwigoff felt the action was real. Most documentarians and viewers would agree; how do you feel about it?

Many times B-roll and recreation sequences can be enhanced with additional sound. Sweetening the sound track with sounds that match action is part of the artistic enhancement of your storytelling. Where the line is in postproduction sound track enhancement isn't always clear, so give all sound enhancement lots of thought.

Stylized sound can be a powerful addition, as Errol Morris has demonstrated for over 20 years in his recreations and B-roll sequences. Some critics think he goes too far, while others enjoy his filmatic approach to enhancing his sound tracks. Once again, you must decide where your limits are.

Paying Subjects to Be in the Documentary

Another area of ethical concern is whether it is OK to pay your on-screen subjects for their time and effort. This is a delicate question and here are some ways that documentarians have grappled with this problem.

In historical documentaries that are fully directed and dependent on interviews with authors, historians, experts, and survivors, it is common to pay these subjects for their travel, lodgings, and food. Sometimes a stipend for their effort is included. An ethical decision can arise if you have a strong point of view about your subject matter and the payment of money might cloud the objectivity of your storyteller. When money enters the relationship of maker and storyteller, it is vital that you remain neutral, and help facilitate an honest interview.

Your point of view will emerge from your completed work, but each of your subjects must be allowed to present his/her point of view freely.

Iconic documentarian Errol Morris has faced this situation many times. In his latest documentary *Standard Operating Procedure* (2008), which is about Abu Ghraib, the Iraqi prison, and the atrocities that occurred there, *Standard Operating Procedure* explores the breakdown of the U.S. military's command of the prison and the story behind the infamous photos of the prisoner abuse. Morris chose to pay American servicemen and women to tell their stories about the incidents. As Morris explained at the Tribeca Film Festival in 2008, he wanted to investigate the use and impact of photography on the perceptions of the world, and paying the military storytellers and photo takers was the only way he could do it.*

Historical documentaries that are made by PBS, HBO, Discovery Channel and other television companies often allow the makers to use part of their budg-

In his documentary *Standard Operating Procedure*, which is a study of the atrocities inside Abu Ghraib prison in Iraq, director Errol Morris's payments to his military storytellers caused a controversy *(2008 Sony Pictures Classics and Participant Productions).*

*On the Tribeca Film Festival web site there is a video of Errol Morris discussing his decision to pay the military storytellers in *SOP*. http://www.tribecafilm.com/festival/.

ets to pay for interview-related expenses. However, only a stipend will ever be paid to subjects directly.

Again, Your Personal Point of View

Documentaries are personal stories of the human condition. Sometimes documentary makers try to maintain a neutral position if their subject matter is controversial. Other times the documentarian makes a conscious effort to persuade the viewer. A passionate belief in your story is what got you into the documentary journey in the first place, so how far you promote your point of view needs to given a lot of thought. If your point of view intrudes too much, you are in the world of propaganda, and this world does not enlighten the audience on the human condition. It forces a viewpoint on the viewer and often distorts truth/reality.

The purpose and effect of two classic documentaries made in the 1930s by the creative German documentary maker Leni Riefenstahl have been debated for 70 years. She specialized in capturing important events during the rise of the Third Reich. Her innovative filmmaking techniques helped capture massive German nationalistic rallies (*Will to Power*, 1934) and the 1936 Olympic Games in Berlin (*Olympia*, 1937). Riefenstahl always claimed she was making art not propaganda for the Third Reich. Many historians and humanitarians disagree. I would recommend that every documentarian watch one or both of these documentaries and try to answer the ques-

tions for him or herself. The documentary *The Wonderful, Horrible Life of Leni Riefenstahl* (1993) is a character study of Riefenstahl and tries to get her to address this contradiction in her life and work.

In the cultural documentary *Lake of Fire*, director Tony Kaye examines the emotional subject of abortion. The documentary was eight years in the making and is obviously a labor of love. There are many spokespeople for both sides of the issue, but it becomes obvious that the filmmaker's heart lies with the pro-life argument. The documentary is beautifully shot and edited, and the spokespeople are eloquent and passionate. But the message seems to be pro-life, not pro-choice.*

Ken Burns, who is one of the great documentarians in our national history, admits he has an agenda that he brings to many of his documentaries. He abhors racism in all of its forms. When he made his epic series *The Civil War*, he tried to show how lethal racism can be. In his series *Baseball*, he highlighted in detail the story of the Negro Leagues and their suc-

Was iconic documentary maker Leni Riefenstahl making art or propaganda? That is the issue in the documentary *The Wonderful, Horrible Life of Leni Riefenstahl (Omega Film, 1993).*

*An excellent, long interview with director Tony Kaye can be found at this web address http://www.cinemawith outborders.com/news/139/ARTICLE/1637/2009–02–22.html.

cess despite the racism of Major League Baseball. In his exploration of the origins and evolution of jazz in his documentary *Jazz*, he gives a lot of time to the story of Louis Armstrong and other black jazz pioneers. Wynton Marsalis, who is black, emerges as the primary expert. Burn's documentary *Unforgivable Blackness* is the story of heavyweight boxer Jack Johnson, and makes a point of presenting all of the racist attitudes and negative consequences this strong, black athlete had to endure.*

When Spike Lee decided to tell the story of the Katrina tragedy, he made the heartwrenching documentary *When the Levees Broke* (2006). Lee was angry about the mismanagement of the disaster and the personal tragedies that resulted. He felt the people who suffered and lost the most needed a voice and he provided it. Using archival news footage and survivors' testi-monies, he crafted a story that reflected not only his point of view, but that of many Americans. Did he go too far in pointing his finger of blame? That is a decision every viewer must make.

Michael Moore always brings his populist, liberal point of view to his documentaries. He is interested in stirring the pot and getting people worked up about some of the United States' biggest problems: corporate flight, gun control, terrorism, healthcare, and rampant capitalism. He uses the documentary form as a hammer to strike against these societal "evils." He is a voice for the little person, even if a lot of the little people don't buy into his agenda.

You will need to articulate to yourself and others your point of view on your documentary subject. The documentary production process often is an enlightening

In the documentary *Sicko,* Michael Moore takes on U.S. healthcare by finding the seemingly endless loopholes in the present system and using real people to make his points *(Dog Eat Dog Films, Inc., 2007).*

*When Ken Burns visited Rowan University for a presentation of his documentary work he discussed his lifelong attempt to address the societal problem of racism in America. During that visit he screened clips from *Unforgivable Blackness*.

one, and you may find that your point of view shifts and reforms. This is a good thing. Self-awareness is one of the keys to developing consistency and confidence.

FAIR USE

"Fair use" is the term given to the free use of audio or video/film that someone else has originally created and copyrighted/ trademarked/registered. This includes music, film clips, archival footage, and company logos, among many other forms of work. The question always is how much can you use and not endanger yourself and your project. Documentarians are often caught up in the rush of telling their stories and overlook material they may have captured that is not theirs to use.

If your objective is to tell your story for a small audience and not make money from the sale of it, then you can probably use copyrighted, trademarked or registered material. But if you are planning to enter your documentary in larger film festivals and/or seek out distribution, then fair use will come into play.

The best resource for understanding fair use and how far you can go before you must gain official permission to use certain material is the Web site at American University's Center for Social Media in Washington, DC. Posted on the Web site is the most up-to-date information on the status of fair use and how documentarians can use their first amendment rights to use footage shot by others.

The Center for Social Media has been an outspoken advocate for documentarians exercising their fair use rights for over 20 years. Patricia Aufderheide, the director of the Center, has been leading a collection of documentarians, lawyers, entertainment industry professionals, students, and teachers in researching and supporting the fair use of sound and visual elements that might otherwise be perceived as unavailable for documentary production. The Web site is a comprehensive and accessible treasure trove of fair use and social media information (http://www.centerfor-socialmedia.org/).

Movie Clips and Music

Movie clips and registered music are the two largest categories for which issues concerning fair use arise. It is often a long, tedious, expensive journey to gain the rights to use these resources, and unless you have a budget line for royalties and rights fees, it would be a good plan to use public-domain archival footage and music by someone you know who will assign you the rights. The department in film and television companies that deals with copyrights and permissions is called "rights and clearances." The people who work in this department are responsible for getting permission from the people, organizations, estates, and companies that own the rights to footage, music, and trademarked visuals.

As filmmakers and artists continue to fight for their rights to use previously recorded music and pictures, the term "repurposed" has emerged as a key concept. If you are using a visual or sound clip in a different way than the originator of the footage used it, then you have a case for fair use. For instance, if you want to use a clip from a Hollywood movie trailer to show how your storyteller loved to watch films as a child, you are repurposing the footage and would have a strong case. Or if you are using a public-domain clip that has a registered song playing on the radio in the shot, and you are using the clip to show how the song influenced the development of your subject's music sensibility, you would have a case.

If you are making a documentary under contract, on a fixed budget for a public TV station or a cable network like Discovery, HBO, or A&E, then you need to understand that these outlets are very gun-shy about lawsuits involving third-party ownership of clips and music. There will be a budget for rights and clearances, and you will have to bring in your documentary for whatever funds you were allotted for music and film clips. If there is any doubt about whether you have cleared permission to use the clip or music, the network will make you replace the image or visuals. TV and cable networks also have departments called rights and clearances, and their whole job is to make sure everything that appears on their air, Web sites, or DVDs has been properly released to the networks for use. Similarly, if distribution companies like Sony, Magnolia, or ThinkFilm want to pay you for distribution rights, they will want to be sure there are no copyright, trademark, or music rights issues in your documentary.

During the late 1990s and early 2000s, the most popular show on VH1 was a documentary series called *Behind the Music* (*BTM*). *BTM* made documentaries about bands that were popular in the 1980s and '90s. The operating budget for each 44-minute episode was approximately $220,000. Within this budget was a specific category for the rights and clearances to use licensed music and video clips. Depending on the band, this line item could expand or contract. Just because *BTM* was making a documentary about a band did not guarantee that it could use the band's music without paying for it.

Paperwork

In order to make sure you have the rights to tell your story, there are some forms you will need to have signed as you progress through your production.

Standard Talent Release

If you are working under contract to a network, TV station, or production company, it will have its own release form it wants you to use. If you are working on speculation, as a student, or for a small company, then you will need a standard talent release for your subjects to sign. This is a one-page form that states the person is releasing his/her rights to any form of ownership of your documentary to you. Since you have won the person's support and trust, and because you are taking all of the financial risk, s/he is usually willing to sign the release. When s/he signs, s/he is giving you, or the company you are working for, the right to use the footage you have of him/her in any way you want. This is a leap of trust for the signee, and a large responsibility for you. You want to protect these subjects who have trusted you to tell their story.

Below is a standard talent release. This form can also be used for the people who have created original music for your documentary. You want to get a signed release form from the person or people who wrote the music and lyrics and performed the music on the CD. Often your musicians have registered their music with ASCAP, BMI, or SESAC. If this is so, then you must contact these organizations and pay a royalty to use the music. The best music is original music that hasn't been registered with these large, international organizations.

It's important to have the signees include their addresses, phone numbers, and e-mail addresses. You never know when you might need to contact them after the documentary is made. You should refer to your documentary by its title, if you are sure of the title. If you're not sure of the title, then call it "Documentary Project."

Standard Talent Release Form

I hereby give my permission to _____ [the production company and/or owner], its agents, successors, assigns, clients, and purchasers of its services and/or products to use my photograph (whether still, audio, film, or video), music, artwork, electronic effects, and recordings of my voice and my name in any legal manner whatsoever.

The Project_____

The Producers/Owners_____

In the case of an interview.

I have agreed (a) to be interviewed, (b) to the recording of this interview in any form and in any media, and (c) to provide information and other materials to be used in connection with the project, including my personal experiences, remarks, incidents, dialogues, actions, and recollections, as well as any photographs and documents that I may give to the producers (collectively, the interview materials).

I hereby grant to the producers, and to the licensees, successors, and assigns of each:

1. The right to quote, paraphrase, reproduce, publish, distribute, or otherwise use all or any portion of the interview materials in the work, and in advertising and related promotion of the work, in all forms and in all media throughout the world and in perpetuity.

2. The right to use my name, image, and biographical data in connection with any use of the interview materials, including as described above.

I hereby acknowledge that I have no copyright or other rights in the project.

I hereby release and discharge the producers, and the licensees, successors, and assigns of each, from any and all claims, demands, or causes of action that I may have against them regarding any use of the interview materials or regarding anything contained in the project or in related advertising or promotional materials, including (but not limited to) any claims based on the right to privacy, the right to publicity, copyright, libel, defamation, or any other right.

Agreed and confirmed:

Signature:_____   Date: _____

Name (print):_____

Address: _____

_____

Phone Number_____

E-Mail Address_____

Because every documentary has its own group of creators and storytellers, it is always good to have a lawyer read and approve your release form. Sometimes the release forms can be customized to your specific project. The above release form is only one example. If you have musicians involved in the project, you should check the Web and with legal experts for a release geared more for music rights.

Sometimes an independently made documentary will find a wider-than-planned audience. If a local TV station is airing it, the station will ask you as the maker to sign a release that says you have handled all of the releases and accept full responsibility if there is a problem. When the station airs the documentary, it is covered if there is a problem. Local TV stations usually pay $100/minute for programming. Many TV stations, for example, have local versions of the PBS documentary series *POV*. If you have someone create special effects and/or graphics you should have them sign releases also.

As you shoot your B-roll, you need to observe closely who might be a recurring figure in the documentary. In *Hoop Dreams* (1994), many family members and friends reappear, and they all signed releases. General rules of thumb are if someone talks during a B-roll sequence or reappears more than once or is on-screen longer than five seconds, it would be a good idea to have him/her sign a release. Bring along lots of releases as you shoot. You need to exercise discretion as you ask for releases to be signed. Waiting until all of the shooting is over is taking a chance. If you don't get the releases as you shoot, it is often hard to find people again to have them sign one.

In the documentary *Ecstasy & Electronica* (2002), which is an underground look at ecstasy use and raves, director Kathleen Berger rented a nightclub for four hours and invited young people to attend a mini-rave. As the people entered the club, the producer explained they would be shooting dance footage and interviewing some of the ravers, and everyone had to sign a release to get in. There was no admission fee. Almost all of the people signed the release and the crew shot B-roll and interviews for four hours.

In the documentary *Rink of Fire* (2005), which profiled a team of female Roller Derby skaters, all ten members of the team signed a release, even though only five of them were interviewed. But the other five members were in most of the B-roll shots, so the producer wisely decided to be safe.

LEGAL CHALLENGES: SHOOTING PERMITS AND OFFICIAL PASSES

Often when you are shooting outdoors in cities and/or near national monuments, security people will approach you and ask if you have official permission to shoot footage there. What they are referring to is whether you have secured an official shooting permit from the city or other entity. Cities will grant official permits for you to shoot footage, but they are very specific about where you shoot and what you plan to do. You must fill out a lot of forms, pay a fee, prove you have insurance, schedule in advance, and jump through a lot of other bureaucratic hoops. If you have a big budget and a lot of time, then it is worthwhile to do this. Most larger cities and states have film offices that can help you through this shooting phase.

The documentary *Man on Wire* (2008) tells the story behind Philippe Petit's dar-

ing walk across a wire suspended between the two World Trade Center towers in 1974. There are many recreations of how Petit's team managed to plan and execute the act. One of the recreations shows a truck pulling up to the "World Trade Center" and the crewmembers unloading the gear and taking it into the building. The block they used was in another part of the city, and it's not clear whether they got permits to shoot where they shot. But if they had gotten official permission from the NYC's Office of Film, which works with the city to issue shooting permits, they could have taken their time and reshot many of the sequences.

Because in many people's minds documentaries are considered a hybrid form of journalism, and TV stations shoot freely throughout the cities and towns they cover, law enforcement understands the need for producers to shoot relevant footage for their stories.

Most documentary makers don't feel comfortable taking this official permit route. Michael Moore never gets permits when he shoots. If he gets rousted or challenged, it becomes part of his vérité story. In many ways, taking your chances in the filming is part of the documentary process. This is another reason to keep your crew small and your subject(s) natural. If a police officer asks you what you are doing, you can give a quick explanation and say you will be not be long, and almost always the officer will walk away for a few minutes and let you finish. People shooting footage with cameras is a common sight today, but if you look like you might be doing some-

thing different than a typical tourist, then you might get approached. The key is to keep your cool and explain who you are and what you are doing quickly and respectfully.

If your story takes you into performance and entertainment venues, even though you may be following a band or other performers, you and your crew will need to have official passes to get in and have all access. The same is true for political and sporting events. Most of the time your subjects will be able to get these passes to you or lead you to the people who can get you the passes. But these are important details. If you don't have the official passes, it is very hard to talk your way in.

FINAL THOUGHTS

Sometimes it's hard to place yourself in the position of having responsibilities for so many details of production. But depending on how far-ranging your documentary is, you might have to accommodate the laws, ethics, and procedures of a world that likes everything to be documented and legal. On the other hand, you

have rights as a documentarian and a journalist. There is a growing body of law that states documentarians are covered by the same shield laws as reporters are. So you can be aggressive in your research and investigations. Similarly, fair use enables you to repurpose clips and music so you can better substantiate and tell your story.

DOCUMENTARY REFERENCES

Each of these documentary references was chosen because it has a creative element or technique that stands out. Some of the most creative filmmaking has occurred while a documentarian is telling his or her story. It is hoped that the curious reader will be motivated to watch many of these documentaries not only for enjoyment, but also for inspiration.

The Civil War: TV Series. 1990. Ken Burns. PBS. In this ten-hour, nine-episode series created for PBS Burns often creates tableaus that combine with music and/or narration to establish the mood he is after. For instance, after describing a bloody battle he will place an authentic civil war era canon on a hill at sunset. The camera composes a beautiful shot while sad, mournful music plays under-

neath and a narrator completes the scene. In another example he will use a dramatically lit table top filled with a map, ink well, oil lamp, a pair of glasses, and some handwritten letters to show how the politicians and generals were limited in their first hand knowledge of the war and rarely up-to-date with critical information. This series is still the most watched series in the history of PBS.

Every aspiring documentarian should watch this film because many of the techniques now considered part of the grammar of documentary storytelling were pioneered in this amazing series.

Crumb. 1994. Terry Zwigoff. Crumb Partners. This Sundance winner was shot in 16mm color film and has a vibrant, dark aesthetic, not unlike the subject, Robert Crumb. Its vérité style captures the strange, intense life of an iconic artist. The director's comments are interesting as Zwigoff explains how odd it is to make a documentary about a friend and iconic cultural figure.

Ecstasy and Electronica. 2002. Kathleen Berger and Erin Plyler. Rowan University. This Cine Golden Eagle winner is an underground look at ecstasy use and raves. Director Kathleen Berger rented a nightclub for four hours and invited young people to attend a mini-rave. As the people entered the club the producer explained they would be shooting dance footage and interviewing some of the ravers, and they had to sign a release to get in. There was no admission fee. Almost all of the people signed the release and the crew shot B-roll and interviews for four hours.

Hoop Dreams. 1994. Steve James. New Line Home Entertainment, Inc. This three-hour, vérité-style documentary took five years to make (1989–1994) and generated 250 hours of raw footage. It was shot on video using a Betacam video camera. This documentary remains a classic example of dedicated vérité filmmaking. It captures the lives of its two subjects as well as the inner city life of Chicago.

Lake of Fire. 2006. Tony Kaye. Above the Sea. This beautifully shot black and white documentary deals with the controversial issue of abortion. Both sides are strongly presented and the filmmaker leaves it up to the audience to decide for themselves. It was a labor of love and took sixteen years to make.

Nanook of the North. 1913, 1921 (DVD 1998, The Criterion Collection). Robert Flaherty. Robert Flaherty is generally agreed to be the first person to make a feature length documentary. It was originally shot in 1913. But the film was destroyed in a fire and Robert Flaherty reshot the documentary in 1921. The film tells the story of Nanook and his family, who are Inuit Indians living in extremely harsh conditions in northern Canada. Flaherty shot the film himself and often risked his own life to capture his footage. Flaherty was concerned with preserving the way of life of a vanishing group of people. He often

told Nanook what to do, and would ask him to repeat an action so Flaherty could film it better. Nanook's own family wasn't interested in the film so Flaherty rounded up a "wife" and "children" to be presented as Nanook's. Flaherty also had Nanook hunting with a spear, although the Inuits had converted to guns years before. Still, Flaherty was a good friend of Nanook's and the Inuits. Sometimes Nanook was doing activities that were common for modern Inuits, and other times he was reenacting what once was. This is a must see, because this is where the documentary form began.

Rink of Fire. 2006. Paul Foster (producer) and David Diperstein (director). Rowan University. This award-winning, intimate exploration of a team of female roller derby skaters features B-roll from a tournament that was shot with six cameras. The wild action footage is nicely mixed with calm interview settings where the women tell who they are and why they do it.

Spellbound. 2002. Jeff Blitz. Blitz/Welch. This first-time documentary was conceived while Jeff Blitz was a student. Almost all of the footage was shot with a low-end digital camera and a crew of two. It is a prime example of how a good story can be told with a minimum of cost and technology.

Standard Operating Procedure (S.O.P). 2008. Errol Morris. Sony Pictures Classics and Participant Productions. This film is a study of the atrocities inside Abu Ghraib prison in Iraq and explores the breakdown of the U.S. military's command of the prison. It is also the story behind the infamous photos of the prisoner abuse. Director Morris chose to pay American service men and women to tell their stories about the incidents. These payments to his military storytellers caused a controversy.

Unforgivable Blackness. 2004. Ken Burns. Florentine Productions and WETA-TV. This is a character study of the turn-of-the-century black heavyweight fighter, Jack Johnson, and the racism he encountered during his life. Director Ken Burns uses period music under most of the interviews and B-roll sequences. His archival stills and moving pictures are sweetened with natural sound that he has created. At one point he recreates with actors' voices some dialogue from a court trial, and matches the dialogue with appropriate pictures. This documentary is a fine study in the mixing of sound elements for story enhancement and emotion.

When the Levees Broke. 2006. Spike Lee. 40

Acres & a Mule Filmworks and HBO. Director Lee was angry about the mismanagement of the Hurricane Katrina disaster and the personal tragedies that resulted. He felt the people who suffered and lost the most needed a voice and he provided it. Using archival news footage and survivors' testimonies he crafted a story that reflected not only Spike Lee's point of view, but that of many Americans. Did he go too far in pointing his finger of blame? That is a decision every viewer must make.

The Wonderful, Horrible Life of Leni Riefenstahl. 1993. Ray Müller. Arte and Channel Four Films. Was she making art or propaganda or both? This is the question that drives director Ray Müller to interview Leni Riefenstahl about her life and career. They play cat and mouse with each other until Müller finally loses it off camera. A fascinating study with pristine archival footage of Riefenstahl's classic documentaries: *Triumph of the Will* and *Olympia.*

10. Funding Your Documentary and Connecting to Your Community

Documentaries usually fall into one of two groups when it comes to funding: funded and on speculation. If you were fortunate enough to have your documentary funded, your funder has certain rights to the project unless these rights were signed away in the contract. Hopefully, you have read the contract and are aware of who owns the rights for television, theatrical presentation, and Web and DVD sales, both national and international. Similarly, there are syndication companies that will place your documentary on television for a fee. This world of distribution, marketing, merchandising, and syndicating is often a cloudy one of deals, grosses, nets, percentages, and negotiated rights. If your contract looks complicated, spend the money on a contract or entertainment lawyer. Here is a quick rundown of how documentaries can be financed.

FUNDED DOCUMENTARIES

These documentaries have been done for companies and networks that have an interest in the content of the documentary and want to control screenings and distribution. Sometimes the makers give up some or all of the rights of ownership. The money is given out in steps as the documentary progresses from the research phase to completion. The documentary makers are under contract and must adhere to the production schedule, budget, and content demands set out in the contract. After completion of the documentary, the entity that has funded the production is guaranteed at least a certain number of airings and a percentage of the DVD sales and income from other distribution avenues. The funding company provides marketing and promotion. When producer and director Arnold Shapiro completed his classic documentary *Scared Straight!* (1978) for KTLA-TV, the PBS station in Los Angeles, he was sure he had a worthy documentary, but he wasn't sure how the public would react to the content. It was filled with profanities and verbal abuse because the story concerned a group of lifers in Rahway State Prison trying to scare at-risk teens straight. Here is Shapiro's brief rundown of the process that took *Scared Straight!* from a small-budget, local program to international success. It's a fascinating study of how socially redeeming content can overcome language/obscenity restrictions.

KTLA decided to show the film to FCC Commissioners before it went on TV. We wanted to let the FCC know we were doing this for the greater good. So that was its first official showing.

Scared Straight! had two disclaimers on it: graphic language and parental discretion advised. It went on the air on November 2, 1978, on KTLA in Los Angeles and caused an uproar unprecedented to this day. KTLA's phones were ringing nonstop for three days. People wanted to know where they could get their child into the program. How they could get a copy of the film. Virtually no complaints about the language.

People saw what the purpose of the documentary was. The inmates were trying to turn the kids around and if they had to speak those words in that harsh tone, then that's what they had to do.

Even before *Scared Straight!* aired locally, we had syndicators interested in distribution. When it aired on Thursday night from ten to 11, it beat all of the LA network stations, which had never happened before or since. Within a week after it aired locally, we had a deal with a syndication company for national distribution. And we made a deal with CBS network to make a TV movie, a dramatized fictional movie inspired by the documentary that I would produce.

In March 1979 *Scared Straight!* aired nationally. Once again, it was number one in every market it aired in. It got even a higher rating in LA the second time. Once again, it caused quite an uproar. The TV movie was made in 1980 and aired in early 1981. It was called *Scared Straight! Another Story*. It was about a group of kids who go through the program and turn their lives around.*

Arnold Shapiro had convinced his executive producer at KTLA to let him make the documentary. Shapiro was a salaried employee. The station owned the rights to the program. KTLA made the money as the documentary was aired in other TV markets. Shapiro didn't make a lot of money from the documentary, but the fame and prestige it received enabled him to strike out on his own, form his own production company, and make hundreds of hours of socially redeeming programs for theatrical and television release.

Speculation Documentaries

These documentaries are funded by the documentary makers, their friends and families, small grants, and fundraisers. All of the financial risks are absorbed by the producer(s)/filmmaker(s). These documentaries rely on the drive and passion of the documentarians. When the documentary is completed, the makers enter it in film festivals and might pitch it to the TV/cable networks. The goal is to land either a distribution deal with a large distributor like Miramax or Magnolia, or sell all or part of it to public TV or a cable network like HBO, A&E, and Discovery Communications. In a speculative documentary the money comes after the production. The vast majority of documentary makers make documentaries on speculation and for the love of the experience. After your documentary is completed, you need to set a plan for giving it a life after production. Here are some ways to get it out there and hopefully make some money.

Have a Premiere

This is important. If you have made the documentary as a labor of love, everyone connected to it, producers, crew, and storytellers, deserves to see the completed documentary on a big screen, surrounded by family and friends.

You can rent a local theater for a night. Local colleges and high schools

*These words were transcribed from an interview I had with Arnold Shapiro on March 26, 2001.

with large auditoriums and big screens will often allow outside projects to screen films in their facilities. Film communities in larger cities have venues for premieres. You can cater food for before or afterwards. Contact media outlets with your story in advance. There will be a buzz and that is always a good thing. You can sell DVDs of your documentary at the premiere. If you don't have enough copies yet, take orders. Try to get people from distribution companies to attend. By providing a classy and fun premiere, you are telling everyone how much you value their hard work and dedication. The storytellers have their moments in the sun, and the overall vibration is a wonderful, upbeat one. For everyone directly involved in the production, it is one of the high points of their lives. For the friends and families, there is a deep pride.

Create a Web Site

In this day and age a Web site dedicated to the documentary is necessary. How large or small is up to you. But there are elements involved in putting the site together. The following elements go from basic to full-blown marketing.

• **Home Page** • This page has all of the basic information about your documentary and maybe links to other pages you have created. The minimum would include: title, synopsis, awards, reviews, and some frame-grab stills or clips from the documentary, contact information and ordering instructions. If you Google "Documentary Home Pages," a wide variety of examples comes up.

• **Trailer** • This is a short, edited teaser that includes the essence of your idea, the main storytellers, exciting/dramatic footage, all in a one to two minute package. As you edit the documentary, you will see the moments, bites, and shots that stick out. Make a note of them and use them in the trailer. The trailer enables you to showcase your documentary in a brief period of time, and can be used beyond the Web site.

• **Online Media Kit** • This takes the Web site a step further. The media kit includes a fact sheet, production people bios, company background, FAQs, graphics and still photos that can be grabbed by the viewer. Clips and special features can be part of the kit.

A speculation documentary, *Invisible Children*, made in 2003 by a small group of just-graduated filmmakers, that documents the tragedy in Uganda of children being used as soldiers, has a comprehensive Web site that is a good model: http://www.invisiblechildren.com/.

Marketing Campaign

If your documentary becomes successful through festival awards, distribution assistance, and media screenings, your Web site can expand into a comprehensive marketing site where you manage DVD sales, book screenings and appearances, sell related items, set up blogs and links to a wide range of related sites. The funded documentary *The Devil Came on Horseback* was made in 2007 and tells the sad story of the orphaned children in war-torn Darfur. The Web site devoted to the documentary, which won many awards, is a full-blown marketing site with donations for a relief fund as part of the plan.

• **Social Networking** • One of the newest methods of promoting films and documentaries is to create a Facebook or MySpace page with information and media clips related to your documentary. Because the social networks expand so quickly, before you know it you will have distributed the news of your film to hundreds/thousands of people who have similar interests. Many new documentaries are presented and marketed through social networking, and DVD orders are part of the marketing.

• YouTube • It is so easy to upload video to YouTube that there is the temptation to upload your clips to a YouTube site. But YouTube is a low-resolution viewing site, and the comments are often made by uninformed people who don't really care about the content. It's a last-resort place where you might get lucky and strike a cyber nerve.

• The Educational Market •

COURSE INCLUSION: HIGH SCHOOLS

Many documentaries tell stories that fit into high-school curriculums. If your documentary is historical, social-studies oriented, or culturally relevant, then you might want to contact schools and pitch your documentary to the curriculum committees. High-school curriculums are carefully controlled by committees that are sensitive to controversial topics and language excesses. But if you feel your documentary belongs in a learning unit within a curricular area, then contact a school and schedule a meeting with the curriculum committee. Often there are state curriculum committees that set the curriculum for all of the high schools. You can contact them for a presentation.

Assembly Screening

Another avenue to take is to request a screening during an assembly. If there is time, you can frame the screening with a presentation and question/answer session. Social-problem documentaries work well in this format. Once again, you need to contact someone at the high school and make your pitch. Principals are usually the ones who make these decisions.

Study Guide

If you feel strongly about the educational value of your documentary, you can create a study guide that integrates the screening and subsequent discussions into an educational format. This would involve activities like essays, papers, media projects, team-led discussions, field trips, and visits from experts. Study guides should be reviewed by a teacher familiar with the structure and content of a study guide.

A historical documentary called *Prisoners Among Us* was made by director and producer Michael DiLauro in 2004. It is a study of Italian-American history in the United States, centered around the discrimination Italians suffered in the U.S. during World War II. It is a thoroughly researched and impeccably presented documentary that reveals how a group has experienced discrimination. The documentary won many film-festival awards, and now provides a valuable resource for history and social studies teachers. On the

This historical documentary, made by director Michael DiLauro, has an educational guide for teachers that goes with the DVD. The web site promotes the many ways to enjoy and learn from the story *(Michaelangelo Productions, 2003).*

Web site for the documentary is a teacher's study guide for using the film in class. The study guide is comprehensive and relevant. There are many other informative links on the film's home page. It is a well constructed and visually attractive Web page that serves as a template for creating an educational audience for your documentary. The web address is http://prisonersamongus.com/.

Another historical documentary that has a study guide for its content is the Holocaust story *Into the Arms of Strangers*. This ultimately upbeat and life-affirming documentary tells the story of the thousands of German-Jewish children who were voluntarily placed with English families during the rise of Nazism in the late 1930s. It is a story of the triumph of the human spirit over horrific tragedy. It won the Academy Award for Best Documentary in 2000. The mother of the producer of the documentary, Deborah Oppenheimer, was one of these Kindertransport children. The Web site for this documentary is rich in historical and teacher/student resources. It is a treasure for a teacher who wants to teach a unit on the Holocaust and use a fascinating story as the jumping-off place. The Web site is http://www2.warnerbros.com/intothearmsofstranger.

Supporting Web Site

If having a study guide and an educational market works for your documentary, then all of the educational and teaching resources need to be integrated into your Web site. This creates a bigger challenge, but also gives credibility to your documentary. If you study the two Web sites mentioned above, you will see the potential of a well-thought-out and well-constructed Web site that functions as both a promotional and educational tool. Securing endorsement quotes from academics who have used the documentary or screened it can also further your educational marketing.

COURSE INCLUSION: COLLEGE

College teachers usually have greater freedom to pick media resources than high-school teachers do. By visiting college Web sites, you can get the contact information of any teacher in the college. If you feel a screening and discussion afterwards would help educate college students in a particular class, contact the appropriate teacher and pitch your documentary. Often college professors like new, exciting media to present to their students. Your Web site can add support to your pitch.

College radio stations often have talk shows that showcase artists and professionals. Maybe you fit into one of those formats. It is worth looking for and contacting the station.

• **Nonprofits** • Another large group of dedicated individuals is the people who work for various nonprofit organizations. These groups almost always need media that address their area of expertise. Social-issue documentaries almost always share issues with nonprofit groups that are dealing with the same problem. If you contact the appropriate nonprofit organization and request a screening, maybe your documentary can become part of its media resources. Often these organizations receive grants and donations, and they can pay you for your involvement or advocate for the sale of your DVDs.

An example of a national nonprofit organization that uses documentaries as a tool for raising awareness is Security on Campus, Inc. This organization is an advocate for preventing crime on college campuses. It gathers crime data, lobbies for legislation, is present at conferences, maintains an information-rich Web site, and is dedicated to warning young people about the dangers that lurk on college campuses. It currently distributes five documentaries that address specific criminal problems at colleges, problems like binge drinking, sexual assault, drug abuse, stalking, and hazing. The organization's Web site is securityoncampus.org. It has distributed the documentaries to over 10,000 high schools, colleges, rehabilitation organizations, law enforcement training centers, and the U.S. military. Organizations like Security on Campus, Inc., often share grants with media makers, including documentary makers.* If your documentary addresses social problems that already have a national presence through a group like MADD or DARE, don't hesitate to contact the organizations and request a screening of your documentary.

• **Edited Versions** • Often you can edit shorter versions of your documentary to fill different needs. PBS stations need 28- and 55-minute versions to fill time slots. Other forms of programming demand shorter versions of your documentary.

• **Talk Shows** • TV and cable stations all have public-affairs talk shows that are always looking for stories and people to showcase. If you can package yourself and clips from your documentary into a 22-minute talk show, local TV stations would be very interested in listening to your pitch.

• **Free Public Screenings** • In many cities the city funds public screenings of locally produced films. For instance, in Philadelphia there is a weekly screening of films in the Headhouse Square section of the city. Libraries and specially focused societies also are looking for reasons to gather their communities together to view a locally made film.

Film Festivals

Film festivals are a logical next step for your showcasing of your documentary. Most film festivals have up to four categories: Narrative, Documentary, Experimental, and Animation. They often break the categories into Comedy, Drama, Shorts, and Feature Length. Some festivals are themed. If your documentary fits the theme, then you have a much better chance of acceptance. It is worthwhile to spend time Web surfing the thousands of film festivals. Every festival has a group of committed film lovers behind it, and they are always looking for new ideas and films.

• **Without a Box** • This is an online-entry application service that almost all film festivals prefer you to use. It is free. All you have to do is go to withoutabox.com, join, then fill out an information profile about your film. When you want to enter a film festival, just go to your Without a Box account and direct your film information to the festival. The festival will receive your application, contact you via e-mail, and explain how and where they would like you to send your DVD entry. Without a Box has simplified the entry process and offers many other benefits to members. One of its best services is to send you daily alerts for hundreds of film festivals. It includes all festivals, from the largest to the smallest. Definitely consider using Without a Box when you begin your festival strategy. Film festivals break into three loosely defined groups.

• **National and International Film Festivals** • These are the biggest and the most prestigious festivals. Often the winners are automatic qualifiers for Academy Award

---

*Security on Campus, Inc., is a non-profit organization committed to reducing crime on college campuses. They have the largest database in the world of college crimes. They use media to aid them in their cause. Their website is large and comprehensive. They use documentaries as one of their tools to educate and prevent crime. Security oncampus.org.

consideration. These festivals are star-studded and attended by thousands of people. The movie companies and distributors attend looking to cut deals and buy distribution rights. Sundance is the largest American film festival. It is also hard to get your film chosen as an official Sundance selection. Other world-class film festivals are Cannes, Toronto, Venice, Berlin, Tribeca, SXSW (South by Southwest), Silverdocs, and Slamdance. If you are a first-time filmmaker, the odds are long on getting accepted. But you never know. If you believe in your documentary, then don't be afraid to submit. Just don't get your hopes up. What you do have going for you is the fact that *all* film festivals are always looking for the new filmmakers who are about to burst onto the scene.

• **National and Regional** • These festivals have earned a reputation for quality and showcasing new filmmakers. There are buyers there from film companies and television looking for product and talent. The crowds aren't as big, but it is easier to get your film accepted into the festival. These festivals attract regional filmmakers who have connections to the regional film community. There are usually some stars there accepting awards or premiering a modest or indy film. They are great places to meet other filmmakers and network.

• **Local and Regional Film Festivals** • These festivals are run by interested local groups and are held in local theaters, auditoriums, and buildings like schools, churches, firehouses, cafes, pubs, and other funky-type venues. Entries from the region are given priority. These festivals usually screen their films over a weekend and don't draw large crowds. People connected to the films are the largest part of the audience. But these are the grassroots festivals and they serve to keep the love of films alive and healthy. The acceptance rate is geared to create an audience for the screenings. There might be a name film person connected to the festival. If your documentary is accepted for screening, that can become part of your marketing plan. No matter what the acceptance rate is, every film festival is competitive. If your film is accepted, then you have proven your film is worthy of being shown to an audience of strangers.

FINAL THOUGHTS

Making a documentary is a huge undertaking and it can leave you exhausted after it is complete. A mistake many beginning documentary makers make is to set the documentary aside after the premiere and first round of festival rejection. If you believe in your documentary and its story, then there are ways to get it out there to the right people. Whether it's through film festivals, television airings, private screenings, Web access, or DVD sales, you want to stay involved with your work after it is done. Sometimes reediting after a break will make it better. Maybe an aggressive marketing campaign can find the right circumstance in which your documentary can have a productive life after completion.

You are now part of that long and extraordinary tradition of people who are driven to explore their worlds and tell others about it. You have contributed to the sum total of human knowledge and the world will always be a better place for your effort.

DOCUMENTARY REFERENCES

Each of these documentary references was chosen because it has a creative element or technique that stands out. Some of the most creative filmmaking has occurred while a documentarian is telling his or her story. It is hoped that the curious reader will be motivated to watch many of these documentaries not only for enjoyment, but also for inspiration.

The Devil Came on Horseback. 2007. Anne Sundberg and Ricki Stern. Break Thru Films. A first-person account of the genocide going on in Darfur, Sudan, by a former Marine who has been engaged as a photographer to record the atrocities. We follow his awakening as he experiences the tragedy. He decides to return to the United States and become an activist to alert the world of the genocide and advocate for help. This personal journey builds to an emotional climax of realization and is very moving.

Into the Arms of Strangers: Tales of the Kindertransport. 2000. Deborah Oppenheimer and Mark Jonathan Harris. This is a moving, inspirational story of how 10,000 children, mostly Jewish, were sent by their families to England to avoid the Nazis in Germany. Spectacular, pristine archival footage is presented from a child's point of view. Judy Dench narrates this Academy Award winner. The web site includes a study guide for teachers. http://www2.warnerbros.com/intothearmsofstrangers/.

Invisible Children. 2003. Bob Bailey, Laren Poole, Jason Russell. Made in 2003 by a small group of newly graduated filmmakers, the film documents the tragedy in Uganda of children being used as soldiers. The documentary has evolved into a national campaign to save Ugandans from oppression. This massive movement shows the power one documentary can have. It has a comprehensive website that is a good model. http://www.invisiblechildren.com/.

Prisoners Among Us. 2004. Michael DiLauro. Michaelangelo Productions. This historical documentary is a study of Italian American history in the United States centered around the discrimination Italians suffered in the United States during World War II. It is a thoroughly researched and impeccably presented documentary that reveals how a group has experienced discrimination. The documentary won many film festival awards, and now provides a valuable resource for history and social studies teachers. On the web site for the documentary is a teacher's study guide for using the film in class. The study guide is comprehensive and relevant. There are many other informative links on the film's home page. It is a well constructed and visually attractive web page that serves as a template for creating an educational audience for your documentary. The web address is http://prisonersamongus.com/.

Scared Straight! 1978. Arnold Shapiro. Golden West Television. This classic vérité documentary has the lifers in a maximum security prison trying to scare a group of at-risk teenagers into walking the straight and narrow. The Oscar-winning film captures an event that is only going to happen once. Shapiro met with the prisoners ahead of time, demonstrated to them that he had researched their program, and won their trust. The raw language and intensity of the lifers creates an atmosphere that is electric. The observational camera captures it all. Beautifully edited.

11. Why We Do It

Hopefully, at this point you are ready to embark on a documentary journey that will result in a special story you have to tell. This book has been created to blend the two worlds of creative storytelling and technical production knowledge. Since it is almost impossible for one person to fulfill both of these roles, there is a need to find others who are committed to your documentary goal.

Documentaries are labors of love. Documentaries are portals into our collective unconscious. They reveal who we are and where we think we are going. The people who make documentaries are committed and driven, and the world always needs all the documentarians it can get. Here are some final thoughts from four world-class documentarians who understand why they go to such lengths to tell their stories.

When I was finishing my interview with documentarian Arnold Shapiro, he wanted me to be sure to include his final thoughts about the process and purpose of making a social-issue documentary. *Scared Straight!* (1978) is a classic vérité documentary that addresses the social issue of saving at-risk teens who have been raised in poor, dysfunctional homes. The lifers in Rahway State Prison ran a program for these teens, and the idea was to scare them so much about life in a maximum-security prison that they would be scared straight. *Scared Straight!* was shot in film and first aired on KTLA-TV, the PBS station in Los Angeles, in 1978. It's 56 minutes long. It launched Arnold Shapiro's national career, but while he was in the midst of making it, he was totally focused on capturing reality for the benefit of all of us.

The reason I made the documentary was to get other prisons to start similar programs. Other prisons did start programs but they weren't successful for a variety of reasons. It takes a unique set of conditions and people to make this work. Rahway had that. You have to be willing to give the prisoners a certain autonomy. You have to realize they will get publicity and attention. Kids are going to have to go inside the prison. There are wardens out there for whom these conditions are not acceptable. Most importantly, you need a group of inmates willing to do it. They get nothing out of it except a feeling of doing something right.

We needed each other. I needed the cooperation of the administration of the prison and the lifers and they needed me to get national exposure for their program. I knew I was safe with them. I knew they were going to cooperate with me.

I'm very proud to have done *Scared Straight!* I didn't go into it knowing it would become what it became. I've done other documentaries that I feel are just as important, especially two on child abuse. One was *Scared Silent*, hosted by Oprah Winfrey. That documentary was the most-watched documentary in the history of TV. It aired on ABC, CBS, NBC and DBS.

I believe in the collaborative approach. A good idea can come from anybody. Somebody has to have a vision, a core idea, but along the way, whether it's camera people, sound people, editors, writers, everybody brings something to the documentary. And the end result will be the better for it.

My advice to young documentary makers is obviously you have to have basic skills and learn how to tell a good story. In addition to that, if you're going to be successful you have to pick topics that are commercial. Meaning that someone is going to want to put your documentary on TV. You have to come up with topics that have broad or universal appeal and you have to know how to market.

I'd advise every person taking a documentary production class to also take a class in marketing so you can learn how to get your idea exposed in the broadest way possible.*

On another note, the VH1 series *Behind the Music,* which aired over 200 episodes between 1997 and 2006, was the first documentary series targeted at a young audience (22–40-year-olds). Perhaps more than any other show on television, *BTM* introduced the documentary form to young Americans. Although the show was tightly formatted, it told stories about the bands and performers that went beyond the musical style they were using. *BTM* was the most watched prime-time show on VH1 for six years. When MTV added two vérité documentary series, *True Life* (1998–2011) and *Made* (2003–2011), that were targeted toward teens and people in their early twenties, it became clear that the most-watched network for teens and young adults understood the power of the documentary form. It is now over fifteen years since this MTV/VH1 documentary explosion, and I can see in my documentary studies and production classes that the students have a foundation in storytelling in documentary form.

Paul Gallagher was the supervising producer for *BTM* during its first six years. He understood the power of telling a compelling story that includes conflict, tragedy, surprises, and redemption. Music was the vehicle that put so many young musicians into situations they couldn't deal with. Here are some closing thoughts Gallagher has about the documentary process and telling stories for a television series.

In the beginning we brainstormed 100 bands that would be *BTM* subjects. It wasn't that easy. We started production in May '97. Our first two shows were MC Hammer and Milli Vanilli. The next two were Boy George and Lynyrd Skynyrd. They were very successful. Viewers and the music world went wild. What we discovered was we had hit a rich vein of gold no one had mined before: journalism and real personal storytelling in the music world.

I was supervising producer from the beginning. These documentaries are different from other *Biography*-type series. What we learned from doing the original four shows was that the personal story works. When we put the story into documentary form, we had storytelling that is dramatic and compelling. People connect with a personal story. What other people had done previously was use a retrospective of the band's history. People who were fans of the artists/bands would tune in to see them. There was no larger/common connection. If you didn't like the music you were out of there.

So many people came to us and said, I hated the band/artist but I watched the show because I felt for the band/artist. They liked the human story. What we did is turn the *Biography* formula on its ear. We came at it: no matter if you liked the band/artist or not, you're going to identify with this person, and Joe and Jane Beercan at home will understand who this person is.

The best producers search down inside themselves to see if there is anything in their subject they identify with. And they put that personal feeling on the screen. It is an emotional medium. A viewer is being pulled in a million different directions with all the pressures in their life and all of the choices that they have. They are going to stop on your show because there is something about that show that has a tangible quality that resonates inside them. That's what makes a success-

---

*These words were transcribed from an interview I had with Arnold Shapiro on March 26, 2001.

ful TV show, or movie, or play. There is something that resonates, that is magical about it.

And the fact we've been able to produce so many episodes of *BTM* and find some way in every one of them to make that resonation, I'm really proud of that. It goes to show you that great storytelling is what the producer brings to *BTM*. There are stories you can't mess up. But there are stories you have to work at. That's what makes a great producer. I'll have producers come to me and say there's no drug addiction, no tragic accident, and I say you're going to have to work a little harder for your story. But I think these stories are the more interesting ones because the producer has to work for it.

The way I look at a TV show, it's an ecosystem. Everything has to make sense. It's its own little environment. TV is a linear medium. It's not like a paper where

you can jump back and forth. You have to know who the characters are, and you have to feel for the characters. It's human interest. In its essence television is simple. It's going from moment to moment. The moments are what you care about. In between is how you get from one moment to the next.

I think so much of what is wrong with television is it's treated and taught like it's a job. But to work, it has to be a passion in order to be really good. For example, you the viewer may not care about Faith Hill, but spend a few minutes and think about what if you didn't know who your mother was, spend a few minutes and think what kind of hole that would make in your life. When you start thinking about that, when you put yourself in her shoes, now you can begin to have empathy for this character and now you can enjoy the show.*

DOCUMENTARIES ON TV

Since the late 1990s the growth of the documentary form can be seen in many places. Television has added many documentary series that continue to be entertaining and informative. Programs include A&E network's *Intervention* and classic *Biography*, which first aired in 1987 and now airs on the Biography channel; Discovery Channel's *Life* series; PBS's *Frontline*, *American Experience*, and *Now*; and ESPN's *30 for 30* series that includes a doc-

umentary on Muhammad Ali made by the Maysles Brothers. The History Channel features over 250 documentaries in its broadcasting queue and the Learning Channel continues to make and air documentaries on a wide variety of topics. Natural-history documentary series like *Nature* and *Nova*, as well as National Geographic's ongoing documentary series, all are part of the documentary world on television, the Web, and DVD.

REALITY TV

Running parallel to these documentary programs are the reality series. While most of the series are exploitative and controlled by producers, there are a few that qualify as vérité-style storytelling. Reality shows seem to break into two categories: pseudo-reality and authentic reality. In the

pseudo-reality world you have *Big Brother*, *The Real World*, *Survivor*, *Flavor of Love*, *The Bachelor* and all of the shows in which people are screened for conflict and the living situation is artificially created. The weekly fare is mean-spirited negativity and bullying. In the authentic-reality

*These words were transcribed from an interview I had with Paul Gallagher on March 14, 2001, at the VH1 production studios in Santa Monica, CA.

category are shows that call on people to meet a challenge and accomplish something. These are shows like *The Amazing Race, Chopped, Pimp My Ride,* and *Property Virgins*.

One huge benefit of all of these pseudo- and authentic-reality shows is that they are good training grounds for documentary makers looking for some seasoning and production experience. Television in the 1950s and '60s was the great training ground for the early, classic documentary makers. Programming like CBS's *CBS Reports* and *See It Now,* NBC's *White Paper,* and ABC's *Close Up!* featured documentaries on every aspect of American life. Giants like documentary makers Albert and David Maysles, Robert Drew, Richard Leacock, Charlotte Zwerin, David Wolper, and many others all began their careers creating documentaries on these series shows.

Now there is another cadre of documentary makers who are working on documentaries that will air on television as well as run in theatrical release and on the Web. Many of the works of this new wave are referenced in this book. We are all the beneficiaries of these times, when making a documentary is something we can all do.

INTO THE ARMS OF STRANGERS

Another one of the documentarians I have had the privilege of interviewing is Deborah Oppenheimer, who won an Academy Award for her documentary *Into the Arms of Strangers*. This uplifting story of children who survived the Holocaust by being sent by their doomed German-Jewish parents to live with families in England was a labor of love. Oppenheimer's mother was one of these Kindertransport children, and the documentary was made to tell the world about this amazing program. Oppenheimer's background is producing television programs. She was one of the producers of *The Drew Carey Show* and has molded a successful career in television. But she had to tell her story, so she embarked on a one-year journey to make her documentary. After it was completed I spoke with her in 2001. *Into the Arms of Strangers* was her first documentary. She has some thoughts for anyone who feels they must tell their story.

> It's totally changed my life and I think what has been so rewarding to me about it is that I felt really good waking up each morning and knowing this was what I was working on. It's a wonderful feeling that not everybody has in their lives and in their careers, so I always hope to have something of significance or meaning in my life now. Whether its volunteer work or I'm not even entirely sure what form it will take, but making the documentary was so rewarding and gratifying that I'm sure that I'll continue to look for that in a project. I was just trying to tell a great story because I believed in it. It's probably the hardest thing I've ever done. I'm still recovering from it. It was really, really, really consuming and really, really hard. But the rewards were so tremendous that I'll do it again.*

STUDENT DOCUMENTARIES

Wasted Youth

Over the years the students in my documentary production classes have made many documentaries. It astounds me how much effort, care, and time they put into their stories. Young people are looking for their voices, ones that can make a dif-

*These words were transcribed from an interview I had with Deborah Oppenheimer on March 10, 2001.

ference in another person's life. Addiction is a phenomenon that exists in their world and many of the best documentaries they have made deal with this tragic and growing social problem. In 2000, a crew of six made a documentary about binge drinking for a target audience of high-school seniors and college students. The documentary was called *Wasted Youth*. The producer was Carolyn Scharf and the director was Rasheed Daniel. The documentary was outstanding and a nonprofit organization called Security on Campus has distributed *Wasted Youth* to over 10,000 high schools and colleges, rehab centers, police academies, and hospitals for over ten years. It has been seen by tens of thousands of young people and prevented thousands of tragedies from happening.

The reason for the success of *Wasted Youth* is that it was made by 21- to 22-year-olds for the same target audience. Although students were experienced production people, they were inexperienced documentary makers. But they understood the basic elements of compelling storytelling. They captured reality and organized their footage into a coherent whole. They added their individual and collective creativity and the result was a moving story of addiction and redemption. For those of you who may be considering making your first documentary in a college setting, Scharf's words should be inspiring.

The origin of the idea...

I wanted to produce a documentary because I felt I could be more creative and have some degree of control over the project. In my other production courses the formats for the projects were pretty specific. But a documentary seemed freer. An open space that I could fill. There weren't any limits. It didn't feel like a class project. It felt like we would be in control the whole time. I liked that.

A documentary on binge drinking seemed important because I could see it going on all around me. I didn't want to preach, I'm not anti-drinking. I wanted to

tell young people that we're not telling you not to drink. We're telling you to be careful when you do. Because if you're not careful, then some bad things can happen. One mistake can kill you.

Research...

I used my computer and surfed the net for information and stories of binge-drinking tragedies. I began to see the scope of the problem. An organization in Philadelphia kept coming up as a resource so I called them up and asked if I could visit them. They had an entire library on the problem of binge drinking. They had a file on every college in the country and in those files were news clippings of binge-drinking episodes.

I read so much. I had to decide what information was useful, which stories were compelling. After we crewed out and there were six of us, my director helped me research further. We would have crew meetings and I would present information for discussion and evaluation. But binge drinking was all around us and everybody was coming up with ideas and new information.

You have to be very organized. And you should never throw anything away or think something is unimportant. Research is critical, and you need to get your hands on it at different times.

Managing the Crew...

At the beginning I had everyone write down their schedules. That included part-time jobs and commuting time. We had enough people to cover everything. One crewmember lived one and one-half hours away, and she ended sleeping over at our campus places a lot.

I asked my crew what they wanted to do in the production. By talking with each other before the class picked their documentaries, we pretty much knew where we would all fit. Beside myself, two crewmembers wanted to be on the creative side, they became codirectors. Two members were interested in camera work, sound, lights and editing. The last member wanted to be our researcher and production assistant.

I was the only one who went on every shoot. I was able to rotate people, which was great for the crew. Sometimes I would want one crewmember more than another, but because this is still college and not the real world, although it felt like the real world sometimes, I made sure to balance everyone's participation.

The directors planned how they wanted the interviews to look. Lighting. Camera placement. Sound. Camera shots. They would bounce their ideas off me, but I trusted their judgment. We were all on the same page.

Structure and Design...

We decided to create a documentary for a target audience: high-school seniors and college freshmen. Since these two groups are the largest binge drinkers. As a result, we wanted to mix visual styles. We wanted that free, MTV-style look. We wanted it "younger" looking. Less conservative. Something this age group would want to pay attention to. Fast pace. Louder music. A lot going on. Quick edits.

During the preproduction planning stage, we worked together to structure the documentary and address the design elements. We started with a structure, but we had to make adjustments as the shooting began. Once we got going, we had to remain flexible.

Originally we thought it would be longer than it turned out. I thought there was so much material we would top out at half an hour. We ended up putting in what we thought was best. We shot at least 20 minutes of interviews with everyone and sometimes only used one to two minutes. We put in what we needed to tell the story effectively.

Each segment had an overall theme. And that theme was "one mistake can change your life." So I picked the stories that would follow this theme the best.

The party scenes...

We needed to get from tragic story to tragic story. We needed some way to do that. We came up with a party scene that, as the party goes on, people drink too much too fast and begin to become affected by the drinking. The party scenes were our bridges between segments. We knew they had to have a fast pace and lots of wild camera angles and movement. We used an improv acting group at the college as our core of people. Then we added our friends and they all acted

out the party scenes. The improv actors were great because we could tell them what we wanted and they would do it. It was like working with professionals.

The party scenes have a MTV feel. Lots of people. The party gets wilder as the documentary moves forward. The editing is fast. We couldn't hang on to a picture for too long. We knew a 16-, 17-, 18-year-old has a short attention span, so we wanted to keep it moving so they would pay attention. If we slowed down we were going to lose them.

My directors decided to shoot the party scenes with no "white" light. So they are either blue or magenta, depending which gels were in the lights. We used one camera and shot for six hours.

Interviews...

I picked the stories and people I wanted to interview by seeing how much tragedy was in each story. Also, I had to determine over the phone in a preinterview if they were willing to talk. Some of the people had already talked to the media and we knew they would be more willing to help us. One woman's son had just died a few months before, and she agreed to talk to us because she was just beginning to deal with her tragedy. The father didn't want to talk because he didn't want his son's legacy to be that he died from binge drinking.

Interview Number One...

Our first interview was with a father whose son had died in a car accident after binge drinking with the driver. The father had spoken with the media before and he was reserved and together. He was on a crusade to alert the world to the dangers of binge drinking. He was very patient with us. His son was buried in Arlington cemetery and I asked him if we could videotape the gravestone. That was an awkward situation. But the father was very cooperative and gave us permission and directions to the gravesite. He didn't want his son to have died in vain. He gave us photos of his son.

Interview Number Two...

Our second interview was with a family whose son had died three months earlier of aspiration pneumonia after binge drinking and swallowing his own vomit.

We weren't prepared for what happened. The interview started and the mother was answering some general questions. When we got to the description of the death, she got hysterical. No one knew what to do. We had gone in expecting someone to cry, but until you see it there just isn't any way to prepare. We didn't know whether we should stop. She didn't want to stop. We offered to stop, but she just wanted to get it out. It was uncomfortable for everyone. But the mother pushed on.

When we edited her segment, I only used the bites that were necessary to tell her story. In some of those bites, she was crying. But we didn't exploit her. That wouldn't have been right. The story was what drove my decision making.

We interviewed the father and the sister and they teared up a little. But the mother was hysterical. On the way home from the shoot, we talked about what happened. We realized how emotional our subject was.

Interview Number Three...

Getting an interview with an inmate at the Garden State Correctional Facility was a nightmare of letters, faxes, phone calls and scheduling. I had to sell the warden, the PR department and Kevin Price, the prisoner I wanted to interview.

We were limited in our time in the prison, so while I was talking to people, the crew shot a lot of jail B-roll. I told the crew to get B-roll and make it interesting. After we were done, we drove around the prison for establishing shots. My director went with a cameraperson and told them what to shoot. But it was collaborative. The cameraperson had a lot of input. She was also our editor, so that helped her find shots.

Design of the interview setups...

One of my directors had a creative vision for the way the interviews would look. I trusted him. He communicated his vision to the technical members of the crew. In meetings, they would tell me their plans and I would approve them. That's one of the things you need to do: trust your crew. You can't get hung up on "I'm the boss." I was happy to listen to them and let them go with it. We were all going for the same goal.

Rape sequence...

On day three crewmembers had an idea and went out and shot lot of shots to use in the rape-segment montage. When they showed it to me, I wouldn't let them use it. It was too over the top. Too graphic. Too much. We ended up shooting scenes that went along with the story the rape counselor was telling about a date-rape incident. Only we used a more impressionistic, abstract approach. We had to be discreet, but we had to get our point across. So the pictures matched the words and weren't offensive. You didn't have to see someone getting raped to feel the impact.

Postproduction...

For the interviews, I would assign the transcription of each interview to someone. We transcribed interviews right after we shot them. Everyone on the crew had to transcribe at least one interview. I would go through the transcriptions and highlight the information I thought was important.

The party footage and the B-roll would be logged by whoever shot it. We started cutting the party scenes right away. We made off-line versions that we would all critique. We had limited memory on our Avid, so we did lots of off-line, linear versions, then would digitize the best version. Then do the final tweaks in the Avid.

I had a large three-ring binder with tabbed sections. My production bible. I kept everything in there. Lots of labeled categories and interviews. As time went on, I got a little sloppy with my paperwork. I could have been more organized. But by keeping everything in one place, I always knew where the information was.

Montages and music...

We needed music that was fast paced and upbeat for the party scenes. It had to appeal to a younger crowd. We needed more soothing music for the introductions. One of the crewmembers had a friend who was in a hard-rock band. They had a CD out and we used one of their songs for the party scenes. Everyone in the band signed a release so I could use their music.

We used montages a lot. The final montage summed up the whole piece.

We were taking you through everything that happened, and nothing that had happened in this whole documentary had been cheerful. We needed to find music that would appeal to a young crowd and suited the situation. The father of one of the crewmembers had composed some slow folk-sounding single-string guitar music many years ago. We brought him into our studio and recorded some tracks and ended up using them. They were perfect.

Narration...

I knew we needed a narrator to begin and end the piece, and to lead into the segments. We wanted a young-sounding voice because the age group we were going for was young and we knew they didn't want a narrator who sounded like their parents. A younger voice would sound like one of their peers. One of our crewmembers asked if he could read for the narration. He had some on-air experience. We all listened to his reading of the narration and agreed he would be fine.

I wrote most of the narration script. Another crewmember helped me with feedback.

Final thoughts...

As a producer, you are going to have to criticize people and their work. You're going to have to say, "I don't like your idea." You really have to learn how to do this and not hurt people's feelings. Because you still need them to come up with new and creative ideas. If you get people mad, they won't work hard for you. Or they will be afraid to have new ideas. I learned that you have to find something of value in everything people do. I may not use their suggestion, but I can find positive value in the person's work. But don't just come out and say, "This sucks."

Don't think because you are the producer you don't have to be open to other people's suggestions. You have to be open to the suggestions of others in order to make the best documentary you can make. Brainstorming really works. You can throw your idea out there, and if everyone feels comfortable with sharing ideas, six minds will be better than one. By the end we were all hanging out with each other.

When I started the course, I thought the only documentaries were historical documentaries. Now I feel documentaries are there to teach you something. And we taught our audience that binge drinking is bad. We found and told stories that helped us teach. At one of our early production meetings, "Scared Straight" came up. Everyone had seen it in high school, and we decided we were trying to scare young people straight about binge drinking.*

What Jeanne Didn't Know

Scharf showed maturity and sensitivity as she led her team through the documentary experience. Another student production that exemplifies the power of a documentary is *What Jeanne Didn't Know* (1990), which was made by a crew of four in my documentary production class in 1990. Keith Gale was the producer/director and his journey led him into an investigation of a brutal murder at Lehigh University in 1986. As he revisited the crime, he realized there was something he could do to prevent similar crimes from happening in the future. His own personal production story is as interesting as his documentary.

The origin of the idea...

I remember my junior year I was cohosting a radio show on Rowan's student radio station, WGLS, called *Campus Call-in*. It was an amazing experience for me. It was like *60 Minutes* on the radio. It made me love sleuthing around and assembling a story.

As I took some TV production courses, I began to enjoy making television. I enrolled in the documentary production course because I wanted to add the visual element to my investigative reporting. The first few weeks of the course required all of us to find a worthy documentary subject and write a pro-

*These words were transcribed from an interview I had with Carolyn Scharf on April 19, 2001.

posal. I knew I wanted to produce one of the documentaries, but I didn't have a subject yet.

I vividly remember sitting down at the desk in my apartment and opening the drawer that contained all of my files on the numerous *Campus Call-in* shows I had made. As I shuffled through the piles of topics, I came across a large white sheet of paper that was not in the place it should have been. It had obviously fallen out of its stapled file and was loose in the drawer. It was a news clipping about a girl who was raped and murdered in her dorm room in college. Her name was Jeanne Clery. I had done a *Campus Call-in* show about her and campus security. It seemed so sad to me that this girl was cut down just as some of the best years of her life were in front of her.

It seemed odd to me that this one piece of paper was not in the place that it was supposed to be. That sounds like an unbelievable story, but one I would not make up out of respect for the people involved. I felt like a story was reaching out to me, asking to be told. I was going to tell that story.

Research...

The reason the documentary happened was because of the intensive research I did. By the time I started to write a proposal and create a structure, I was already an expert on the case. I realized I couldn't do the story justice unless I became a research nut. My research of the murder and the aftermath was the single most important thing I did.

I met the parents and I was touched by their tragedy, which was the murder and the loss of their child. Then I saw what they had been doing since the murder, which was beginning their Security on Campus organization to prevent campus tragedies. The story was bigger than the tragic death.

The prosecuting attorney, Richard Pepper, turned over everything he had on the case. He allowed my crew to have access to items the national media had not seen. Most of the people, because of their involvement in the case, were willing to help. The arresting officers and the district attorney agreed to be interviewed. They saw this as an opportunity to help the grieving family.

But the coroner who did the autopsy wasn't cooperative. I wanted his information for shock value. I wanted his analytic description of the cadaver. He was key. He would drive home the point of the brutality of the murder. He turned me down four times. Finally I called him up and told him that he was critical to the piece and if he didn't agree to an interview I would sleep on his front lawn until he agreed. He laughed, then said OK for an interview.

The documentary was a lot like a jigsaw puzzle. I was always prepared for my preinterviews on the phone because of my extensive research. Each interview was one of the puzzle pieces, and I wanted to know everything there was to know about that person and their role in the story I was telling.

Then, as we shot interviews, we added more information, and now the pieces were all there and I had to assemble them in the right order. But if you haven't taken the time to learn your topic inside and out, you don't have a chance to put the pieces together in the most effective order.

The documentary unit...

I have never thought that I am smarter than anyone else. But I will put my work ethic up against anyone else. I was blessed with three other smart, talented people. They were experienced production people who were motivated at all times to make the best documentary we could. They accepted me as their leader, but many times I did what they suggested. There was a true chemistry that developed.

I was the producer, research guy and the interviewer. We had a director, a cameraman, and a sound and light technician who was also the editor. They all had busy lives and a full load of courses. Advance planning became critical. I had their schedules. I had to always make sure that everyone was current with information. Meetings. Shoots. Editing sessions. By planning in advance, everyone can make adjustments to their lives. But there are always last-minute tapings and you just to the best you can.

On a shoot, I would go right to the interview subject and try to relax them and prepare them for the interview. It's all about trust. I trusted my crew and they busted their butts to prepare themselves.

Designing and shooting the interviews...

When we arrived for an interview, there were almost always four people. The cameraperson and technician set up the camera, lights, monitor and sound systems. They would make sure there were plenty of batteries nearby.

The director would select the shooting environment in the home, always looking for depth in the frame. This resulted in the camera shooting at an angle to the subject. He would arrange objects within the frame that helped tell the story, often providing a foreground and a background. He would use two- and three-point field lighting setups. We would discuss the "look" on the way to the shoot. Everybody would contribute. But ultimately, the way the interviews looked was the vision of my director. One of the strengths of my documentary is the shot composition of the interviews. My director had a great eye. There were a few last-minute shoots he couldn't make and they aren't up to the visual standards of the others.

Logging and B-roll...

I logged and transcribed every second of footage we shot. We taped over ten hours of footage. I had the footage dubbed onto VHS tapes with a time-code window on it. I would come home from my part-time job and log every night. I was familiar with all of the interviews and all of the B-roll. When I needed to cover up an edit point or break away from a talking head or narration, I just used my B-roll logs and found a shot. If there wasn't a shot that matched what was being said, we would create one.

From day one in the course, the teacher stressed the need for B-roll. So B-roll was always on my mind. We shot floor plans, headlines, newspaper articles, old family photos, neighborhoods, work environments, you name it. When I started the course, I thought I was just going to sit down and interview people and everything would be great. I didn't realize that I needed B-roll to more effectively tell the story.

Writing...

I wrote the narration from my extensive knowledge of the details of the murder case and the family story. I knew things that the parents didn't know. I knew I wanted a certain message to be delivered. The documentary wasn't going to be just a depiction of a tragedy and roll the credits.

I wrote late at night. Sometimes, while I was logging tape, I would write some narration. I had a vision that the documentary would be in two parts. The first would be the telling of the tragic rape and murder of Jeanne Clery at college. The second part would be the courageous fight of the parents to start an organization that was dedicated to making college campuses safer.

Narrator selection...

I was so deeply immersed in the project, I thought I should do the narration. But when I told my crew, they thought I should consider other voices. I recorded some of the narration tracks myself, and the feedback from my crew and teacher was not positive. They suggested I try some local media people. I was able to sell one of the local Philadelphia news anchors on the value of the project, and he recorded the narration. During the recording session, the anchor was reading the copy that described in graphic detail the rape and murder. Right in the middle of recording it, he stopped and stepped back and wiped a tear from his eye. He didn't know it at the time, but that was the biggest compliment I could have ever received.

Music...

I realized that there were parts of the documentary that needed music to create a mood and have more impact. Some segments were dry and fact driven. Statistics and legalese. Then there were some segments that were supposed to reach out and touch your heart. Those were the parts that lent themselves to music.

My editor was a musician and had lots of suggestions as far as where the music should be and what it should sound like. Where and how to use music was definitely a collaborative effort.

I eventually used piano instrumentals from an artist named George Winston. My roommate was a music buff and I came home one day and heard him playing George Winston and really liked the sound. I went out and bought a few of his CDs and found the tracks I used. In my mind and heart, I knew what kind of tone and texture I was looking for. When I heard Winston I knew he was right. It was just piano. No lyrics. No other instruments.

Final thoughts...

I think if you are going to commit yourself to making a meaningful documentary, you need to commit yourself as you've never committed yourself before. You may think you have achieved success in other projects, but a documentary is probably more complex than anything you have done so far. And it is a direct reflection of the effort of the people involved.

What Jeanne Didn't Know has stood the test of time. The dedication of the crew, the support of the teacher and

Clery family, all these surrounded the project. But at the center is the commitment of the producer.

Here is an example of what I mean. I wanted to interview a congressman in Washington, DC, because I thought the Washington setting would lend credibility to the story I was telling. I usually got off work from my part-time job at 2 A.M. in the morning. To accommodate my crew we had to leave at 5:30 A.M. to make the two-and-a-half hour drive to DC. It would have been easy to scrap the shoot, write some narration and use a still of the Capitol building. Or wait and interview him in his New Jersey office. But I wanted the congressman in front of the Capitol building with cherry blossoms over his shoulder.

Half an effort probably won't produce an effort you are proud of. Prepare to make a huge effort.*

FINAL THOUGHTS

So, we finish with two student documentaries that are still impacting the world around them. As we have seen, the documentary universe is large and diverse. The filmmakers who want to make documentaries about the people, issues, and events in our world are invested in the stories and driven toward success. There are two characteristics of a documentarian that stand out more than any other qualities. The pro-

fessional documentary makers agree, as do the independent and student documentarians. These qualities are passion for the project and a collaborative approach to production. If you can identify with these qualities and are burning to explore your world using the documentary form, then you are ready for your documentary experience.

DOCUMENTARY REFERENCES

Each of these documentary references was chosen because it has a creative element or technique that stands out. Some of the most creative filmmaking has occurred while a documentarian is telling his or her story. It is hoped that the curious reader will be motivated to watch many of these documentaries not only for enjoyment, but also for inspiration.

Behind the Music series. 1997–2006. George Moll and Paul Gallagher. VH1 Productions. This legendary, one-hour documentary series has made over 200 documentaries about musical artists and performers. For many

Americans now in their thirties and forties, *BTM* was their first exposure to the documentary form. Although the episodes followed a strict formula, they often broke through the barriers many of the artists put

*These words were transcribed from an interview I had with Keith Gale on April 10, 2001.

up and mined raw emotions. The drama the show uncovered through well researched interviews was always real.

Scared Straight! 1978. Arnold Shapiro. Golden West Television. This classic vérité documentary has the lifers in a maximum security prison trying to scare a group of at-risk teenagers into walking the straight and narrow. The Oscar-winning film captures an event that is only going to happen once. Shapiro met with the prisoners ahead of time, demonstrated to them that he had researched their program, and won their trust. The raw language and intensity of the lifers creates an atmosphere that is electric. The observational camera captures it all. Beautifully edited.

Wasted Youth. 2000. Carolyn Scharf and Rasheed Daniel. Rowan University. Binge drinking and its tragic consequences are the subject of this social issue documentary that has been viewed by tens of thousands high school and college students. Creative use of a recurring surreal party reenactment enhances the message, and provides a counterpoint to the heartbreaking stories of binge drinking.

What Jeanne Didn't Know. 1990. Keith Gale. Rowan University. This Emmy Award–winning film was made by a crew of four in my first documentary production class in 1990. Keith Gale was the producer/director and his journey led him into an investigation of a brutal murder at Lehigh University in 1986. As he revisited the crime he realized there was something he could do to prevent similar crimes from happening in the future. He found a small, non-profit organization that was dedicated to making campuses safer and told their story also.

Bibliography

This bibliography reflects my favorite print and electronic resources. These authors and documentarians have given themselves to the art and craft of making and studying documentaries. History, production, aesthetics, and storytelling are all covered in these works. The documentaries tell the stories of a wide spectrum of human experience. The books analyze and explain the documentary form. The Web sites expand our knowledge of the elements of storytelling and present the bodies of work of some of our most accomplished documentarians.

BOOKS

Barnouw, Erik. *Documentary: A History of the Non-Fiction Film*. London: Oxford University Press, 1993.

Coles, Robert. *Doing Documentary Work*. New York: Oxford University Press, 1997.

Douglass, John, and Glenn P. Harnden. *The Art of Technique: An Aesthetic Approach to Film and Video Production*. Boston: Allyn and Bacon, 1996.

Ellis, Jack C. *The Documentary Idea: A Critical History of English-Language Documentary Film and Video*. Englewood Cliffs, NJ: Prentice Hall, 1988.

_____, and Betsy McLane. *A New History of Documentary Film*. New York and London: Continuum, 2005.

Giannetti, Louis. *Understanding Movies*. 10th ed. Upper Saddle River, NJ: Pearson, 2005.

Lowell, Ross. *Matters of Light & Depth*. Lowell-Light Manufacturing, Inc., 1999.

Rabiger, Michael. *Directing the Documentary*. 5th ed. Oxford: Focal Press Elsevier, 2009.

Rosenthal, Alan. *Writing, Directing, and Producing Documentary Films and Videos*. Carbondale: Southern Illinois University Press, 2007.

Rysinger, Lisa. *Exploring Digital Video*. Clifton Park, NY: Thomson Delmar Learning, 2005.

_____. *Digital Video Essentials*. Clifton Park, NY: Delmar Cengage Learning. 2009.

Stubbs, Liz. *Documentary Filmmakers Speak*. New York: Allworth Press, 2002.

DOCUMENTARIES

Almost all of these documentaries have special features in which the documentary makers discuss both the story and the production process. I would recommend that when you find a documentary that moves you, you make it a point to hear the documentary maker discuss his or her work.

4 Little Girls. DVD. Directed by Spike Lee. [New York]: Home Box Office, 1998.

All Grown Up. DVD. Directed by Andrea Whiting. [Howell, NJ]: Psyko Punk Productions, 2007.

American Hardcore. DVD. Directed by Paul Rachman. West Hartford, CT: Envision Films, 2006.

American Movie. DVD. Directed by Chris Smith and produced by Sarah Price. Culver City, CA: Columbia TriStar Home Video, 1999.

Anvil!. DVD. Directed by Sacha Gervasi. [N.p.]: VH1 Films, 2008.

Behind the Music. DVD. Produced by George Moll and Paul Gallagher. [N.p.]: VH1 Productions, 1997–2006.

Blowing Smoke. DVD. Directed by Laura Cava and William Donald Kaufman. [N.p.]: WDK Films LLC, 2006.

Born Into Brothels: Calcutta's Red Light Kids. DVD. Directed by Zana Briski and Ross Kauffman. [New York]: ThinkFilm, 2004.

Bowling for Columbine. DVD. Directed by Michael Moore. [New York]: Dog Eat Dog Films, 2002.

The Boys of Baraka. DVD. Directed by Rachel Grady and Heidi Ewing. [New York]: Think-Film, 2005.

Broken Glass. DVD. Directed by Jonathan Waller and produced by Jennah Trocchia. Glassboro, NJ: Rowan University, 2006.

Buena Vista Social Club. DVD. Directed by Wim Wenders. [N.p.]: Film Produktion, 1999.

Capitalism: A Love Story. DVD. Directed by Michael Moore. [New York]: Dog Eat Dog Films, 2009.

Capturing Reality: The Art of Documentary. DVD. Directed by Pepita Ferrari. [Montreal]: National Film Board of Canada, 2008.

Capturing the Friedmans. DVD. Directed by Andrew Jarecki. [New York]: HBO Video, 2003.

The Civil War. DVD. Directed by Ken Burns. Alexandria, VA: PBS Video, 1989.

Crazy Love. DVD. Directed by Dan Klores and Fisher Stevens. [N.p.]: Shoot the Moon Productions, 2007.

Crips and Bloods. DVD. Directed by Stacy Peralta. [New York]: Docuramafilms; distributed by New Video, 2009.

Crumb. DVD. Directed by Terry Zwigoff. [N.p.]: Superior Pictures Productions, Crumb Partners, 1994.

The Curse of King Tutankhamun. DVD. Directed by Connie Bottinelli. Silver Spring, MD: Discovery Communications, Inc., 1999.

The Devil Came on Horseback. DVD. Directed by Anne Sundberg and Ricki Stern. [N.p.]: Break Thru Films, 2007.

Devil's Playground. DVD. Directed by Lucy Walker. [New York]: Wellspring Media, 2002.

Dogtown and Z-Boys. DVD. Directed by Stacy Peralta. Culver City, CA: Sony Pictures Classics; distributed by Columbia TriStar Home Entertainment, 2002.

Ecstasy and Electronica. DVD. Directed by Kathleen Berger and produced by Erin Plyler. Glassboro, NJ: Rowan University, 2002.

Encounters at the End of the World. DVD. Directed by Werner Herzog. Silver Spring, MD: Discovery Communications, Inc., 2008.

Enron: The Smartest Guys in the Room. DVD. Directed by Alex Gibney. Los Angeles: Magnolia Pictures, 2006.

Fahrenheit 9/11. DVD. Directed by Michael Moore. [New York]: Dog Eat Dog Films, 2004.

Fatal Mistakes. DVD. Directed by Cheryl Kurn and produced by Jason Kitchen. Glassboro, NJ: Rowan University, 2005.

Finding the Light. DVD. Directed by Lauren McGarry and produced by Ziporah Paskman. Glassboro, NJ: Rowan University, 2004.

The Fog of War. DVD. Directed by Errol Morris. Culver City, CA: Sony Pictures Classics, 2004.

Food, Inc. DVD. Directed by Robert Kenner. Los Angeles: Magnolia Home Entertainment, 2009.

Generation Rx: Prescription for Pain. DVD. Directed by Harry T. Fleckenstein III and produced by Steven A. Klink and Missy Stankowski. Glassboro, NJ: Rowan University, 2008.

Gimme Shelter. DVD. Directed by Albert and David Maysles and produced by Charlotte Zwerin. [New York]: Maysles Films, 1970.

Gonzo. DVD. Directed by Alex Gibney. Los Angeles: Magnolia Home Entertainment, 2008.

Grey Gardens. DVD. Directed by Albert and David Maysles. [New York]: Maysles Films, 1975.

Grizzly Man. DVD. Directed by Werner Herzog. Santa Monica, CA: Lionsgate Home Entertainment, 2005.

Hard Choices. DVD. Directed by Marian Lipschutz. New York: New York University, 1984.

Harlan County U.S.A. DVD. Directed by Barbara Kopple. [Irvington, NY]: The Criterion Collection, 2006.

Hoop Dreams. DVD. Directed by Steve James. [N.p.]: New Line Home Video; Turner Home Entertainment, 1995.

Intimate Portrait: Jessica Savitch. DVD. Directed by Connie Bottinelli. [N.p.]: Lifetime Home Video; Seattle, WA: Unapix Entertainment, 1995.

Into the Arms of Strangers: Tales of the Kindertransport. DVD. Directed by Mark Jonathan Harris and produced by Deborah Oppenheimer. Burbank, CA: Warner Bros. Pictures, 2000.

Invisible Children. Directed and produced by Bob Bailey, Laren Poole, and Jason Russell. [El Cajon, CA]: Invisible Children, 2003.

Jesus Camp. DVD. Directed by Heidi Ewing and Rachel Grady. Los Angeles: Magnolia Home Entertainment, 2006.

King of Kong: A Fistful of Quarters. DVD. Directed by Seth Gordon. Burbank, CA: New Line Home Entertainment, 2007.

Lake of Fire. DVD. Directed by Tony Kaye. Los Angeles: Anonymous Content. Chatsworth, CA: distributed by Image Entertainment, 2006.

Leonard Cohen: I'm Your Man. DVD. Directed by Lian Lunson. Santa Monica, CA: Lionsgate Home Entertainment, 2005.

Madonna: Truth or Dare. DVD. Directed by Alek Keshishian. Van Nuys, CA: LIVE Home Video, 1992.

Man on Wire. DVD. Directed by James Marsh. Los Angeles: Magnolia Home Entertainment, 2008.

Man with a Movie Camera. DVD. Directed by Dziga Vertov. 1929. [N.p.]: Film Preservation Assoc. Inc., and Kino International Corp, [n.d.].

Meeting David Wilson. VD. Directed by David A. Wilson and Daniel J. Woolsey and produced by Barion Grant. [N.p.]: Official Pictures, MSNBC; distributed by NBC Universal, 2008.

Movement X. DVD. Produced by Cindy Lewandowski. Glassboro, NJ: Rowan University, 2007.

Murderball. DVD. Directed by Henry Alex Rubin and Dana Adam Shapiro. Santa Monica, CA: Lionsgate Home Entertainment; distributed by ThinkFilm, 2005.

My Architect. DVD. Directed and produced by Nathaniel Kahn. [New York]: New Yorker Video, 2004.

Nanook of the North. DVD. Directed by Robert Flaherty. 1913, 1922. [Irvington, NY]: The Criterion Collection, 1998.

No Direction Home: Bob Dylan. DVD. Directed by Martin Scorsese and produced by Jeff Rosen. Hollywood, CA: Paramount, 2005.

Overnight. DVD. Directed by Tony Montana and Mark Brian Smith. [New York]: ThinkFilm, 2005.

The Personals. DVD. Directed by Keiko Ibi. [Boston]: Fanlight Productions, 1998.

Prisoners Among Us. DVD. Directed by Michael DiLauro. Scranton, PA: MichaelAngelo Productions, 2003.

Red Darkness Before Dawn. DVD. Directed by Diana Nicolae. [N.p.]: Cineluci, 2005.

Rink of Fire. DVD. Produced by Paul Foster and directed by David Diperstein. Glassboro, NJ: Rowan University, 2006.

Roger and Me. DVD. Directed by Michael Moore. [New York]: Dog Eat Dog Films, 1989.

Salesman. DVD. Directed by Albert and David Maysles. [New York]: Maysles Films, 1968.

Scared Straight! DVD. Arnold Shapiro. Santa Monica, CA: Pyramid Films, 1978.

Seabrook Farms Remembered. DVD. Directed by Ned Eckhardt. Seabrook, NJ: Seabrook Educational and Cultural Center and New Jersey Historical Commission, 2002.

Sicko. DVD. Directed by Michael Moore. [New York]: Dog Eat Dog Films, 2007.

Spellbound. DVD. Directed by Jeff Blitz. Culver City, CA: Columbia TriStar Home Entertainment, 2002.

Standard Operating Procedure (S.O.P). DVD. Directed by Errol Morris. Culver City, CA: Sony Pictures Home Entertainment, 2008.

Supersize Me. DVD. Directed by Morgan Spurlock. New York: Hart Sharp Video, 2004.

Taxi to the Dark Side. DVD. Directed by Alex Gibney. Chatsworth, CA: Image Entertainment, 2008.

The Thin Blue Line. DVD. Directed by Errol Morris. [N.p.]: Third Floor Productions, 1988.

Tonal Colors. Produced by Samantha Cressen. Glassboro, NJ: Rowan University, 2005.

Townes Van Zandt: Be Here to Love Me. DVD. Directed by Margaret Brown. [N.p.]: Rake Films, 2004.

Unforgivable Blackness. DVD. Directed by Ken Burns. [Alexandria, VA]: PBS Home Video; distributed by Paramount Home Entertainment, 2004.

The U.S. vs. John Lennon. DVD. Directed by David Leaf and John Scheinfeld. Santa Monica, CA: Lionsgate Films; distributed by Lionsgate Entertainment, 2007.

Wasted Youth. DVD. Directed by Rasheed Daniel and produced by Carolyn Scharf. Glassboro, NJ: Rowan University, 2000.

The Weather Underground. DVD. Directed by Sam Green and Bill Siegel. [N.p.]: The Free History Project, 2002.

What Jeanne Didn't Know. DVD. Produced by Keith Gale. Glassboro, NJ: Rowan University, 1990.

When the Levees Broke. DVD. Directed by Spike Lee. [New York]: HBO Video, 2006.

Who Killed the Electric Car?. DVD. Directed by Chris Paine. Culver City, CA: Sony Pictures Classics, 2006.

Why We Fight. DVD. Directed by Eugene Jarecki. Culver City, CA: Sony Pictures Home Entertainment, 2006.

The Wonderful, Horrible Life of Leni Riefenstahl. DVD. Directed by Ray Müller. [N.p.]: Arte and Channel Four Films, 1993.

Woodstock. DVD. Directed by Michael Wadleigh. Burbank, CA: Warner Home Video, 1994, © 1969.

WEB SITES

These are Web sites that have information and personalized commentary beyond Imdb.com, Wikipedia.com, and the home page for the sale of the DVD.

GRANTS

National Endowment for the Humanities. http://www.neh.gov/grants/guidelines/AmMedia-Makers_production.html.

This site explains how to apply for production grants from NEH (National Endowment for the Humanities). It is inclusive and written in a language that is reader friendly. Collaborative projects and programs aimed at young audiences are in demand.

AWARDS

Academy Award for Best Documentary Feature. http://en.wikipedia.org/wiki/Academy_Award_for_Best_Documentary_Feature. This site is a quick reference for every feature-length documentary that has won an Oscar since this category began in 1942.

TEACHERS' SITES

Into the Arms of Strangers. http://www2.warnerbros.com/intothearmsofstrangers/. This Holocaust story has been integrated into teaching tools that are exceptional.

Prisoners Among Us. http://prisonersamongus.com/. This site explores the story of Italian-American immigrants in the U.S. The prejudice they encountered is a cautionary tale and worthy of study so it doesn't happen again.

Unforgivable Blackness. http://www.pbs.org/unforgivableblackness/teachers/. This is the site that uses Ken Burns' documentary *Unforgivable Blackness* as a key to studying racism and American history. Well researched and full of media, it is a good way for a teacher to create a unit on racism and civil rights.

DOCUMENTARIANS

Blitz, Jeff. http://www.njstatefilmfestival.com/pr-spellbound2.htm. A detailed recounting of the documentary *Spellbound*'s production, featuring director Jeff Blitz. Fascinating reading, especially for rookie documentary makers.

Burns, Ken. http://www.answers.com/topic/ken-burns. This site gives in-depth background on Ken Burns and lists his filmography. There are many sites dedicated to his documentaries, with *The Civil War* sites being the most common.

Ewing, Heidi, and Rachel Grady. http://www.mtv.com/videos/true-life-resist-the-power-saudi-arabia/1639546/playlist.jhtml. *True Life* is a documentary series that has been running on MTV since 1998. It has produced over a hundred documentaries. This Web site features a special 2010 edition of *True Life* titled *Resist the Power: Saudi Arabia.* The one-hour documentary was made by Heidi Ewing and Rachel Grady, who made *Jesus Camp. True Life* has introduced the documentary form to hundreds of thousands of Americans.

Gibney, Alex. http://www.filmmakermagazine.com/issues/winter2008/taxi.php. A long, interesting interview with Alex Gibney, who gives insight into how he brings art and an aesthetic to his documentaries (*Gonzo* and *Taxi to the Dark Side*).

Greenspan, Bud. http://budgreenspan.com/index.html. Bud Greenspan was unique as a documentarian. He specialized in capturing the drama and action of 13 Olympic Games during his life, and loved finding the small, moving stories that everyone else missed. He died in 2010 and his work is worth knowing.

Kaye, Tony. http://www.avclub.com/articles/tony-kaye,14158/. A long, informative, revealing interview with eclectic documentarian and film director Tony Kaye. His documentary *Lake of Fire* is a personal exploration of abortion, and his movie *American History X* is a cult classic.

Made. http://www.mtv.com/shows/made/series.jhtml. *Made* is a reality show that focuses on the problems of teenagers. It has been in continuous production since 2003. Although many of the situations are manipulated, for many viewers this is their first exposure to a camera documenting real life. *Made* often leads to an appreciation of *True Life*.

Moore, Michael. http://www.michaelmoore.com/. A deep and information-rich home base for Michael Moore. You can find out how he has been spending his millions.

Morris, Errol. http://www.newyorker.com/reporting/2008/03/24/080324fa_fact_gourevitch. In this *New Yorker* article, Errol Morris tries to get to the bottom of why Abu Ghraib happened and profiles one of the women who took many of the photos. This is a sidebar to Morris' documentary *Standard Operating Procedure.*

The Real World. *New York Times*. http://query.nytimes.com/gst/fullpage.html?res=9E0CE3DE1631F93AA35754C0A964958260. This is a 1992 article written for the *New York Times* that reviews and describes the first season of the still on-going documentary/reality series *The Real World*. It's fascinating to see how innocent the roommates seem to our now jaded and cynical eyes and sensibilities.

HISTORY

The March of Time. http://www.filmreference. com/Films-Ma-Me/The-March-of-Time.html. This site fills in a lot of the details about the pioneering film documentary series *The March of Time*, made for movie theaters from 1935 to 1951. The format created for this series is still very much alive and seen every night on television in documentary series programs.

Vertov, Dziga. http://dziga.perrybard.net/. This is a fascinating site where people reshoot Dziga Vertov's 1929 classic, *Man with a Movie Camera*. The site has every frame of the original. You can upload your version of a scene, shot, or frame. You can watch the ever-changing global remake right next to the original.

MEDIA

Jump Cut. http://www.ejumpcut.org/currentis sue/index.html.

Jump Cut is an online review of contemporary media. The writers are mostly academics and critics. It is interesting to get a different take on the structure and meaning of films and documentaries. This issue features experimental documentaries circa 2010.

Index